Co-teaching and co-research in contexts of inequality

Using networked learning to connect Africa and the world

Edited by

Phindile Zifikile Shangase
University of the Free State, South Africa

Daniela Gachago
University of Cape Town, South Africa

Eunice Ndeto Ivala
Cape Peninsula University of Technology, South Africa

Series in Education

VERNON PRESS

www.vernonpress.com

In the Americas:	*In the rest of the world:*
Vernon Press	Vernon Press
1000 N West Street, Suite 1200,	C/Sancti Espiritu 17,
Wilmington, Delaware 19801	Malaga, 29006
United States	Spain

Series in Education

Library of Congress Control Number: 2023932594

ISBN: 979-8-8819-0192-9

Also available: 978-1-64889-578-4 [Hardback]; 978-1-64889-685-9 [PDF, E-Book]

Every effort has been made to trace all copyright holders, but if any have been inadvertently overlooked the publisher will be pleased to include any necessary credits in any subsequent reprint or edition.

Cover design by Vernon Press using elements designed by Freepik and pikisuperstar / Freepik.

Table of contents

Cheryl Hodgkinson-Williams
University of Cape Town, South Africa

Daniela Gachago
University of Cape Town, South Africa
Phindile Zifikile Shangase
University of the Free State, South Africa
Eunice Ndeto Ivala
Cape Peninsula University of Technology, South Africa

Sonja Strydom
Stellenbosch University, South Africa

Simone Titus
University of the Western Cape, South Africa

Faiq Waghid
Cape Peninsula University of Technology, South Africa

Daniela Gachago
University of Cape Town, South Africa

Cheryl Brown
University of Canterbury, New Zealand

Proscovia Namubiru Ssentamu
Uganda Management Institute, Uganda

Emily Bagarukayo-Ngabirano
Makerere University, Uganda

Rehema Baguma
Makerere University, Uganda

Tabisa Mayisela
University of Cape Town, South Africa

Jolanda Morkel
STADIO Higher Education, South Africa

Eunice Ndeto Ivala
Cape Peninsula University of Technology, South Africa

Lone Poulsen
Open Architecture, South Africa

Rodney Harber
Open Architecture, South Africa

Nokukhanya Noqiniselo Jili
University of Zululand, South Africa

Mfundo Mandla Masuku
University of KwaZulu Natal, South Africa

Dina Mashiyane
University of the Free State, South Africa

Pauline Ngimwa
Partnership for African Social and Governance Research, Kenya

Proscovia Namubiru Ssentamu
Uganda Management Institute, Uganda

Connie Nshemereirwe
Actualise Africa, Uganda

Busisiwe Alant
University of KwaZulu-Natal, South Africa

Rowan Thompson
STADIO School of Education, South Africa

Kristian D. Stewart
University of Michigan Dearborn, United States of America

Siddique Motala
University of Cape Town, South Africa

Leah Sikoyo
Makerere University, Uganda

Nompilo Tshuma
Stellenbosch University, South Africa

Antonia Liguori
Loughborough University, United Kingdom

Daniel Onyango
Hope Raisers, Kenya

Melaneia Warwick
Loughborough University, United Kingdom

Michael Wilson
Loughborough University, United Kingdom

Daniela Gachago
University of Cape Town, South Africa

Mark Dunford
Digitales, Goldsmiths College, University of London, United Kingdom

Maha Bali
American University in Cairo, Egypt

List of tables

List of figures

Abbreviations

AECT	Association for Educational Communications and Technology
ALS	Architectural learning site
APSE	Access, participation, success and employability
AR	Augmented reality
ASNS	Academic social networking sites
AT & ID	Architectural Technology and Interior Design
BAE	Basic adult education
BBB	BigBlueButton
CAE	Collaborative autoethnographic
CBPAR	Community-based participatory action research
CEDP	Corporate Engineering Degree Program
CIET	Centre for Innovative Educational Technologies
CIfA	Cape Institute for Architecture
CLT	Culture, learning and technology
CMiiST	Creative Methodologies to Investigate Sustainable Transport
COIL	Collaborative online international learning
CoPs	Communities of practice
COVID-19	Coronavirus
CPD	Continuing professional development
CPUT	Cape Peninsula University of Technology
DUT	Durban University of Technology
ECR	early-career researchers
ERLT	Emergency remote learning and teaching
FB	Facebook
GCRF	Global Challenges Research Fund
GIS	Geographic information systems
HDGs	Historically disadvantaged groups
HDIs	Historically disadvantaged individuals
HE	Higher education
HEIs	Higher education institutions
HESA	Higher Education South Africa
HOCS	Higher-order cognitive skills

HOTS	Higher-order thinking skills
HSRC	Human Sciences Research Council
ICDL/ECDL	International Computer Literacy Licence/European Computer Driving Licence
ICT	Information and communication technology
IBSS	International Bibliography of the Social Sciences
IRCEES	International Research Collaborative for Established and Emerging Scholars
IREC	Institutional Research Ethics Committee
ISI	Institute of Scientific Information
IT	Information technology
LMS	Learning management system
MCC	Monroe Community College, New York
MECP	Mulamula Education Centre Project
MoA	Memorandum of Agreement
MS	Microsoft
NGO	Non-governmental organisation
NRF	National Research Foundation
OA	Open Architecture
ODA	Official Development Assistance
OECD	Organisation for Economic Cooperation and Development
PAR	Participatory action research
PASGR	Partnership for African Social and Governance Research
PGDip	Postgraduate Diploma
PGIS	Participatory mapping
PI	Principal Investigator
QUT	Queensland University of Technology
REMEDI	Regenstrief National Center for Medical Device Informatics
RPL	Recognition of Prior Learning
SA	South Africa
SACAP	South African Council for the Architectural Profession
SAIA	South African Institute of Architects
SAMHSA	Substance Abuse and Mental Health Administration
SEL	Social emotional learning
SHM/UL	Supporting historically marginalised and underserved learners
SRC	Student Representative Council
SUNY	State University of New York

SURMs	Single, unemployed, rural mothers
ToC	Theory of Change
UEL	University of East London
UFPE	Federal University of Pernambuco, Brazil.
UIC	University-industry collaboration
UK	United Kingdom
UKZN	University of KwaZulu-Natal
UMU	Uganda Martyrs University
UNICEF	United Nations International Children's Emergency Fund
USA	United States of America
VC	Virtual classroom
VEP	Virtual exchange project
VR	Virtual reality
VREs	Virtual research environments
WHO	World Health Organization
WISH	Widening Access and Success in Higher Education

Editors

Phindile Zifikile Shangase is Senior Lecturer in the Faculty of Health Sciences at the University of Free State, South Africa. Her current role also involves leading the Master's Programme in Health Professions Education as well as handling the staff development portfolio in the Faculty. She holds a PhD in Public Health, with a special interest in smoking cessation as well as social determinants of health. She has over ten years of teaching, supervision and research experience in higher education. Technology is her current passion in the form of technology-enhanced learning, including blended learning and multimodal pedagogies that contribute towards innovative and interactive teaching, learning and assessment practices. She is also enthusiastic about the use of technology to understand community issues and the development world. Her current research projects focus on digital learning in the form of creating virtual classrooms in order to share and create knowledge that will transform the curriculum in Higher Education towards inclusivity and decolonisation thereof. Contact: Mashukushangase@gmail.com

Daniela Gachago is an Associate Professor at the Centre for Innovation in Learning at Teaching at the Centre for Higher Education Development at the University of Cape Town. Her research focuses on academic staff development to transform teaching and learning in higher education, with a particular focus on socially just pedagogies such as digital storytelling. She is also interested in innovative course and curriculum design drawing from co-creative approaches such as design thinking. She received a PhD from the School of Education at the University of Cape Town. She is a C1 NRF-rated scholar and has published more than 50 peer-reviewed articles and book chapters and is the managing editor of *CriSTaL*, the journal for Critical Studies in Teaching and Learning in higher education. Contact: daniela.gachago@uct.ac.za

Eunice Ndeto Ivala is an Associate Professor and Director of the Centre for Innovative Educational Technology at the Cape Peninsula University of Technology (CPUT) located in Cape Town, South Africa. Her research focus is on information and communication technology (ICT)– mediated teaching and learning in developing contexts. She is a C2 NRF-rated scholar and has published/co-published more than 90 research papers and co-edited/edited two conference proceedings and four books. In 2018 she won an award for excellence in e-learning from Global Learn Tech for her research impact on changing educational and individuals' practices. Recently she was a team member in an international digital storytelling project dealing with foreign youth experiences abroad, which was supported by the European Union, a team leader of the ICT curriculum appraisal of the National Senior Certificate for Adults, and an institutional coordinator for the Council for Higher Education quality enhancement project in the area of learning environments. She was also a team member in a National Research Fund–British Council Workshop Links project on widening access, success and employability, a collaboration between CPUT and the University of East London, UK. She is a Donald H. Wulff Diversity Fellow. She holds a BEd Honours degree from the University of Nairobi, Kenya, an MEd degree in Computer-based Education from the University of Natal, Durban, South Africa, and a PhD in Culture, Communication and Media Studies from the University of KwaZulu-Natal, Durban, South Africa. Contact: ivalae@cput.ac.za

Contributors

Busisiwe Alant is currently Chief Editor of the *African Journal of Research in Mathematics, Science and Technology Education* (*AJRMSTE*) and an Associate Professor of Technology Education. For three years (2017–2020), she served as the Academic Leader in the Science and Technology Education Cluster in the School of Education at the University of KwaZulu-Natal (Edgewood Campus). Busisiwe holds a PhD in Physics Education (University of the Western Cape) and a Master's in Science Education (University of Durban-Westville – Cum Laude). She recently completed two certificates, one an Energy Efficiency and Sustainability Certificate (2019) with the Faculty of Engineering and the Built Environment at the University of Cape Town, and the other a Solar Professional Certificate in Residential & Commercial PV Systems (2017) with the American-based Solar Energy International. She also has an engineering qualification, the Advanced Diploma in Mechanical Engineering (2014) from the Australian-based Engineering Institute of Technology. She has co-authored more than 35 publications with colleagues and students. She has successfully supervised to completion of 19 Master's and 8 PhD students in Science and Technology Education. Contact: alantb@ukzn.ac.za

Emily Bagarukayo-Ngabirano is a lecturer, researcher, and consultant on computing and ICT issues at the College of Computing and Information Sciences, Makerere University. She holds a PhD in Information Science, PGDip (Educational Technologies), Master of Science in Computer Science and Bachelor of Computer Science (Hons). She is a research associate at the International Center of IT and Development, USA. She undertook her doctoral research in the area of e-learning, specifically on the impact of digital learning environments and multimedia in education and industry on learning. For her doctoral research, she developed the Learning by Construction Approach for the improvement of higher-order cognitive skills, building capacity and infrastructure in developing countries. She has researched the impact of social software on learning and ICT4D. Her specific research interests include the use of technology to support personalised learning and the development of instructional content. She is an external reviewer, external examiner and has authored over 20 peer-reviewed journals, conference papers and book chapters. Contact: ebagarukayo@gmail.com

Rehema Baguma is a Senior Lecturer in the Department of Information Systems and Coordinator of the Development Informatics Research Group in the College of Computing and Information Sciences, Makerere University. Before that, she headed the Department of Information Systems in the same college. She holds a PhD in Information Systems from Radboud University in the Netherlands and a PGDip (Educational Technologies) from the University of Cape Town. She has over 20 years of professional experience in research, teaching and leadership. Her research expertise is in digital inclusion, digital governance, digital education and human-centred design. She has authored over 40 research articles, conference proceedings and book chapters. She also consults for government, local and international NGOs/agencies in Uganda and East Africa, providing solutions for making e-government and e-learning services fit the reality of contexts where they are to be used and more usable and accessible to diverse groups of the target population. Contact: rbaguma@cis.mak.ac.ug

Maha Bali is an Associate Professor of Practice at the Center for Learning & Teaching at the American University in Cairo. She also teaches digital literacies and intercultural learning. She is a co-founder of virtuallyconnecting.org (a grassroots movement that challenges academic gatekeeping at conferences) and co-facilitator of Equity Unbound (an equity-focused, open, connected intercultural learning curriculum, which has also branched into academic community activities Continuity with Care and Inclusive Academia). She writes and frequently speaks about social justice, critical pedagogy, and open and online education. She has a PhD in Education from the University of Sheffield in the UK. She tweets a lot @bali_maha and blogs at http://blog.mahabali.me. Contact: bali@aucegypt.edu

Fábio Barbosa de Souza is a dentist who earned his Master's degree in Dentistry / Integral Clinics at the Federal University of Pernambuco (UFPE), Brazil. His PhD was earned in Dentistry/ Operative Dentistry from the University of Pernambuco in Brazil. He has specialised in Teaching Higher Education and Health Surveillance. He is an Associate Professor at the Maxillofacial Surgery Department of UFPE, where he teaches Biosafety and Ergonomics to undergraduate students. He has obtained students' engagement in infection prevention, creating information dissemination actions using communication technologies. He is the creator of the Instagram account @odontologia_biossegura, where photos and videos with content related to infection control in dentistry are published. He is dedicated to studying how to apply social media in an active learning approach. He has published many articles in scientific journals, book and book chapters, text in newspapers/magazines, and a summary in conference proceedings. Contact: Fabio.souza@ufpe.br

Alice Barlow-Zambodla is the e/Merge Africa Research Support Convenor and Network Development Consultant based in South Africa. She is also Landscape Director at Conservation South Africa (an affiliate of Conservation International) in its Umzimvubu Demonstration Landscape. She comes from a multidisciplinary background (Agriculture/Botany/Science Education/Teacher Education/e-learning) involving over 24 years of research and lecturing experience in the African HE sector. Since 2007, she has used her varied skills and experience to support the implementation of collaborative research, sustainable development and capacity-building interventions (for e-learning, as well as environmental restoration for climate change resilience in biodiversity hotspots) working in the African non-profit sector. Contact: alicebarlowzambodla@gmail.com

Cheryl Brown is an Associate Professor in e-learning in the School of Education Studies and Leadership at the University of Canterbury and co-Director of the Digital Education FuturesLab. She has worked in the HE sector for the past 20 years in South Africa, Australia, and now New Zealand. Her PhD (from the University of Cape Town) was in Information Systems and explored how inequality influences university students' digital experience and, consequently, their digital identities. In the past few years, she has explored the role that technological devices (cell phones and laptops) play in students' learning and in the development of students' digital literacy practices. She teaches Digital Citizenship in a pre-service teacher's programme, postgraduate courses in e-learning and convenes and teaches in the PGCert in Tertiary Teaching programme. She has been involved in the Commonwealth of Learning Digital Education Leadership in Action (C-Delta) project since its inception and is passionate about developing a healthy and critical awareness of both the opportunities and challenges of living and learning in a digital world. Contact: cheryl.brown@canterbury.ac.nz

Lindy Osborne Burton was originally educated in South Africa but later moved to Australia, where, as a registered architect, she specialised in the design of complex public and institutional buildings. Following 12 years of practice, during which she received 15 professional design awards, Lindy pivoted to an academic career. Now an Associate Professor in architecture and the Design for Health programme leader at Queensland University of Technology, Lindy's research interests centre on transformational architectural education, the design of innovative learning environments, the integration of biophilic and salutogenic architecture approaches to support mental well-being, and diversity, equity and inclusivity in architecture. Lindy is a member of the Board of Architects of Queensland and a Senior Fellow of the Higher Education Academy. Her teaching excellence has been recognised through Dean and Vice-Chancellor Performance Awards and through an Australian Office for Learning and Teaching citation for 'outstanding contributions to student learning'. Contact: lindy.burton@qut.edu.au

Mark Dunford is an academic, researcher and practitioner. He has held senior academic roles at Goldsmiths, University of Brighton, where he completed his PhD, and the University of East London. He has written widely on media policy and practice and established DigiTales as a specialist media research and production company at Goldsmiths in 2008. Mark's academic publications include *Digital Storytelling: Form and Content* (Palgrave Macmillan, 2018). He is chair of the International Steering Group for the biennial International Visual Methods Conference. His career outside academia includes time at the BBC, British Film Institute and Arts Council England. Contact: Mark@Digi-Tales.org.uk

Steven Feast studied architecture at Curtin University in Perth, Australia, before entering practice and working on commercial, education and multi-residential projects. After gaining professional registration as an architect in Western Australia, he returned to Curtin to take on coordination of the newly commenced fully online architecture programme. Steven guided the online programme through an accreditation assessment in 2018 which led to Curtin's online Master of Architecture, delivered through Open Universities Australia, becoming Australia's first (and at the time of writing only) fully online accredited architecture programme. Steven leads the digital portfolio of the Association of Architecture Schools of Australasia and is a member of the AACA Accreditation Standing Panel. His research interests include online learning in architecture, and he has presented on the subject at various AASA workshops and seminars. Contact: Steven.feast@curtin.edu.au

Hannah Grossman is an instructional designer and design-based researcher at the UCLA/Duke University National Center for Child Traumatic Stress. Her instructional design work centres around adult collaborative experiential learning that makes use of a cognitive load framework. Hannah's research and practice agendas include multimedia skill-based learning, cross-cultural collaboration, social emotional learning, trauma-informed instructional and process design, and problem-based learning. Her expertise began during her service as a forestry Peace Corps volunteer in The Gambia, developed during her time as a classroom biology teacher, and has continued to grow during her service as a non-profit worker and professional learning designer. In 2016 she received her PhD from the University of California Santa Barbara in Cultural Perspectives and Comparative Education with an interdisciplinary Cognitive Science emphasis. Contact: hmgrossman@ssl-mail.com

Rodney Harber is currently practising as Arch Urban Plan Architects, Urban and Regional Planners and Heritage Consultants based in Durban and Cape Town, South Africa. Rodney has been recognised by the International Union of Architects for his 'exceptional promotion of architecture'. Nationally he holds a Medal of Distinction from the South African Institute of Architects, as well as provincially. He retired after teaching at the University of KwaZulu-Natal for over four decades. Rodney has lectured and been a visiting professor all over the globe. He is one of the founders of Open Architecture. Contact: Rodneyharber@mweb.co.za

Cheryl Hodgkinson-Williams (Emeritus Associate Professor) taught Online Learning Design, Advanced Research Design and Researching Higher Education courses to postgraduate students and supervised Master's and PhD students in Educational Technology, Open Education and Higher Education Studies. She holds a PhD in computer-assisted learning and has taught and supervised in the field of information communication technologies in education since 1994, first at the University of Pretoria, then at Rhodes University in Grahamstown and then at the University of Cape Town. In addition, she was Principal Investigator of the IDRC-funded Research in Open Educational Resources for Development project, which investigated the adoption and impact of the use of open educational resources in 21 countries in the Global South. She was an advisor on the Digital Open Textbooks for Development project, the former Principal Investigator of, and now an advisor on, the Cases on Open Learning project that is investigating the readiness towards open learning of Technical and Vocational Education and Training and HEIs in South Africa. She was a UNESCO Chair of Open Education and Social Justice at UCT. In November 2019, Cheryl was awarded the Open Education Consortium Leadership Award and was interviewed for the Leaders and Legends of Online Learning podcast. Cheryl took early retirement at the end of January 2020 but is still active as a consulting researcher and an Open Education and Social Justice advocate. Contact: cheryl.hodgkinson-williams@uct.ac.za

Nokukhanya N. Jili is currently an Associate Professor and Head of the Department of Public Administration at the University of Zululand. She is a cum laude graduate of her Honours and Master's degrees, both obtained at the University of Zululand. She has presented papers at both local and international conferences and has published a number of articles in accredited journals and book chapters, and edited a book. She has won several research awards and has graduated a number of Master's and PhD candidates. She is a board member of the South African Association of Public Administration and Management. She has reviewed papers for different accredited journals, such as the *Journal of Public Administration* and *Ubuntu - Journal of Conflict and Social Transformation*. Her research interests include public management and governance, local economic development, public policy analysis and service delivery in the public sector. JiliN@unizulu.ac.za

Neil Kramm practises and researches at the Educational Technology Unit in the Centre for Higher Education Research, Teaching and Learning, Rhodes University. The centre offers professional development opportunities for academics. Neil specialises in advising and supporting academics on how to approach the use of technologies effectively in their roles as educators and researchers and the role of technology in the teaching and learning process. Neil supports learning design thinking with academics to provide online and blended learning engagements that are transformative. Contact: n.kramm@ru.ac.za

Antonia Liguori is a Senior Lecturer in Applied Storytelling at Loughborough University, UK. She is an advisory board member of the INTELLECT Centre, Centre for Research into Heritage Education, Well-being and Teaching Technology, Department of Education and Humanities, Università di Modena e Reggio Emilia, Italy. Her academic background is in History and Computer Science. Since 2008, she has been involved in a variety of international research projects to develop tools and methods to foster innovation in education, to explore the role of storytelling in today's digital world, and to investigate and trial ways of using digital storytelling as a participatory methodology for interdisciplinary research. Over the past seven years, her research has been focused on three main strands: applied storytelling on environmental issues, digital storytelling in (cultural/heritage) education, and storytelling and urban design. More recently, after having joined HEART – Healing Education Animation Research Therapy, she has been exploring digital storytelling as therapeutic intervention. Contact: a.liguori@lboro.ac.uk

Juhong Christie Liu is an Associate Professor and Director of Instructional Design in Libraries at James Madison University. She leads programmes to provide instructional design support for teaching and learning in technology-enhanced environments. She teaches graduate and undergraduate classes. Her research focuses on instructional design and development, design-based and cross-cultural research, and intersections between culture, learning and technology. Juhong has published peer-reviewed journal articles, book chapters, OER textbooks, and edited IEEE-published international conference proceedings, and served as an investigator in projects funded by the National Science Foundation, Virginia Board for People with Disability, and Virginia Academic Libraries Consortium. Christie has a Ph.D. degree in Curriculum and Instruction/Instructional Design and Technology from Virginia Tech. She serves in leadership roles at the Association of Educational Communications & Technology, Culture, Learning, and Technology Division and the American Educational Research Association Instructional Technology Special Interest Group. She serves on the National Science Foundation review panels and Editorial Boards of *TechTrends* and *the Journal of Educational Technology Development and Exchange*. Contact: liujc@jmu.edu

Dina Mashiyane is an Assistant Director (Campus Librarian) at the University of the Free State, with a demonstrated history of working in HE library and information services. She is skilled in electronic resources, knowledge management, digitisation, information literacy, research methodology, library marketing and liaison. She is also a researcher who has published in reputable academic journals and is an accredited facilitator. She was one of the candidates for the Carnegie CPD Programme' Enhancing librarians' ICT skills for research enablement in African universities'. Her research interests include information literacy, information ethics, inclusive education and social media in libraries/ teaching and learning. She has presented papers at both local and international conferences. Contact: Mashiyanedm@ufs.ac.za

Mfundo Mandla Masuku is an Associate Professor in Development Studies at the School of Built Environment and Development Studies at the University of KwaZulu-Natal. His areas of research interest include inclusive education, food security, scholarship of teaching and learning, African Studies, and gender. Contact: profmmasuku@gmail.com

Tabisa Mayisela is a senior lecturer and coordinator of the Academic Staff Development cluster at the Centre for Innovation in Learning and Teaching, University of Cape Town, South Africa. Tabisa also convenes and co-teaches courses within both of the Postgraduate Diploma in Education streams: Higher Education Studies and Educational Technologies. Her research interests are academic staff (professional) development; students' development of digital literacies; integration of educational technologies and digital literacies into course curricula; and online learning design. In addition to her digital literacies focus in her PhD, she has been involved in the development of the Commonwealth Digital Education Leadership Training in Action concept document. Tabisa is currently the principal investigator of the Cases on Open Learning project funded by the Department of Higher Education and Training of South Africa. Contact: tabisa.mayisela@uct.ac.za

Jolanda Morkel is the Head: Instructional Design at STADIO Higher Education and a licenced architect. She has co-designed, coordinated and facilitated various transformative learning and teaching innovations aimed at broadening access to HE. Jolanda's research interests include studio-based learning, flexible, blended and online learning, technology-mediated and work-integrated learning, learning experience design, and design-thinking for staff development. Jolanda championed the part-time blended Cape Peninsula University of Technology BTech programme in Architectural Technology offered in collaboration with Open Architecture as one of the flagship transformation projects of the South African Institute of Architects and the first of its kind in Africa. Contact: JolandaM@stadio.ac.za

Siddique Motala is an academic development senior lecturer in the Department of Civil Engineering at the University of Cape Town, South Africa. He is a trained land surveyor and holds a PhD in Education. His research is focused on posthumanism, the scholarship of teaching and learning, spatio-temporal mapping, storytelling and innovative practices in engineering education. He was a recipient of the 2017 HELTASA/CHE National Excellence in Teaching and Learning Award. Contact: siddique.motala@uct.ac.za

Pauline Ngimwa is the Programme Manager for the Professional Development and Training Programme at the Partnership for African Social and Governance Research, responsible for conceptualising and guiding the development and delivery of training programmes in policy-oriented research to early- and mid-career researchers and policy actors in Africa. She has extensive work experience in the African HE sector, where she has led academic and training programmes, including technology-enhanced learning initiatives. Her research interests include the design and use of digital educational resources, including open educational resources, in African HE. She has published in this area and has peer-reviewed for international journals. She holds a PhD and Master of Research in Educational Technology from the Open University of the UK; and a BSc and Master's in Information Science from Moi University, Kenya. She is also a fellow with the African Science Leadership Programme at the University of Pretoria. Contact: pngimwa@pasgr.org

Connie Nshemereirwe is an independent science and policy facilitator and acts at the science-policy interface as a science writer, trainer, and speaker. She divides her time between her role as the Director of the Africa Science Leadership Programme at the Future Africa campus of the University of Pretoria and Actualise Africa, a company that she set up in 2016, and through which she provides training in leadership, research methods, and communication. Beyond this, she is active in various civil society organisations through which she speaks and writes on the adequacy and relevance of formal education in Uganda as well as Africa at large. Her undergraduate studies were in Civil Engineering, which she followed with a Master's degree in Education and Training Systems Design at the University of Twente, and later a PhD in Educational Measurement in 2014. She also spent 15 years at Uganda Martyrs University with a dual appointment as an academic in the Faculty of Education and the Faculty of the Built Environment. Contact: cnshemereirwe@gmail.com

Mark Olweny is currently Senior Lecturer in the School of Architecture and the Built Environment at the University of Lincoln and Research Associate Professor in Architecture in the Faculty of the Built Environment at Uganda Martyrs University. Mark holds professional degrees in architecture and urban design and a PhD in architectural education. He has been engaged in architectural practice and education for the past two decades. His research currently focuses on curriculum development and teaching practices in architectural education, as well as social-cultural factors and sustainable architecture, with an emphasis on sub-Saharan Africa. Contact: molweny@lincoln.ac.uk

Daniel Onyango is the founder of Hope Raisers Initiative, a community youth-led organisation. Daniel has continued to support collaborative development and art projects, highlighting the importance of arts and cultural expression as a tool to inspire change, with the overall objective of strengthening and encouraging youth involvement in their community. He has great experience working with marginalised youths and children in his community and brings in knowledge on a strategic level. He holds a BA in Political Science and Sociology from the University of Nairobi. Contact: daniel.onyango@hoperaisersinitiative.com

Nicola Pallitt coordinates the efforts of the Educational Technology Unit in the Centre for Higher Education Research, Teaching and Learning at Rhodes University and offers professional development opportunities for academics to use technologies effectively in their roles as educators and researchers. Nicola provides learning design support and consultation in relation to teaching with technology (technology integration) and blended and online teaching and learning. She also supports lecturers to design appropriate technology-mediated learning experiences for their students. Nicola supervises postgraduate students and co-teaches formal courses in HE. She enjoys meeting EdTech practitioners and researchers from across the globe and is part of the e/merge Africa team. Contact: n.pallitt@ru.ac.za

Lone Poulsen holds a Bachelor of Architecture and a Master's in Town and Regional Planning from the University of Natal, Durban. She practiced and taught in Durban until 1991, when she joined the School of Architecture and Planning at Wits University, eventually serving as Assistant Dean for the Built Environment disciplines and Director of the Architecture Programme. Lone was the Programme Director for the SAIA-initiated OpenArchitecture programme from 2013 to 2019. She has served on the judging panels of architectural and urban design competitions, adjudicated national Merit Awards in South Africa and in Zimbabwe and acted as external examiner and critic for architectural, urban design, housing and planning courses at a number of universities. Contact: lone@poulsen.co.za

Krista M. Rodriguez is an adjunct Associate Professor in the Dental Studies Department at Monroe Community College in Rochester, New York, since retiring from her full-time position. She earned associate degrees in both dental assisting and dental hygiene, a bachelor's degree in Allied Health Education and a Master's degree in Liberal Studies with a focus on culture and communication. She taught didactic and clinical courses for both of the dental studies programmes and developed a course: Multicultural and Diversity Influences on Health and Wellness. She has lectured to professional organisations on topics of diversity and culture in the health professions, concepts of cultural competence and impacts of culture/diversity on healthcare communication and management of health and wellness. She has been involved with online collaborative learning (COIL) since 2015, developing a number of global partnerships and collaborative projects and presenting workshops on the implementation of global cultural collaborations. Contact: krodriguez@monroecc.edu

Leah Sikoyo is a teacher educator and curriculum specialist currently serving as a Senior Lecturer at the School of Education, Makerere University in Uganda. She holds a PhD in Education and a PG Dip in Educational Technology, both from the University of Cape Town, South Africa, and an MEd (Curriculum Studies) and BA with Education from Makerere University, Uganda. Her research interests include transformative pedagogy, online learning design, curriculum design and teacher professional development, with publications in high-impact international journals. Since 2019, she has co-facilitated modules on Curriculum and Learning Design for online and blended learning contexts with the Pedagogical Leadership in Africa (PedaL) project to cascade training for academic staff in African universities. Contact: leah.sikoyo@mak.ac.ug

Proscovia Namubiru Ssentamu is an associate professor of education and head of the quality assurance department at Uganda Management Institute (UMI). She facilitates education-related Master's and PhD programmes and supervises graduate research. She is an external examiner on PhD programmes and a member of three Editorial Advisory Boards within and beyond Uganda. She has a Doctorate of Philosophy of Education (University of Bayreuth, Germany), MA in Curriculum Studies (London), MEd in Curriculum Studies (Makerere), PGDip in Human Resource Management (UMI), PGDip in Education Technology (Cape Town); Graduate Certificate in Quality Assurance (Melbourne), and BA/ED - Literature in English, English Language, Education (Makerere). Proscovia is a scholar, practitioner, trainer, researcher and consultant in quality assurance in education; curriculum design, development and evaluation; pedagogy and andragogy; educational research, monitoring and evaluation; and teacher professional development, and has published in these areas. Contact: psnamubiru@umi.ac.ug

Kristian D. Stewart is a Fulbright Scholar Candidate for Greece (2023) and a King Chávez Parks Faculty Fellow in the Department of Language, Culture, and the Arts at the University of Michigan-Dearborn, USA. Kristian is a digital storytelling and literacy practitioner, and in this context, she conducts research around 'glocal' literacy, transnational course collaboration and design, and critical and discomforting pedagogies as methods to reshape and decolonise curriculum. Kristian has authored research grant proposals, peer-reviewed journal articles, and book chapters in these areas. She was also the recipient of the Collegiate Lectureship Teaching Award (2022) for her outstanding teaching of writing. Contact: kdstew@umich.edu

Sonja Strydom is a Deputy Director (Academic Development & Research) at the Centre for Learning Technologies and a Research Fellow at the Centre for Higher and Adult Education at Stellenbosch University. She holds a PhD in Education from the University of Stellenbosch and a DLitt et Phil in Psychology from the University of South Africa. Sonja teaches a number of short and postgraduate HE courses and is also involved in the delivery of the MPhil in Higher Education at Stellenbosch University. She was instrumental in the establishment and further development of the African Digital University Network (ADUN) that originated in the Centre for Learning Technologies. Her current research interest is in the field of technology-augmented curriculum development, academic development, digital well-being and alternative methodologies for furthering the field of higher education research. Contact: sonjas@sun.ac.za

Rowan Thompson completed an Honours Degree in Industrial Design at Napier University, PG Dip in Energy Systems at the University of Strathclyde and PGCE Technology Education at Edinburgh University. Attracted to education following a research project in Zimbabwe, he has taught and trained educators in various technology curricula in Botswana, England, Scotland, and South Africa. Rowan works for STADIO School of Education as HOD for Maths, Science and Technology. He has an MEd in Technology Education from UKZN and is completing a PhD investigating the integration of CAD in ICT courses for teacher education. He advocates for technology education to have a permanent place in the national curriculum, creating an entrepreneurial society using engineering and design professions. He co-authored the OUPSA publication *Teaching Technology*, integrating modern pedagogies for technology education with indigenous knowledge systems. He recently authored an article for *Educational Research for Social Change* journal based on his MEd study. Contact: rowant@stadio.ac.za

Simone Titus is a teaching and learning specialist in the Interprofessional Education Unit at the Faculty of Community and Health Science at the University of the Western Cape in South Africa. She graduated with a PhD in Education from the University of Cape Town, where she developed an interest in the use of emerging technologies as a tool to mediate learning. Her special research interests are focused on game-based learning and using emerging technologies to foster cross-cultural interaction, learning, and engagement in higher education. Contact: sititus@uwc.ac.za

Nompilo Tshuma is a Lecturer in the Centre for Higher and Adult Education at Stellenbosch University in South Africa. She has been working in educational technology since 2005 in student (extended studies) and staff development and as a researcher. She has been involved in academic staff development, where she supported lecturers as they integrated technology into teaching and learning through workshops and presentations, contributing to formal qualifications and individual support. She is also a researcher in educational technology and academic staff development and is passionate about challenging academics to be critically reflective about their use of educational technology, particularly in light of the calls for a transformation of HE in South Africa. Nompilo holds a PhD in Information Systems from Rhodes University, which focused on the culture of resistance to educational technology practices of academic staff. Contact: ntshuma@sun.ac.za

Anisa Vahed is a Dental Technology academic, researcher and practitioner in the Dental Sciences department at the Durban University of Technology. A Fulbright Fellow and Y2 National Research Foundation-rated researcher. Her research interests include undergraduate research, scholarship and creative inquiry, unfurling the post-school education and training sector, and internationalising the curriculum through collaborative online international learning, which uses digital technologies to infuse intercultural and global dimensions into curriculum content. Dr. Vahed has delivered numerous papers, workshops and seminars nationally and internationally. She is currently participating in the Future Professors Programme, an initiative of the Department of Higher Education in South Africa. Contact: anisav@dut.ac.za

Faiq Waghid is an academic at the Cape Peninsula University of Technology's Centre for Innovative Educational Technology. His research interests include the use of participatory action research towards improving teaching and learning practices, augmented through the use of educational technologies. Faiq's noteworthy research endeavours include the publication of three international co-authored books, *Educational Technology and Pedagogic Encounters: Democratic Education in Potentiality* (Sense, 2016), *Rupturing African Philosophy on Teaching and Learning: Ubuntu Justice and Education* (Palgrave-MacMillan, 2018), and more recently *Cosmopolitan Education and Inclusion: Human Engagement and the Self* (Palgrave-MacMillan, 2020). He is rated by the National Research Foundation as a promising young researcher (Y2). Contact: waghidf@cput.ac.za

Melaneia Warwick holds a PhD in Participatory Arts from the University of Brighton. Melaneia has worked extensively on diverse projects in East Africa, in unofficial settlements and at the region's leading research institutions. She employs a range of participatory visual methodologies to undertake practice-led research, including digital storytelling, photovoice and wearable camera technologies. She is currently exploring the ways in which the qualitative data collected via these methodologies can be combined with quantitative data for research and policy engagement purposes. Melaneia is a Winston Churchill Fellow and a Fellow of the Royal Society of Arts. Contact: M.Warwick2@lboro.ac.uk

Michael Wilson is Professor of Drama and Head of Creative Arts at Loughborough University, where he leads the Storytelling Academy, a research team in Applied Storytelling. His main research interests lie broadly within the field of popular and vernacular performance, and over the past 15 years, he has led numerous RCUK/UKRI cross-council and European Commission projects that explore the application of storytelling to a variety of social and policy contexts, especially around environmental policy, health, education and social justice. More recently, this has included GCRF and Newton Fund projects on environment and health in Kenya, Uganda, India and Colombia. He has been a member of the Advisory Boards for the Digital Economy Programme (RCUK, led by EPSRC), Connected Communities (AHRC) and Digital Transformations (AHRC). He is also Chair of the Arts and Humanities Panel for the British Council's Newton Fund programme. Contact: M.Wilson2@lboro.ac.uk

Preface

The power of networked learning to connect staff and students across the world has never been more evident than during the last few years, during which higher education (HE) globally pivoted to online learning. Over the shortest period of time, lecturers redesigned their courses to teach and support their students remotely. For many, this was a difficult process leading to increased demands on both staff and students, with a major impact on workload, research careers, and mental health.

The call for contributions to this book was shared before the pandemic, inviting colleagues known for their passion for online collaboration to share their experiences and reflections on teaching and researching across institutional and geographical boundaries. This edited collection consists of 15 contributions by more than 40 international authors from Africa, Europe, the United States, South America and Australia. The book provides a diversity of views and perspectives on co-teaching and co-research, including conceptual and reflective papers and empirical research on African lecturers' experiences with co-research and co-teaching courses using networked learning in and beyond the African continent. As such, it provides unique insight into opportunities and challenges when engaging in inter-institutional and intercultural collaborations online across unequal contexts.

While the topic of this book was still a rather niche research interest during the time of conceptualisation, with very little available research published in our context, COVID-19 has made this book an essential reading for all academics. Co-teaching and co-research across unequal contexts entail so much more than thinking about access and connectivity (although these are still important issues). What the contributions to this book show are that what really counts when working online are the connections, engagement, relationships and friendships that we form when reaching out to and learning from colleagues beyond our immediate context.

What makes these experiences so valuable (but also difficult) is what we can learn when we engage with different world views and experiences; it's the critical citizenship we facilitate among ourselves and our students when we truly open ourselves to difference. The lessons emerging from these contributions are that it takes time, patience, self-reflection, and the willingness to make mistakes and try again to sustain these collaborations across differences.

This book was a labour of love, created during difficult times, and we hope that you will find it as inspirational and thought-provoking as we do.

Daniela, Phindile and Eunice

Foreword

Cheryl Hodgkinson-Williams

University of Cape Town, South Africa

The global pandemic has thrown into sharp relief the economic, sociocultural and geopolitical challenges in our society. Written and published before and during this challenging time, this volume presents compelling cases for engaging in co-teaching and/or co-researching to advance more socially just, supportive and mutually favourable practices in HE, among local and international academics and their students as well as practitioners. The particular perspective being explored is the value of networked technologies to enable, broaden and sustain team teaching and/or collaborative research within and beyond Africa. This theme is most apt, given the racial strain, rising nationalism and growing inequality globally, as well as the coerced move to online teaching and research during the COVID-19 tumult.

The collection contains a cornucopia of international, transcontinental, pan-African, inter-institutional, institutional and university-industry cases, each accentuating an aspect of the complexity of co-teaching, co-learning and/or co-researching across a range of dimensions, including levels of seniority, nationality, race, ethnicity, gender, class, and rurality, among others. The cases also highlight an array of networked technologies that varyingly enable or constrain co-teaching and/or co-researching, ranging from very general use of information communication technologies (e.g. social media) to specific pedagogic approaches to employing technology (e.g. digital storytelling).

As alluded to in the volume, teachers, practitioners and researchers from different and even related disciplines draw upon varying conceptual and/or theoretical frameworks to describe, interpret, explain and make normative judgements about a similar phenomenon under the spotlight. Likewise, authors of the chapters hold varying ontological, epistemological, pedagogical and methodological positions–implicitly or explicitly–about what constitutes the seminal constructs of co-teaching and co-researching. Far from detracting, these epistemically rich conceptualisations and the spectrum of theorisations inherently reveal the usually undeclared ontological assumptions about the social contexts in which co-teaching and co-researching are seen to be operating. They showcase the wide range of primarily qualitative research methodologies used to investigate (e.g. case studies, participant action research, autoethnographies). However, axiologically, the notion of collaboration in the chapters appears to be underpinned by a remarkably similar set of deep-seated, socially just values across the geographically dispersed sites of implementation and research.

Inspired by the use of Appiah's (2006) Cosmopolitanism: Ethics in a World of Strangers in Chapter 8 of this volume, I wholeheartedly endorse the idea that we "can learn [from] each other's arguments and beliefs without trying to bend the other to his or her will". This edited volume exhibits 'cosmopolitanism' in action, and I trust that readers entering this conversation will be provoked by each case and, in turn, be galvanised into action to extend collaborative practices to encourage economically, culturally and politically inclusive teaching and research.

Chapter 1

Introduction

Daniela Gachago

University of Cape Town, South Africa

Phindile Zifikile Shangase

University of the Free State, South Africa

Eunice Ndeto Ivala

Cape Peninsula University of Technology, South Africa

Collaboration in a global world

There has been a recent surge of interest in the concept of co-teaching across institutions of HE, globally and locally, as a response to limited international mobility due to COVID-19. Traditionally, co-teaching emerged in fields such as teacher education, where pre-service teachers had to practice team teaching as part of their postgraduate training (Guise et al., 2017). More recently, co-teaching has been introduced as a response to the massification of access to HE (Morelock et al., 2017), but also in the context of internationalisation and globalisation. For this book, however, we use a broader definition of co-teaching (and co-research) following Murphy and Martin (2015), who see co-teaching as "two or more teachers teaching together, sharing responsibility for meeting the learning needs of students, and, at the same time, *learning from each other*" (emphasis added). We see co-teaching and co-research as teaching and research that connects educators and learners across different institutions and different contexts, be it across South Africa, Africa or the world. We very deliberately linked co-teaching and co-research to the term 'networked learning', following the Networked Learning Editorial Collective's (2021) emphasis on relationships and collaboration rather than technology and foregrounding our strong commitment to social justice.

As such, our definition of co-teaching has much in common with what the literature terms 'Collaborative Online International Learning' (COIL), which connects classrooms across geographical locations to create an environment that fosters the development of intercultural competence skills with the use of technology (Appiah-Kubi & Annan, 2020), although some of the contributions in this edited collection move beyond the classroom, involving community-based organisations and other partner institutions.

Co-teaching in such a 'global classroom' (Kahn & Agnew, 2017) gives students the opportunity to hear multiple perspectives on the same topic and to learn from experts within and outside their institutions (Minett-Smith & Davis, 2019). This supports global citizenship education (Stewart & Gachago, 2016), broadens the potential student base, can extend a university brand, and offers cross-institutional networking and research opportunities (Clark & Wilson, 2017).

These partnerships have great potential to bring together students, teachers and community partners from widely differing backgrounds, cultures and locations to combine global perspectives and local relevance (Stewart & Gachago, 2016). Co-teaching and co-research can support institutions' efforts of internationalisation, a critical component of institutional culture, by creating academic mobility while 'staying at home'(Tanhueco-Nepomuceno, 2019). Most importantly, however, it can establish mentoring relationships (Cordie, Brecke, Lin & Wooten, 2020), allowing us to *learn from each other.* Despite the above advantages, over half of the universities' collaborative teaching ventures have failed, with participants blaming bureaucratic administration, departmental silo mentality, work ethics, lack of flexibility and cultural barriers to working together (Morelock et al., 2017). Furthermore, collaboration between universities is difficult and often fails due to a lack of a shared vision, poor administrative support and difficulties with funding arrangements (ibid). Also, while online co-teaching is expanding, its use at the undergraduate or graduate level is still not widely spread (Clark & Wilson, 2017).

Co-teaching and co-researching in the Global South

Co-teaching and co-research are of particular interest to African countries, as they often lack the funding to allow international academic mobility for their lecturers and students. Technologies such as institutional learning management systems (LMS), as well as shared collaboration spaces, such as Google Drive, web-conferencing tools, such as Zoom and MsTeams, and social media, such as WhatsApp and Facebook, have allowed international connection and engagement that was previously hard to achieve. The world has become smaller but not less complex. While technically, solutions are here to connect academics and students across the globe, there is little research on *how* to connect them in a way that recognises and values differences while being conscious of how these differences affect academics and students in different ways.

Local studies we found in our literature review include Cloete et al.'s (2015) paper on four universities' attempts at facilitating creative engagements between students and educators in theatre and performance classrooms. This project involved Massey University (New Zealand), the University of Cape Town (South Africa), UWC Mahindra College (India), and the University of the Witwatersrand (South Africa). Shared syllabi that enabled the co-production of a visual/digital archive were developed, supported by online forums to facilitate discussions and collaborative learning between students. Based on student requests, a closed Facebook group page allowed student interaction and the sharing of course materials. Some of the challenges students reported were the need for live interaction for a more productive collaboration since this was a theatrical project; the lack of motivation, as this was not a graded component, as well as of non-virtual interactions; different time zones; as well as limitations of access and availability of resources that were exacerbated by different geopolitical learning environments.

A partnership project between two large Schools of Education in Australia (Edith Cowan University) and South Africa (Stellenbosch University) engaged in collaboration to promote the integration of technology-enhanced learning in initial teacher education programmes and the empowerment of staff to integrate blended learning in their curriculum (Lane, Carl & Strydom, 2015). In this project, collaborators applied a socio-constructivist approach combining face-to-face visits (a series of collegial professional visits) and online collaboration. A blended model was adopted that allowed researchers to gather data via face-to-face semi-structured interviews on the design and implementation of an ICT-rich mode of delivery in undergraduate teacher education programmes. This study concluded that while students were able to use online tools in a social context, they were not competent in integrating these in the academic context. Institutional support was therefore identified as essential within the following components: infrastructure, content, human resources, management, and policy.

Moving beyond the South African border, a project involving high school students from Colombia, the Czech Republic, Turkey, and Guinea created an open-source Java-based course-in-a-box curriculum to co-teach Computer Sciences across borders while adapting to a wide variety of local teaching practices and languages (powered by Google Translate and human translators), to translate the entire course into non-English languages and cultures (Piech et al., 2020). In this model, students experienced high-quality learning being taught by instructors from different countries. This initiative has also proven to be a high-impact professional development experience for university instructors and undergraduate teaching assistants from different universities. It facilitated the open transfer of pedagogical ideas, cultural understanding, and technical know-how to both students and instructors.

Finally, a COIL project between engineering technology students from the University of Dayton (UD) and environmental engineering students from the University of Ghana (UG) showed that these students not only valued the international collaboration but also improved their performance in their project work by drawing on students' different perspectives leading to better solutions (Appiah-Kuby & Annan, 2020).

While these are interesting studies and provide important pointers as to how co-teaching and co-research can be successful, there is little research that tackles differences beyond the expected ones, such as technical access or digital literacies. In particular, issues around unequally distributed issues of power and influence – often linked to international funding bodies' agendas and interests – are not adequately explored and discussed widely as yet (Boughey & McKenna, 2021; Mkwananzi & Cin, 2021).

Our passion for co-teaching and co-research

As editors of this book, we have been passionate about co-teaching and co-research for many years. Some of our earliest publications focus on lessons learnt from bringing together students from Botswana and the United States of America to discuss issues on adult education using an online discussion forum (Giannini-Gachago & Seleka, 2005). We have reflected on what happens when we create a Facebook group for South African and American students to share their assumptions and beliefs about the *other*, and how engaging with their (digital) stories challenged some of these (Stewart & Gachago, 2016). We have written about the difficulties of engaging in co-research with lecturers and students (Ngoasheng et al., 2019) and how important it is to set up guidelines and rules of engagement in advance and create enough space and time to work within and continuously reflect on how these highly uneven power structures impact on our relationships.

This book came about through a conversation about co-teaching between Zifikile and Daniela, where Zifikile shared her experiences in setting up a pilot synchronous virtual classroom (VC) to facilitate the co-teaching of Research Methods to Master's students, a collaboration between the University of KwaZulu-Natal (UKZN) and the University of Botswana. This was before COVID-19 made Zoom a common learning platform across the world. Extensive consultation and planning took place prior to setting up the VC, which involved ensuring availability and access to appropriate infrastructure for the project. Since both universities used Moodle as their learning management system, the VC was set up via the BigBlueButton (BBB) web-conferencing technology. Upon reflecting on this project,[1] Zifikile noted many challenges, such as network interruptions during the day due to the size of bandwidth, especially at the University of Botswana. But she also recognised the need for facilitation skills as well as confidence in using technology among facilitators. Despite these challenges, she clearly saw the potential of co-teaching using existing resources and infrastructure, leading to capacity building of academics as well as enhancement of students' 21st century literacy skills, which led to the conceptualisation of this book project.

Our collective experiences have shown that co-teaching and co-research are not easy endeavours, especially when they involve differently positioned and differently resourced contexts, students and academics. These collaborations are enriching and exciting but need careful support, preparation and time for sustained relationship building – topics that we find are not necessarily discussed in the literature around co-teaching and co-research.

Contributions to co-teaching and co-researching in this book

This book is an attempt towards closing this gap in knowledge, providing a range of chapters documenting personal experiences of academics and practitioners engaging in co-teaching and co-research across the African continent and beyond, facilitated by various networked learning tools and technologies. Some of the insights the book provides are on the benefits and challenges of such collaborations, affordances of technologies to bridge unequal divides, emerging practices of continental collaboration and beyond, framed by a spirit of sharing and connection. The book is divided into two main sections: *Connecting Africa through co-teaching and co-research* and *Connecting Africa and the world through co-teaching and co-research*. Both sections offer a mix of conceptual, empirical and reflective/autoethnographic chapters.

Section 1 consists of six chapters, connecting both institutions within South Africa and across the African continent. The first two chapters reflect on inter-institutional experiences of teaching and learning within Postgraduate Studies. Employing Therborn and Aboim's (2014) three categories to define inequality, Archer's (1995) meta-theoretical concept of social change, Rancière's (2006) concept of democratic education, Brown's (2009) notion of design thinking and Berger's (2004) use of liminality, Chapter 2 describes and explores the complexities of inter-institutional collaboration among academics from contextually different HE institutions in the Western Cape province in South Africa. The authors highlight the value of negotiating different worldviews, accommodating

---

[1] https://sobeds.ukzn.ac.za/news/2019/02/setting-up-a-virtual-classroom-explored-in-workshop/

different contexts, valuing co-creation, embracing uncertain spaces and taking steps towards the shared ownership of learning.

Through the methodology of narrative research (Kyratzis & Green, 1997), Chapter 3 provides a reflection on a case of blended co-teaching, co-learning and co-researching among academics and students in cross-cultural contexts to facilitate inter-institutional collaborative spaces, with the support of a range of networked technologies. This chapter draws on Colbry et al.'s (2014) collaboration theory as a framework for interpreting their findings, which highlights the competencies of turn-taking, observing or doing, status-seeking/collegiality, building group consensus, organising and influencing others.

Chapter 4 describes a university-industry collaboration (UIC) motivated by the shared pursuit of demographic transformation of the architectural profession. Using a critical action research approach, the authors reflect on the collaboration of the Cape Peninsula University of Technology with Open Architecture, a non-profit transformation unit linked to the South African Institute of Architects. Guided by Zavale and Langa's (2018) UIC model, which addresses 1) the modes or channels of interaction, 2) the kind of knowledge and resources that universities and firms exchange, and 3) the outcomes yielded from these processes, they show that industry can play a catalytic role where university systems fall short, to implement educational innovation for transformation. This case revealed a different kind of bi-directional educational UIC: one that follows an irrational process that relies on the informal social interactions between the organisations, producing results that were not possible through the individual efforts of the respective collaborators and relying on the unique contributions of individuals and teams.

Moving from co-teaching to co-research, Chapter 5 provides a broad sweep of current literature to explicate the concept of 'co-researching', and highlights some of the benefits, implications and challenges of this practice. Although networked technologies are mentioned as a way of facilitating co-research, it is the attention drawn to the socio-cultural practices of publishing embedded in the rules of engagement between students and their supervisors, interdisciplinary partnerships and/or networks that are most insightful.

Chapter 6 creatively combines Bower's (2008) affordance analysis for e-learning design and Sharples et al.'s (2009) generative framework for new modes of learning as a design methodology to interrogate the match between affordances of technology and the co-creating, co-teaching and co-research activities undertaken by the Partnership for African Social and Governance Research (PASGR) in collaboration with various scholarly, pedagogic, commercial and civic communities. Their personal reflections incisively highlight the key contextual challenges (e.g. affordability, capacity, connectivity, motivation, rapid technological development) as well as possible mitigating strategies (e.g.

mobile technologies, virtual communities of practice and funding for data, when necessary and where possible).

Finally, the last chapter in Section 1, Chapter 7, adapts a community-based participatory action research (Balazs & Morello-Frosch, 2013) methodology with elements of community of practice (Lave, 1991; Wenger 1998) and appreciative inquiry (Kevany & MacMichael, 2014) elements, to describe a community-based intervention for young mothers in a resource-constrained rural area in northern South Africa. Of interest is that after finishing this combined custom-created Information and Communications Technology (ICT) and basic adult education nutrition skills training course, the young mothers were alert to the benefit of ICT skills to improve their employment prospects. The findings of this study highlight the powerful effect of a cooperative co-research and co-teaching community education intervention for young mothers in a resource-limited rural area of South Africa and show affordances as "possibilities for action" that can be "both enabling and constraining".

Section 2 moves beyond the African content to connect African institutions of higher learning with the rest of the world, critically reflecting on the opportunities such collaborations can offer to partners but also highlighting issues of power and inequalities. The first chapter in this section, Chapter 8, draws upon a number of feminist, new materialist, critical race, critical pedagogy and cultural theoretical perspectives to thoughtfully expose economic, cultural and political tensions, resonances, dissonances and silences in an international collaboration between South African engineering students and students of composition in the United States. Two of the discernible benefits of this deliberately arranged "pedagogy of discomfort" (Boler & Zembylas, 2003) via WhatsApp were the students' increased spatial gaze and glints of cultural awareness.

Chapter 9 adopts a quantitative case study methodology to explore South African, Brazilian and American students' perspectives of professional practice in dental disciplines and their cultural differences, competency and co-constructed knowledge in a Collaborative Online International Learning (COIL) virtual exchange project (VEP). The authors adopt Boschma's (2005) distance/proximity dynamics theory to provide a conceptual framework to discern more sharply the intertwined geographic, social, cultural, cognitive, institutional and organisational relationships among students from globally diverse geo-locations. An important insight is the need for the faculty of the co-developed and co-taught modules to provide additional interaction and oversight to ensure overtly defined and consistent expectations and outcomes for all student groups in the VEP.

Applying a collaborative autoethnographic research methodology, the authors of Chapter 10 explore co-learning and co-teaching in online and blended modes at two South African and two Australian Schools of Architecture. As a response to some of the pressing challenges related to architectural studio education globally, the authors use collaborative autoethnography to describe the design and implementation of this inter-institutional collaboration across economic, cultural and geopolitical boundaries. They discuss seven themes that emerged from their reflections, connecting: online and on-ground spaces; the university and the profession; digital learning and teaching tools; students and educators; educators locally and globally; students and international experts; and students through peer-to-peer learning. From these themes, they derive four principles for the conceptualisation and implementation of connected co-learning and co-teaching in online and blended global architecture studios: employ relevant technologies and techniques through learning design; acknowledge students as partners to promote student agency and well-being; consider flexibility through multiple interlinked learning settings and modes; and recognise humanity, humour, culture, and community.

Chapter 11 focuses on another under-researched topic: the investigation of collaborative processes among researchers. As members of an international collaborative research group, the authors use a team ethnography approach to examine their research practices following the ABCs of collaboration shared by Amundsen et al. (2019): Acknowledging the Affective, Becoming Bolder and Cultivating Creativity. The authors discuss the research process and their theoretical lenses, ethos and practices that they used to design that process. This is followed by emerging principles to ensure committed and sustained engagement in collaborative research online. They emphasise the importance of recentring researchers by creating a flexible and equitable space for collaborators and putting effort into building relationships, rather than being output driven.

Applying a participatory action research (cf. Martin et al., 2019) approach to a collaboration between a grassroots organisation based in a slum in Nairobi and the Storytelling Academy at a university in the United Kingdom (UK), Chapter 12 discusses the potential of digital storytelling through a range of case studies of community-led solutions to the design of urban spaces. Drawing upon the notion of communities of practice (Wenger-Trayner et al., 2014), the authors critically highlight digital storytelling's potential to affirm the local knowledge of community members. They also highlight the importance of recognising each partner's strengths and working towards structures to empower the local NGO to sustainably continue the work in their communities, allowing the HE partner to withdraw from the project.

Chapter 13, informed by design thinking principles (Von Thienen et al., 2017), and framed by a theory of change as proposed by O'Flynn and Moberly (2017), reflects on a short-term cross-country project with early-career researchers and practitioners from South Africa and the UK to explore the different ways in which HE could improve students from marginalised communities access, completion and success in their studies. The authors provide both a useful critique and a perspicacious appreciation of the challenges they faced in organising the SA-UK engagement across many geographical, socio-cultural and socio-political boundaries, highlighting the need for reflexivity within the partners who were positioned as more powerful.

Finally, the afterword by Maha Bali offers a critical gaze on 'Scholarly Collaboration', highlighting both the pains and the gains of such engagements, and concludes this edited collection.

We are particularly proud of this book, which provides an unusually honest and nuanced view on co-teaching and co-research across contexts of inequalities, foregrounding relationship- and community-building rather than technology and emphasising the importance of sustained connection and reflection in these collaborations. Applying a wide range of critical theoretical frameworks, these evidence-based but also reflective and reflexive contributions are a unique and important reminder that behind and through our screens, we connect as humans who yearn to learn from each other but also need to learn *how* to learn from each other when we do not share the same world views. As Maha Bali so aptly writes, this book invites you to ask yourself: "As you read through these chapters, what messages resonated most with you? How might you approach collaboration differently now?"

While this edited collection by no means answers all the questions in relation to co-teaching and co-research across contexts of inequality and has limitations, such as the strong focus on South Africa, we are hoping that it will encourage others to enter co-teaching and co-research opportunities but also to contribute to a much-needed conversation around collaborating across unequal contexts and add to the growing body of knowledge in this field.

References

Amundsen, D., Ballam, N., & Cosgriff, M. (2019). The ABCs of collaboration in academia. *Waikato Journal of Education, 24*(2), 39-53.

Appiah-Kubi, P. & Annan, E. (2020). A Review of a Collaborative Online International Learning. *Engineering Management and Systems Faculty Publications*, 2. https://ecommons.udayton.edu/enm_fac_pub/2

Archer, M.S. (1995). *Realist social theory: The morphogenetic approach.* Cambridge: Cambridge University Press.

Balazs, C.L. & Morello-Frosch, R. (2013). The three Rs: How community-based participatory research strengthens the rigor, relevance, and reach of science. *Environmental Justice, 6*(1), 9-16.

Berger, J. G. (2004), Dancing on the threshold of meaning: Recognizing and understanding the growing edge. *Journal of Transformative Education, 2*(4), 336-351. doi: 10.1177/1541344604267697

Boler, M. & Zembylas, M. (2003). Discomforting truths: The emotional terrain of understanding differences. In P. Trifonas (Ed.), *Pedagogies of Difference: Rethinking education for social justice*. New York, NY: Routledge.

Boschma, R. (2005). Proximity and innovation: A critical assessment. *Regional Studies, 39*(1), 61-74. doi: 10.1080/0034340052000320887

Boughey C. & McKenna, S. (2021). Interrogating the power dynamics in international projects. Critical Studies in Learning and Teaching (CriSTaL), 9(2), 64-82. https://www.cristal.ac.za/index.php/cristal/article/view/448/317

Bower, M. (2008). Affordance analysis–matching learning tasks with learning technologies. *Educational Media International, 45*(1), 3-15.

Brown, T. (2009). Change by Design. New York, NY.: HarperCollins. http://books.google.com/books?id=x7PjWyVUoVAC&pgis=1

Clark, C.H., & Wilson, B.P. (2017). The potential for university collaboration and online learning to internationalise geography education. *Journal of Geography in Higher Education, 41*(4), 488-505. doi: 10.1080/03098265.2017.1337087.

Cloete, N., Dinesh, N., Hazou R.T. & Matchett. S. (2015). E(Lab)orating performance: transnationalism and blended learning in the theatre classroom. *Research in Drama Education: The Journal of Applied Theatre and Performance, 20*(4), 470-48. doi: 10.1080/13569783.2015.1065723.

Colbry, S., Hurwitz, M. & Adair, R. (2014). Collaboration theory. *Journal of Leadership Education, 13*(14), 63-75.

Cordie, L. et al. (2020). Co-Teaching in Higher Education: Mentoring as Faculty Development. *International Journal on Teaching and Learning in Higher Education, 32*(1), 149-158.

Giannini-Gachago, D., & Seleka, G. (2005). Experiences with international online discussions: Participation patterns of Botswana and American students in an Adult Education and Development course at the University of Botswana. *International Journal of Education and Development using ICT (IJEDICT), 1*(2). http://ijedict.dec.uwi.edu/viewarticle.php?id=42&layout=html

Guise, M., Habib, M. Thiessen, K. & Robbins, A. (2017). Continuum of co-teaching implementation: Moving from traditional student teaching to co-teaching. *Teaching and Teacher Education,* 66.

Kahn, H.E., & Agnew, M. (2017). Global learning through difference: Considerations for teaching, learning, and the internationalization of higher education. *Journal of Studies in International Education,* 21(1), 52-64. doi: 10.1177/102831531562202

Kevany, K.M., & MacMichael, M. (2014). Communities of knowledge and knowledge of communities: An appreciative inquiry into rural wellbeing. *Gateways: International Journal of Community Research and Engagement,* 7(1), 34-51

Kyratzis, A., & Green, J. (1997). Jointly constructed narratives in classrooms: Co-construction of friendship and community through language. *Teaching and Teacher Education, 13*, pp. 17-37.

Lane, J., Carl, A.E., & Strydom, S. 2015. The integration of technology enhanced learning in initial teacher education programmes: Collaborative research from Australia and South Africa. *AARE Conference,* Western Australia 2015.

Lave, J. (1991). Situating learning in communities of practice. *Perspectives on Socially Shared Cognition, 2*, 63-82.

Martin, S.B., Burbach, J.H., Benitez, L.L., & Ramiz, I. (2019). Participatory action research and co-researching as a tool for situating youth knowledge at the centre of research. *London Review of Education, 17*(3), 297-313.

Minett-Smith, C. & Davis, C.L. (2019). Widening the discourse on team-teaching in higher education. *Teaching in Higher Education, 0*(0), 1-16. doi: 10.1080/13562517.2019.1577814

Mkwananzi, F. & Cin, M. (2021). Equal research partnerships are a myth – but we can change that. *THE Campus (Times Higher Education)*. https://www.timeshighereducation.com/campus/equal-research-partnerships-are-myth-we-can-change?s=03

Morelock, J.R., Lester, M.M.G., Klopfer, M.D., Jardon, A.M., Mullins, R.D., Nicholas, E.L., & Alfaydi, A. S. (2017). Power, perceptions, and relationships: A model of co-teaching in higher education. *College Teaching, 65*(4), pp. 182-191. doi: 10.1080/87567555.2017.1336610

Murphy, C., & and Martin, S. (2015). Coteaching in Teacher Education: Research and Practice. *Asia-Pacific Journal of Teacher Education, 43*(4), pp. 277-280.

Ngoasheng, A., Cupido, X., Oyekola, S., Gachago, D., Mpofu, A. & Mbekela, Y. (2019). Advancing democratic values in higher education through open curriculum co-creation: Towards an epistemology of uncertainty. In L.E. Quinn (Ed.), *Reimaging Curricula: Spaces for Disruption* (pp. 324-344). Stellenbosch: African Sun Media. doi: 10.1093/0198294719.001.0001

Networked Learning Editorial Collective (NLEC) et al.(2021). Networked Learning in 2021: A Community Definition. Postdigital Sciiences in Education, *3*, pp. 326–369. https://doi.org/10.1007/s42438-021-00222-y

O'Flynn, M. & Moberly, C. (2017). *Theory of Change.* Rovigo, Italy: Intrac. https://www.intrac.org/wpcms/wp-content/uploads/2017/01/Theory-of-Change.pdf

Piech, C., Yan, L., Einstein, L., Saavedra, A., Bozkurt, B., Sestakova, E., Guth, O. & McKeown, N. (2020). Co-teaching computer science across borders: Human-centric learning at scale. *L@S '20*, Virtual Event, USA.

Rancière, J. (2006). *Hatred of democracy.* New York, NY: Verso.

Sharples, M., Crook, C., Ian, J., Kay, D., Chowcat, I., Balmer, K. & Stokes, E. (2009). *New Modes of Technology-enhanced Learning: Opportunities and challenges.* http://www.becta.org.uk on 18-02-16.

Stewart, K. & Gachago, D. (2016). Being human today: A digital storytelling pedagogy for transcontinental border crossing. *British Journal of Educational Technology, 47*(3), pp. 528-542. doi: 10.1111/bjet.12450.

Tanhueco-Nepomuceno, L. (2019). Internationalization among selected HEIs in the ASEAM region: Basis for a proposed framework for an internationalized campus. *International Journal of educational Development, 65*, pp. 153-171.

Therborn, G. & Aboim, S. (2014). The killing fields of inequality. *Análise Social, 212*, pp. 729-735.

Von Thienen, J., Royalty, A. & Meinel, C. (2017). Design thinking in higher education: How students become dedicated creative problem solvers. In Zhou, C. (Ed.), *Handbook of research on creative problem-solving skill development in higher education* (pp. 306-328). Hershey, PA: IGI Global.

Wenger, E. (1998). Communities of practice: Learning as a social system. *Systems Thinker, 9*(5), pp. 2-3.

Wenger-Trayner, E., Fenton-O'Creevy, M., Kubiak, C., Hutchinson, S.& Wenger-Trayner, B. (Eds). (2014). *Learning in Landscapes of Practice: Boundaries, identity, and knowledgeability in practice-based learning.* Abingdon: Routledge. http://www.routledge.com/books/details/97811380221.

Zavale, N. & Langa, P. (2018). University-industry linkages' literature on Sub-Saharan Africa: Systematic literature review and bibliometric account. *Scientometrics, 116*(1), pp. 1-49. doi: 10.1007/s11192-018-2760-4

Section 1:
Connecting Africa through
co-teaching and co-research

Chapter 2

Enabling inter-institutional co-design and co-facilitation of a postgraduate diploma module in educational technology: Uncovering sites of struggle, negotiation and accommodation among course facilitators

Sonja Strydom

Stellenbosch University, South Africa

Simone Titus

University of the Western Cape, South Africa

Faiq Waghid

Cape Peninsula University of Technology, South Africa

Daniela Gachago

University of Cape Town, South Africa

Abstract

The development of a curriculum for a diverse group of students is challenging, whether at the undergraduate or postgraduate level. Various social, organisational, political, cultural, and personal factors are at play in the process of designing a curriculum that is learning-centred and responsive to societal needs. The notion of learning-centred curriculum development has been addressed extensively in the literature; however, scant research focuses on the interests of agents, as well as the cultural and structural considerations at play, when designing a postgraduate module for participants from diverse and unequal backgrounds. Analysing written reflections and reflective conversations on the various events, mechanisms, and structures encountered during the process of curriculum development, we shed new light on the covert issues facilitators have had to acknowledge when designing a learning-centred curriculum for participants across vastly diverse higher education contexts in South Africa. Drawing on sociologist Margaret Archer's research, we seek to provide insight into the interplay between structure, culture, and agency when course facilitators from different institutional backgrounds collaboratively designed and facilitated a postgraduate module in educational technology.

Keywords: curriculum design, co-design, inter-institutional collaboration, co-facilitation, PGDip, educational technology, structure, culture and agency, South Africa

***

Introduction

We present facilitators' reflections on inter-institutional conceptualisation and facilitation of a module that forms part of the Postgraduate Diploma (PGDip) in Teaching and Learning in Higher Education offered by three differently positioned institutions in the Western Cape, South Africa. As authors and course facilitators, we have worked together for many years and have offered this module three times since 2015. In the Western Cape, there is a drive to support such inter-institutional collaboration, driven by the Cape Higher Education Consortium (see www.chec.co.za), instituted to support systemic collaboration between the four higher education institutions (HEIs) in the region, namely the University of the Western Cape, Cape Peninsula University of Technology, Stellenbosch University and the University of Cape Town. This is one way of sharing resources and redressing some of the historical inequalities in terms of student access and success in the Western Cape.

Collaboration across such differently placed institutions is not without its challenges. We use our experiences to unpack some of the opportunities and tensions in inter-institutional collaborative postgraduate teaching. In the conceptualisation of the elective module 'ICTs in Teaching and Learning in Higher Education,' we, as facilitators, had to consider a number of factors. While we occupy similar positions at our institutions, namely, supporting academics in the acquisition of digital literacies, course/curriculum development, and advancing the scholarship of teaching and learning, our institutions have different histories and cultures. These contextual factors impact our approach to curriculum development, possible theoretical frameworks to consider, understanding of how learning transpires, and how facilitators subsequently respond to creating learning experiences.

One particular challenge is the inequalities observed within all of the represented HEIs, manifested to varying degrees of prominence. We define inequalities here as avoidable, morally unjustified, hierarchical differences (Therborn & Aboim, 2014). Therborn and Aboim (2014) refer to three forms of inequality: vital inequality, resource inequality, and existential inequality. Vital inequality refers to survival rates and life chances. Studies indicate that educated people generally live longer (Meara, Richards & Cutler, 2008), as do their parents, since they have the socioeconomic resources to take better care of themselves and their children (Friedman & Mare, 2014; Ingraham, 2014). HEIs in South Africa are characterised by heterogenous student cohorts, with many being first-generation students. Retention of some of these first-generation students is often at risk, as they are unable to draw on the socioeconomic support of their parents (Bui, 2002). Failure to succeed in university studies as a consequence of being inadequately supported may diminish their life chances and further exacerbate prevailing vital inequality.

Therborn and Aboim (2014) also refer to existential inequality, another form of marginalisation or discrimination. For example, teacher-centred pedagogical practices may be deemed inadequate to address the higher-order learning needs of students in general and first-generation students in particular (Waghid, 2019a). Such pedagogical practices are still prominent at many of the aforementioned HEIs. Finally, resource inequality refers to the unequal distribution of resources (Therborn & Aboim, 2014). Although primarily concerned with the uneven distribution of material resources, this has been expanded to include the lack of skills and competencies to function effectively in higher education (HE) and beyond (Waghid, 2019b). Given the presence of participants from different HEIs in South Africa, we had to acknowledge how these intersecting inequalities were playing out at the different institutions and consider participants' attempts to mitigate them. Not just the participants' contexts had to be considered, but also the respective levels of inequality in the institutions of the facilitators.

We offer a reflection on the facilitators' teaching and learning practices in the PGDip module, which interrogates these processes as they relate to the co-design and co-facilitation of the curriculum. This involves being cognisant and intentional about negotiating differences, contextual accommodation, embracing co-creation of learning, adapting the approach to uncertain spaces, and sharing ownership. This chapter also outlines a theoretical lens through which we consider how structure, culture, teaching and learning, as well as curriculum, could shape an inter-institutional curriculum design and facilitation process.

Structure, culture, and agency: An overview

The interplay and interrelatedness of structure, culture, and agency need to be considered in terms of the way facilitators acknowledge the interaction between themselves and the collaborative teaching environment. We offer insight into the dualism between structure, culture, and agency to describe various social and cultural phenomena that occurred in the conceptualisation and implementation of this collaborative design module.

In terms of our understanding of structure and agency, we draw on the research of sociologist Margaret Archer (1995) and her morphogenetic approach; she argues that both structure and agency consist of emergent powers, which are distinguished from each other. Archer (1995, 2000) warns against limited approaches to understanding social behaviour and suggests that individuals, as well as the social world in which they act, have powers and influences that should be acknowledged. Mutual interaction between the two entities results in relational interaction with one another. This implies that there is "no difference between the individual and society, rather there is a continuous and ubiquitous interaction and symbiosis between these two" (Banifatemeh et al., 2018, p. 59). This implies that we had to acknowledge that as agents in our different social contexts, we are not separated from the structural contexts we emanate from because there is a link between ourselves and the social world we represent.

To explain the social world and the interrelated nature of structure, culture, and agency, Archer (1995) posits that the social world could be either dynamic (morphogenesis) or stable and an extension of the current societal systems (morphostasis). To be enabled to uncover the processes of morphogenesis or morphostasis, the process of analytical dualism was useful.

Through the process of analytical dualism, structure and agency could be separated analytically over a period of time to interrogate the interplay between them (Zeuner, 1999). This enabled the relationship between them to be analysed further (King, 2010). It implies that, as authors, we could separate our own experiences of structure and agency over a period, to consider the relationship between the two entities. Although, according to Archer (1995), structure and agency are closely linked, the impact on each other could really only be understood when these notions are analytically separated (Zeuner, 1999). Through the separation of structure and agency, the agents are better able to understand the opportunities and challenges in their respective structural contexts (Newman, 2017). Additionally, reflexive activities afford agents the opportunity to duplicate or expand on structural components (Newman, 2017). We used reflexive activities in our methodology to establish an awareness of unique structural components that we had experienced in our various institutions, and how these impacted on our choices and agency in the design and facilitation of the module.

Archer (1995) emphasises two aspects of structure: first, the assumption that structures are emergent and impacted by "material resources, both physical and human" (p. 175), and second, that in practice structures are aligned with "roles, organizations and systems" (Archer, 1995, p. 175, also cited in Leibowitz et al., 2015). Through this insight of Archer (1995) we established a close link between the differently resourced institutions (which we represent), as well as the cultural dimensions of each.

Culture refers to our "common beliefs and conventions which are unique to a particular group" (Van Wyk, 2011, p. 337). According to Archer, society further consists of a "cultural system" or "sociocultural layer" (Banifatemeh et al., 2018, p. 61). This implies that the social world consists of different knowledge forms, as well as a variety of belief systems. Therefore, agents have the capacity to influence one another through the sociocultural level of epistemic views and positions (Banifatemeh et al., 2018). To understand the difference between agency and culture, Archer's research explains that *culture* is a collective endeavour, whereas *agency* implies what we choose to do, or react towards, individually (Banifatemeh et al., 2018). In the context of this chapter, it was necessary to examine the aspects of the collective, which were evident in our various institutions, and the manner in which we decided to act in relation to the cultures we represent, while collaborating with each other and with participants in the course.

Human agency can be explained by an individual's ability to reflect on his/her actions, which is closely aligned with a process of "internal deliberation in which concerns, commitments and knowledgeability play a role" (Leibowitz et al., 2015, p. 318). Personal agency implies that we each have the ability to action activities through a series of choices, possibilities, and duties. According to Archer (2007), agency is further understood through the process of reflexivity and internal deliberations that people employ to reflect on their current structural context, as well as how they are to further their association with such (Newman, 2017, p. 5). Archer's (1995) three levels of agency could be explained in terms of interest groups, social action, and personhood. Interest groups relate to the structures in which agents live and are reared, while social action refers to the different positions agents occupy in society. Lastly, personhood suggests that "any individual who changes roles or interest groups maintains their sense of selfhood as a single person, knitting together their past and present lives into a single life-story" (Newman, 2017, p. 6).

When considering our own practices, many structures and mechanisms are at play that will impact our experiences (Khan, Qualter & Young, 2012). Archer (1995) suggests a deeper understanding and acknowledgement of the interplay between structural elements, our own agency, and the institutional culture. To respond to the notion of emergence, as underscored by critical realism, the morphogenetic approach accentuates the need to interrogate relations between various emergent properties, namely the structural emergent properties, cultural emergent properties, and personal emergent properties (Mogashana, 2015).

Through the process of curriculum development based on our own teaching philosophies, personal and institutional backgrounds, and the contexts of the course participants, the structural, cultural, and agentic elements were evident in our curriculum decisions.

Curriculum decisions

We embraced a learning-centred approach to the curriculum development of this module; this veers away from facilitator-led initiatives, to thinking carefully of "how and how well students are learning" (Blumberg, 2016, p. 303). This requires facilitators to reconsider aspects such as the role of content; the responsibility of the teacher (or facilitator) and student (or participant); the reason for and approaches associated with assessment; and the power relations between teachers and students (Blumberg, 2016). A learning-centred approach emphasises the process of learning, and not–as seen in many HE practices–the transmission of knowledge (Von der Heidt & Quazi, 2013). A common misconception in HE suggests that students need to be *taught*, instead of highlighting what they could contribute to the teaching and learning process. These teacher-centred pedagogical practices leave little room for student engagement, and may be deemed undemocratic. A form of democratic education was proposed throughout this PGDip, which would leverage participants' involvement while drawing on the ideas of French philosopher Jacques Rancière (2006).

Rancière (2006) offers a progressive understanding of democratic education. Traditional practices involve organising teachers and students to engage with one another critically. As a student of Louis Althusser, during the 1960s Rancière dissociated himself from his teacher's work due to his understanding of the notion of equality (Simons & Masschelein, 2011). Rancière (2006) argues that Althusser viewed equality as a promise or reward to attain through democratic education practices (Simons & Masschelein, 2011, p. 3). Consequently, a void is maintained between inequality and a distant equality, resulting in student and teacher remaining separated. Thus students, who are incapable of deliberating, and those who can deliberate remain apart. Rancière (2006) challenges the aforementioned view of equality, and argues that equality is an entitlement for all. By implication, democratic education "is no longer a process of inclusion of excluded parties into the existing [democratic] order; it rather is a transformation of that order in the name of equality . . . [and the] impetus for the transformation does not come from inside but from the outside" (Biesta, 2009, p. 110). In a way, democratic education is about those who have no or little power, are less qualified, or less competent, but nevertheless intervene to install a momentary disruption and dissensus. For Rancière (2006, p. 18), democratic education is sporadic. It affords individuals from the *outside*, with less powerful voices, the opportunity to disrupt or interrupt the practices claimed as democratic education, in the name of equality.

Design thinking is a design approach that values collaboration, experimentation, and contextualisation as driving forces for innovation (Brown, 2009). Moving from designing *for* participants to designing *with* participants promotes a make-do mind-set, working from a position of strength and viewing challenges as opportunities to innovate. Instead of pointing out the resources that are inaccessible, it starts to list which resources are available, and builds solutions around those (Brown, 2009; Kelley & Kelley, 2014). This refers to the importance of considering resource inequality. Design thinking also allows us to understand learning in places of uncertainty, in ill-defined contexts, while attacking wicked problems (Buchanan, 1992) with no simple answers. A design mind-set embraces this uncertainty, and sees it as a space to grow and be creative. This links to Berger's (2004) ideas around innovation in teacher education. She argues that innovation and transformation happen in liminal spaces, on the edges of knowing (p. 338). These are spaces outside our normal practices that push us into the unknown. This learning on the edge of our knowledge could be enjoyable as well as produce anguish in participants. It is essential that facilitators of such processes are aware of this continuum and offer careful facilitation, providing, as Berger explains, openings for participants to push against the edge, and being company for them as they stand at the edge; once they are there, the growing edge is its own teacher.

Figure 2.1 illustrates the iterative nature of our learning design process, and the importance of empathetic, learning-centred approaches, by placing the learner at the centre of our curriculum design and facilitation process.

Figure 2.1. CPUT's learning experience design model

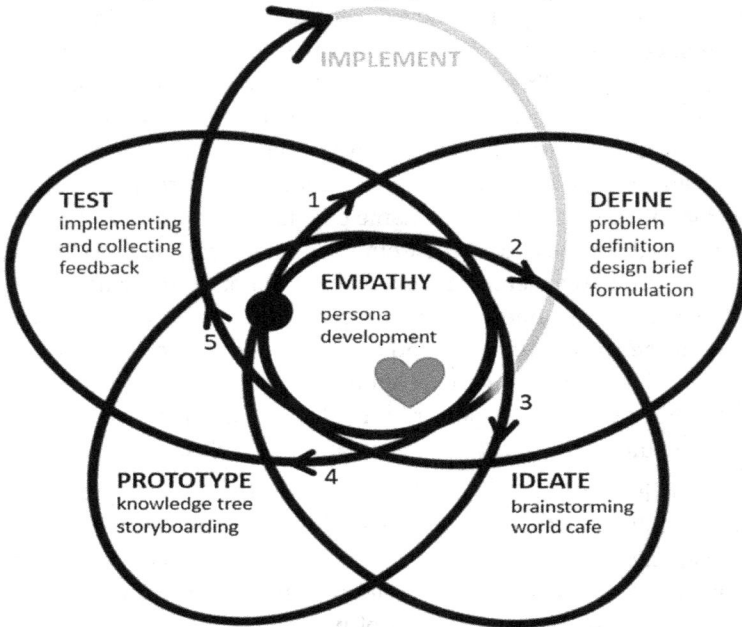

TEST
implementing
and collecting
feedback

DEFINE
problem
definition
design brief
formulation

EMPATHY
persona
development

PROTOTYPE
knowledge tree
storyboarding

IDEATE
brainstorming
world cafe

IMPLEMENT

(Gachago, Morkel, Van Zyl & Ivala, 2021)

Methodology

Our chapter aims to uncover various factors associated with structure, culture, agency, the curriculum and pedagogy, and provide a deeper understanding of inter-institutional collaborative design and co-facilitation, by attempting to make meaning of notable categories as described in the literature, following an exploratory research design (Marshall & Rossman, 2011). We adopted a deductive reflective approach to interrogate underlying factors that impact inter-institutional co-designing and co-facilitation of a module. We chose to engage in critical reflective conversations in the form of written individual reflections, which we shared and commented on, as well as ongoing conversations via MS Teams, which we recorded and transcribed, during the process of writing this chapter (Mezirow, 1990). As mentioned previously, through internal deliberation and reflexivity we started to uncover the different levels of agency, as well as the interrelation between it and the structural and cultural contexts of ourselves as module facilitators and participants. The topics that guided our reflections were based on the contexts we emanate from, an overview of the institutions we represent, reflections on our own identities, different theories we draw on, our different reasons for joining the collaborative course design and teaching initiative, as well as what we have learnt through the collaboration, and how it resonated with structure, culture, agency, curriculum, and pedagogy.

This collective engagement vis-a-vis similarities, sites of struggle, and examples of negotiation/accommodation in our practice of co-designing and co-facilitating, continued throughout data collection and analysis. Through thematic analysis the following findings could be observed as a product of our similarities, sites of struggle, and instances of negotiation, while mirroring our collective sense-making. A holistic overview of our experiences would go beyond the scope of this chapter, but we exemplify moments in our engagement based on a collective sense-making of our individual reflections. Pseudonyms were used to ensure anonymity. Table 2.1 provides some context of the facilitators.

Table 2.1: The facilitators' contexts

Facilitator	Context
Facilitator 1	Academic staff developer in a central support unit at a University of Technology, which serves predominantly underprivileged students. Been in this role for 20 years.
Facilitator 2	Academic developer at a centralised professional support centre, focusing on scholarly integration of learning technologies in the HE curriculum. Working at a historically advantaged institution which is research-focused. Has worked across further and higher education for 17 years.
Facilitator 3	Teaching and learning specialist with a focus on educational technology as a pedagogical practice at a University of Technology. Working in HE for 10 years across a range of different HEIs. Some of the roles include lecturer, staff developer, learning designer, project manager, and researcher.
Facilitator 4	Academic learning and teaching specialist at a historically disadvantaged institution. Has 12 years' experience in HE, with key focus areas in curriculum development in health professions education, learning with technologies, and professionalisation of learning and teaching.

Results

The results provide an analysis of our reflections on co-designing and co-facilitation of a module, involving the five categories explored above, namely structure, culture, agency, curriculum, and pedagogy.

Structure

In terms of structure, we agree that our collaboration in the module is situated outside our normal practices, within in-between, or liminal spaces (Berger, 2004). This allows freedom to innovate and push boundaries that may be less flexible in our own institutional contexts, as shown later. We see these liminal spaces as the origin for innovation, experimentation and learning, which we could transfer into our own individual practices, as Facilitator 1 reflects:

> Working outside one's own context and practice does allow sometimes innovation that would usually not be possible within one's context. You are allowed to experiment, push boundaries, challenge existing routines and practices more easily than within one's own context.

> Working outside our institution helps with moving beyond our comfort zones. I have been in the same institution–in the same position for 10 years and one can become comfortable in what one does. Having to expose myself to outside colleagues, helps me stay on my toes, innovate my practice.

In these liminal spaces, there is opportunity to work on a range of capabilities and concepts:

> I think it goes beyond curriculum and it goes beyond what you are able to do in a class. You know sometimes there are softer skills or softer social competencies that you are able to evoke onto people who cross your path, whether they are students or whether they are staff. (Facilitator 4)

What is also evident are the stark differences regarding resources from which individual lecturers and institutions can draw, be it facilities, internet access, devices, digital literacies, or epistemic access to the discourse of teaching and learning, as well as curriculum and course design. Although inequality exists across all institutions, this is experienced to different intensities by staff and students at the various institutions. Our colleagues from previously disadvantaged institutions indicated that they primarily provide support to more vulnerable students, who have little to no access to teaching and learning resources. In contrast, colleagues from more established institutions commented that it is, to an extent, potentially easier for them to support students with resources, if required.

Unequal resource access raises issues of social justice and equitable access, and emphasises the importance of creating learning spaces and experiences that allow equitable access and engagement, where possible. The shared face-to-face workshop spaces and online learning platforms and tools chosen for the cross-institutional application in this module helped to bridge some of these divides. The face-to-face interactions were crucial to support participants in the more unfamiliar online space:

> The initial [face-to-face] sessions set the scene and provided a safe and secure platform from which the unfamiliar and often frightening online space could be explored. (Facilitator 2)

However, the question of how to transfer what we and our course participants were exposed to within a relatively well-resourced PGDip module, into their own practices, needed constant negotiation and consideration. As discussed under pedagogy, this strongly impacted our learning design.

Culture

We represent HEIs ranging from older, well-established institutions to those that only recently achieved university status. In terms of managerial styles, we work in institutions that engage a more centralised approach, and some with more dispersed decision-making powers. Within these distinct contexts, innovation in teaching and learning is driven in different ways. For the more mature, centrally governed institutions, flexibility in teaching and learning could potentially be impacted by well-established institutional policies and structures:

> I did mention the fact that it's a–very much a privileged work environment that we have access to [with] quite a lot of funding that we have ... [with] different projects that are institutionally driven as well (Facilitator 2)

This context is atypical to those of us from less privileged and younger institutions. Here innovation in teaching and learning is driven by the need to accommodate vulnerable students, many having restricted access to teaching and learning resources as well as limited institutional support:

> We are definitely the lowest, we're the institution with the lowest resources and with the less privileged students. We also have the Technikon history so our, you know, we are still trying to understand what it means to be an institution of higher learning, a university. (Facilitator 1)

> This has necessitated that technology-enhanced teaching and learning activities take into cognisance that staff and students may not have access to the most state-of-the-art technologies. This means, many times, we just have to make a plan. (Facilitator 3)

The module drew on our knowledge and experience as academics and academic developers. Our staff development activities are predominantly based on the ideas of experts in the field of curriculum development and educational technology, namely Gilly Salmon and Diana Laurillard. Our adoption of their views was contextualised very differently, due to the institutional cultures we found ourselves in:

> For me it was interesting to observe the similarities but also differences in our approaches to curriculum development during our planning processes. It is here where our own institutional and personal perspectives come to the fore and it then becomes a space of deciding what to include in the curriculum. (Facilitator 2)

This could be considered a site of negotiation:

> We bring with us the shadow of our institutions that we represent. Perhaps it sounds as a negative metaphor, but I actually try to explain that we cannot escape where we come from. It is part of us, and it influences our choices and approaches to working with others outside of our institution. (Facilitator 2)

We all concurred that the module represented an opportunity for cross-institutional learning, not only between facilitators but also between facilitators and participants:

> I'm always of the opinion that–and it's a saying that learning is a life-long journey and I think in our field of educational technology, it's ever-evolving. It's ever-changing, there's always new things and to keep abreast of all the developments, we attend conferences. We read papers and I see this facilitating with colleagues on a PGDip as another way in which I can continually also improve my understanding in the field of educational technology. ... if I may be confronted with a similar context that some of the–for instance, the Venda[1] students encountered and then it gives me that experience to be able to advise effectively. So that was my approach, you do not know everything, and you will never know everything, and you can always learn from others. (Facilitator 3)

Agency

Our reflections strongly suggested a shared passion for social justice and acute sensitivity for inequalities. We discussed our drive to create caring learning experiences that are equitable, and consider context and learning needs. We

---

[1] Participants from the University of Venda joined the PGDip for the first time in 2018. This is a South African comprehensive rural-based university located in Thohoyandou in Limpopo province. Throughout the course these participants struggled with access to reliable internet connectivity.

share an understanding of the importance of individual differences and positionalities, as well as how these impact the way we engage with each other. We acknowledged what these differences bring to the teaching and learning space, and how we shape learning experiences for ourselves and others.

Remarkably, though, the drive for social justice stems from the facilitators' diverse disciplinary fields and theoretical approaches. Some of us are teachers at the core, having worked in secondary education prior to joining academia. Some view themselves as teachers and scholars, or teachers and academic staff developers, while others have a more vocational background (for example, health professions educator), or are positioned firmly within adult education and academic staff development. The theoretical frameworks that we draw on range from social realism (Archer, 1995), and social constructivism (Vygotsky, 1978), to Rancière's (2006) democratic teaching, Deleuze and Guattari's (1987) rhizomatic learning, as well as critical feminist care theories, such as Tronto's (1993) ethic of care, and Fraser's (1999) participatory parity. These impact our world view, as well as the way we interact with each other and our participants. Some of us talk about learners or students when referring to our PGDip participants, while others view them as participants or colleagues. What helps to bridge these different views of the world is a shared recognition of the messiness and complexities of teaching and learning, and openness to listen and engage with each other's world views. We all believe in collective problem-solving, trusting in each other's expertise and strengths:

> In this way, we are able to draw on each other's expertise and experience in the field of educational technology, across a range of different higher education institutions. (Facilitator 4)

> I've learnt through participating in these programmes that it's okay to share what you know without sounding like the bastion of knowledge, but it's also okay to share what you don't know and it speaks to the safe space that this PGDip environment has been built. (Facilitator 4)

> We as facilitators were comfortable enough with each other to draw on each other's strengths during the course. Some of us are much more technologically inclined and inquisitive towards the technical parts of the course. Others prefer the theoretical perspectives, approaches towards care or to continuously engage with participants via different mediums. I once again realised that such an approach contributes to levels of trust as well as an ability to further learn from each other. (Facilitator 2)

Curriculum

Throughout the offering of the course, the facilitators viewed educational technology as a pedagogical practice, instead of merely referring to the use of digital technology. The facilitators agreed that a one-size-fits-all solution to address the complex contextual factors at play does not exist. Viewing education as a practice allowed the module to be more responsive to the needs of the enrolled participants. A potential challenge related to the fact that the participants were not on an equal footing in terms of integrating technology into teaching and learning. For some participants it was quite easy to devise a method of integrating digital technology to augment their teaching and learning practices. This was primarily due to the institutions they were connected to and related infrastructure, knowledge, and pedagogical support. Some participants lacked necessary resources to support technology-augmented teaching and learning activities. Facilitators needed to be continually sensitised to the fact that participants were not all on an equal footing:

> It was very much an engagement between the participants and ourselves and we came to an understanding of what would possibly work for them …]. (Facilitator 3)

The design thinking process adopted for this module encouraged all facilitators and participants to problem-solve collectively, to generate innovative ideas on responding to the unique needs of participants.

Teaching and learning (pedagogy)

An aspect that was quite prominent throughout our reflections was the notion of learning-centeredness, as we are all strong proponents of learning-centred pedagogical practices:

> I've always seen education as this engagement between a teacher and a student and a lot of my writing also then centres around [this]–about moving away from teacher-centred pedagogical practice towards more democratic teaching and learning practices and that is why I can link a lot of my ideas to social justice, equality, autonomy, rhizomatic learning. (Facilitator 3)

There was a strong emphasis on social forms of learning, as proposed by Laurillard (2012), such as learning through discussion, and through collaboration:

> Whether we use technology to support that or we use conventional methods, it's just about that engagement between a teacher and a student and that conversation that I feel we should be focusing on because that is where the learning for me happens. (Facilitator 3)

The shift in the elective module, from being theoretically intensive to being far more practical in nature, was also quite prominent:

> It was so interesting how [things] shifted when some of the older professors left because it was suddenly so much less theoretical and there was suddenly so much space to innovate and a bit more practice. You know the whole design thinking all of that only came in you know after and I'm not saying theory is not important, but I think it's that theory-practice [link] and the ... and the experimenting. For me, the PGDip especially is such a fantastic space to innovate and experiment because we are given the space to do things but to do things in a credit-bearing course you know. (Facilitator 1)

Discussion

The interplay between structure, culture and agency was evident in our reflections. Not only did this impact our choices, it also prompted us to consider the design of a responsive curriculum as well as implementation of innovative pedagogical practices in the module. We discuss the findings under themes that we observed to be particularly important.

Negotiating different world views

Considering that we facilitators are from diverse cultures, our social worlds comprise various interconnected disciplinary fields, which provide richness of knowledge and experiences for ourselves and participants. Our views of the world are shaped, produced, and reproduced based on our personalities, cultures, institutions, and institutional boundaries. We possess different transformative capacities, based on our different backgrounds, contexts, and quest for social justice and equitable access for our participants (Bozalek & Leibowitz, 2012; Waghid, 2014). Our approach to curriculum development could therefore be considered a product of collective cultures and structures, shaping our actions in the design and facilitation of the module.

In many ways, this realisation provided the structure in which we were able to negotiate and accommodate one another, through our own world views that shaped our actions. Our collaboration led to co-construction of an innovative and responsive curriculum, and allowed us to cut across cultural and institutional differences to produce this outcome. We developed collective agency through the engagement we had with one another as well as with our participants, who were mostly colleagues.

This demonstrates the relational interaction (Archer, 1995) between ourselves as individual facilitators and our practice within our learning environments, evidenced in the ways we were able to acknowledge differences within our inter-institutional spaces. Our responsiveness to the varied dynamics of diverse social systems has in many ways transformed learning spaces into settings that fostered inter-institutional, cross-cultural learning and engagement, for both the facilitators and the participants.

Accommodating different contexts

Most prominently, these differences emerged in the considerations of our different contexts. For example, consideration of the types of knowledge appropriate for this module, or the kinds of tools and technologies appropriate to our contexts, created the opportunity for negotiation and contemplation of numerous contexts as well as the participants' needs. We represented three different HEIs, where academic development and training in educational technology are offered and engaged with differently. In the process of designing and facilitating this module we had to reflect on our own institutional practices, and negotiate approaches and tools that we believed would contribute to the quality of the collaboration. Decisions had to be made regarding the importance of theoretical perspectives, the course platform to serve as a basis for communication as well as teaching and learning, not to mention the type of educational technology tools we felt would empower our participants in their own unique contexts.

Through these emergent powers of structure, culture and agency (Archer, 1995) we were afforded the opportunity to accommodate diverse contexts. Our institutional structures, cultures, and beliefs related to agency motivated us towards the agreement that we would like to explore and embed innovative and creative pedagogical practices. For us, pedagogical innovation implied that we move beyond conventional approaches of professional development towards the notion of experimentation, and creation of a safe learning environment. We wanted participants to reflect on their own contexts, while simultaneously drawing on the expertise and collective knowledge of the whole group. We encouraged the practice of collective reflection, where participants had the opportunity to share their ideas as well as to act on feedback received from their peers (Colet, 2017). Design thinking supported this, with its emphasis on participatory methodologies.

Importance of co-creation

Our awareness that our participants' context and learning needs were important and different (Council on Higher Education, 2017) impacted our actions and deliberations, emphasising the importance of co-creating curricula with them (Bovill & Woolmer, 2019). Conceptualisation and implementation of the module were based on the process of collaborative curriculum development. We argue that the participants bring their own expectations to such a course, which are rooted in their own unique circumstances and motivation for module participation, their personal experiences, and what they believe such a module should entail (Pauler-Kuppinger & Jucks, 2017). We drew on their previous knowledge and expertise, as much as on our own. This approach underlines democratic values as well as acceptance of the multi-faceted nature of learning (Bergmark & Westman, 2018), and requires flexibility and the ability to respond with agility to participants' feedback. Design thinking, with its iterative nature and focus on rapid feedback cycles, helped create a responsive learning space.

Embracing uncertain spaces

The liminal spaces (Berger, 2004) we found ourselves in allowed the freedom to explore, examine, ideate, design, and experiment, which subsequently is transferred back into our own practices. The module design and implementation phases evolved into spaces where we stretched ourselves and our participants to move beyond existing practices and beliefs, in order to actively engage with the multifaceted elements associated with integration of technology into different curricula and contexts. Our own agency was highlighted in the way we acknowledged and considered our own structural backgrounds in terms of culture (Archer, 1995). Our approach and openness to experimentation and responsiveness to participants' needs paved the way for a safe learning environment, in which they felt comfortable and encouraged to dip into the unknown and spaces of discomfort (Berger, 2004). From the facilitators' perspective it also provided conditions to experiment, draw on each other's expertise, and create and nurture a collective and collaborative space (Colet, 2017). Our main quest remained to encourage participants to consider their unique contexts, and not shy away from innovation within their institutions– moving away from a deficit approach to identifying challenges as design opportunities, while drawing from the collective wisdom of the participants and facilitators. Here the design thinking process was again helpful in engaging participants in critical reflection on their own contextual needs, placing these at the centre of the design process, to create an intervention which formed part of their final assignment and that could benefit their own institution or individual practice.

Towards shared ownership of learning

What we agreed on as facilitators is that we wanted to embed our course in a learning-centred approach. This approach moves the emphasis away from teachers and their actions towards questions related to how well students are learning (Blumberg, 2016). A learning-centred method focuses on learning, and not on the process of knowledge transmission so often prevalent in HE (Von der Heidt & Quazi, 2013). This underlined the importance we as facilitators placed on attempting to understand how participants (i.e. students) learn. Learning-centred pedagogical approaches view students as independent learners who take responsibility for their own learning (Von der Heidt & Quazi, 2013). In the process of creating an enabling environment (Von der Heidt & Quazi, 2013), the participants demonstrated agency while we teachers became facilitators, and not only content transmitters. Being facilitators meant embodying different roles at different times in the course. On the one hand, we were formal facilitators who taught an accredited postgraduate course, while on the other we were also working with colleagues and peers engaged in professional development, and positioned as experts in their own fields and institutional contexts. Although this was not always an easy tension to handle, and required release of control and trust in a co-creative process, it allowed us to share the responsibility and ownership of learning with our participants, to create more participatory and democratic learning spaces.

Conclusion

Working across institutions can be a highly enriching experience. It is not an easy task, and needs an appreciation of difference as well as a willingness to work across cultural, disciplinary, and institutional boundaries. In particular, when working with technology integration into teaching and learning, differences in resourcing become marked and could potentially be frustrating and disruptive. Working with a learning design process that is focused on the learner/participant, their context and needs, and that affirms complexity and diversity, allows for collective problem-solving. This positions each participant as an expert knowledge holder of their disciplinary content, acknowledges student needs and context, and leads to the kind of innovation that is sensitive to our contexts and circumstances.

The use of educational technology espoused throughout the module characterised support for the less powerful, or previously less included voices, whether those of facilitators or participants. The facilitators were encouraged to realise their autonomy, thinking innovatively to create new learning experiences that would afford participants their equality and contribution to the pedagogical process. We would argue that the democratised, learning-centred pedagogical practice advocated for in this module may mitigate existential inequality, as participants' perspectives and ideas were continually taken into consideration. This causal relationship between democratisation and the mitigation of inequalities was not sporadic, but a product of a design thinking approach underpinned by a concern and empathy for the learner.

Our journeys in working collaboratively on an inter-institutional co-teaching (and now co-researching) project will always be unique, due to our different experiences and disciplinary backgrounds. Being willing to draw a picture of these similarities and differences through a reflective process of negotiation is an essential ingredient of such collaborations. It encourages us to become reflective practitioners, and to continuously re-evaluate and redesign our own practices in this module, as well as in our own individual contexts, in ongoing deliberations for identifying similarities and sites of struggle, accommodation, and renegotiation.

References

Archer, M. S. (1995). *Realist social theory: The morphogenetic approach.* Cambridge: Cambridge University Press.

Archer, M. S. (2000). *Being human: The problem of agency.* Cambridge: Cambridge University Press.

Archer, M. (2007). Making our way through the world: Human reflexivity and social mobility Cambridge: Cambridge University Press

Banifatemeh, H., Shields, R., Golabi, F., Ghoreishi, F. & Bayani, F. (2018). The ontology of social realism from critical realism's perspective: Focusing on the ideas of Margaret Archer and Andrew Sayer. *Mediterranean Journal of Social Sciences, 9*(3), pp. 57-70.

Berger, J. G. (2004), Dancing on the threshold of meaning: Recognizing and understanding the growing edge. *Journal of Transformative Education, 2*(4), pp. 336-351. doi: 10.1177/1541344604267697

Bergmark, U. & Westman, S. (2018). Student participation within teacher education: Emphasising democratic values, engagement and learning for a future profession. *Higher Education Research and Development, 37*(7), pp. 1352-1365.

Biesta, G. (2009). Sporadic democracy: Education, democracy, and the question of inclusion. In M. S. Katz, S. Verducci & G. Biesta (Eds.), *Education, democracy, and the moral life*, pp. 101-112. Dordrecht: Springer.

Blumberg, P. (2016). Factors that influence faculty adoption of learning-centered approaches. *Innovative Higher Education, 41*(4), pp. 303-315.

Bovill, C. & Woolmer, C. (2019). How conceptualisations of curriculum in higher education influence student-staff co-creation in and of the curriculum. *Higher Education, 78*, pp. 407-422. doi: 10.1007/s10734-018-0349-8

Bozalek, V. & Leibowitz, B. (2012). An evaluative framework for a socially just institution In B. Leibowitz (Ed.), *Higher Education for the Public Good*, pp 59-72. Stellenbosch: SUN Press.

Brown, T. (2009). *Change by Design.* New York, NY.: HarperCollins. http://books.google.com/books?id=x7PjWyVUoVAC&pgis=1

Buchanan, R. (1992). Wicked problems in design thinking. *Design Issues*, 8(2), pp. 5-21.

Bui, K. V. T. (2002). First-generation college students at a four-year university: Background characteristics, reasons for pursuing higher education, and first-year experiences. *College Student Journal, 36*(1), pp. 3-12.

Council on Higher Education. (2017). *Learning to Teach in Higher Education in South Africa: An investigation into the influences of institutional context on the professional learning of academics in their roles as teachers.* Higher Education Monitor 14. Pretoria: Council on Higher Education.

Colet, N. M. (2017). From content-centred to learning-centred approaches: Shifting educational paradigm in higher education. *Journal of Educational Administration and History, 49*(1), pp. 72-86.

Deleuze, G. & Guattari, F. (1987). *A thousand plateaus: Capitalism and schizophrenia.* (B. Massumi, Trans.). Minneapolis, MN: University of Minnesota Press.

Fraser, N. (1999). Social justice in the age of identity politics: Redistribution, Recognition, and Participation. In L. Ray & A. Sayer (Eds.), *Culture and Economy - After the Cultural Turn,* pp. 25-52. London: Sage Publications.

Friedman, E. & Mare, R. (2014). The schooling of offspring and the survival of parents. *Demography, 51*(4), pp. 1271-1293. doi: 10.1007/s13524-014-0303-z

Gachago, D., Morkel, J., Van Zyl, I. & Ivala, E. (2021). Promoting design thinking in course design among academics: reflections on a staff development programme on blended course design in design thinking to design doing: Experiences from an academic staff development programme for blended course design. In E. Dohn, J. Hansen, S. Hansen, T. Ryberg & M. de Laat (Eds.), *Conceptualizing and innovating education and work with networked learning,* pp.19-35. Cham: Springer International Publishing.

Ingraham, C. (2014, July 31). Want to live longer? Send your kids to college. *Washington Post.* http://www.washingtonpost.com/blogs/wonkblog/wp/2014/07/31/want-to-live-longer-send-your-kids-to-college/

Khan, P., Qualter, A. & Young, R. (2012). Structure and agency in learning: A critical realist theory of the development of capacity to reflect on academic practice. *Higher Education Research & Development, 31*(6), pp. 859-871.

Kelley, T. & Kelley, D. (2014). *Creative Confidence - Unleashing the creative potential within us all.* London: William Collins.

King, A. (2010). The odd couple: Margaret Archer, Anthony Giddens and British social theory. *British Journal of Sociology, 61,* pp. 1-8.

Laurillard, D. (2012). *Teaching as a Design Science: Building Pedagogical Patterns for Learning and Technology.* New York & London: Routledge.

Leibowitz, L., Bozalek, V., Van Schalkwyk, S. & Winberg, C. (2015). Institutional context matters: The professional development of academics as teachers in South African higher education. *Higher Education, 69,* pp. 315-330.

Marshall, C. & Rossman, G. B. (2011). *Designing qualitative research* (5th ed.). London: Sage.

Meara, E., Richards, S. & Cutler, D. (2008). The gap gets bigger: Changes in mortality and life expectancy. *Health Affairs,* March, pp. 1981-2000. doi: 10.1377/ hlthaff.27.2.350

Mezirow, J. (1990). How critical reflection triggers transformative learning. In J. Mezirow & Associates (Eds.), *Fostering critical reflection in adulthood – A guide to transformative and emancipatory learning,* pp. 1-20. San Francisco, CA: Jossey-Bass.

Mogashana, D. G. (2015). *The interplay between structure and agency: How academic development programme students 'make their way' through their undergraduate studies in engineering* (Unpublished doctoral dissertation). University of Cape Town.

Newman, J. (2017). *Re-addressing the cultural system: Problems and solutions in Margaret Archer's theory of culture*. Paper presented at the Political Studies Conference, Glasgow, 2017. https://www.psa.ac.uk/sites/default/files/conference/papers/2017/JACK%20NEWMAN%20-%20Paper%20to%20the%20PSA%202017%20-%20Re-addressing%20the%20 20Cultural%20System.pdf

Pauler-Kuppinger, L. & Jucks, R. (2017). Perspectives on teaching: Conceptions of teaching and epistemological beliefs of university academics and students in different domains. *Active Learning in Higher Education, 18*(1), pp. 63-76.

Rancière, J. (2006). *Hatred of democracy*. New York, NY: Verso.

Simons, M., & Masschelein, J. (Eds.). (2011). *Rancière, public education and the taming of democracy*. Chichester: Wiley-Blackwell.

Therborn, G., & Aboim, S. (2014). The killing fields of inequality. *Análise Social, 212*, pp. 729-735.

Tronto, J. (1993). *Moral boundaries: A political argument for an ethic of care*. New York, NY: Routledge.

Van Wyk, B. (2011). Universities as organisations or institutions? The culture debate in one institution. In E. Bitzer & N. Botha (Eds.), *Curriculum inquiry in South African higher education: Some scholarly affirmations and challenges*, pp. 331-347. Stellenbosch: SUN MeDIA.

Von der Heidt, T. & Quazi, A. (2013). Enhancing learning-centeredness in marketing principles curriculum. *Australasian Marketing Journal, 21*(4), pp. 250-258. https://doi.org/10.1016/j.ausmj.2013.08.005

Vygotsky, L. S. (1978). *Mind in society: The development of higher psychological processes*. Cambridge, MAZ: Harvard University Press.

Waghid, Z. (2014). (Higher) Education for social justice through sustainable development, economic development and equity. *South African Journal of Higher Education, 28*(4), pp. 1448-1463.

Waghid, F. (2019a). Towards decolonisation within university education: On the innovative application of educational technology. In C. Manthalu & Y. Waghid (Eds.), *Education for decoloniality and decolonisation in Africa*, pp. 139-153. Cham: Palgrave Macmillan.

Waghid, Z. (2019b). The need for South African (higher) education institutions to be attuned to Education 4.0. *South African Journal of Higher Education, 33*(5), pp. 1-6.

Zeuner, L. (1999). Margaret Archer on structural and cultural morphogenesis. *Acta Sociologica, 42*(1), pp. 79-86.

Chapter 3

Translating learning into collaborative research: Reflections from a postgraduate cohort

Cheryl Brown

University of Canterbury, New Zealand

Proscovia Namubiru Ssentamu

Uganda Management Institute, Uganda

Emily Bagarukayo-Ngabirano

Makerere University, Uganda

Rehema Baguma

Makerere University, Uganda

Tabisa Mayisela

University of Cape Town, South Africa

Abstract

This chapter shares the reflections of a group of colleagues from three institutions who began collaborating during a one-year Postgraduate Diploma in Educational Technology course at the University of Cape Town. The course design is based on a modular approach, and taught using a blended mode of delivery, with intensive blocks of face-to-face engagement, combined with extended online and distance learning. Authentic learning through use of emerging technologies provides opportunities to support team teaching, hands-on group learning, and self- and peer assessment. Each of the four modules on the course has a project or research-based assignment. Students work closely with their peers and facilitators to design and develop individual research- and practice-based projects that seek to provide proactive educational and technological solutions to teaching and learning in their home institutions. Woven throughout the chapter are reflections, by the authors (comprising students and course facilitators) on how their learning on the course translated into practice in their respective contexts, and consequently how their practice developed into publishable research outputs. The authors provide in-depth reflection on their collaboration with each other during and after the course, unpacking how they moved beyond individual assignments to collaborative research and publication. The scope and forms of collaborative teaching, learning and research, tools and technologies used to collaborate with and support each other, and skills needed to nurture this collaboration are explored. This provides an example of blended co-teaching, co-learning and co-researching in cross-cultural contexts to facilitate inter-institutional collaborative spaces, with support from a variety of educational technologies and tools. The chapter contributes to the discourse on emerging collaborative teaching and research approaches that may inform and shape strategies to advance Africa's research agenda. It will also explore the advantages of and challenges faced in inter-institutional collaborative teaching and research engagement using technologies in multicultural settings, and reflect on how the challenges can be managed.

Keywords: co-teaching, co-learning, co-researching, emerging technologies, inter-institutional collaboration, postgraduate diploma, South Africa

***

Introduction and background

Co-teaching has been a regular pedagogical practice in the schooling sector, particularly in the area of inclusive education (Lava, 2012), where it has been viewed as two (or more) teachers working as a team. However, it is a relatively recent development in a tertiary context (Kelly, 2018). With increasing focus on student engagement and blended learning (Brown, Davis & Eulatth-Vidal, 2019), the concept of co-teaching has expanded to include participatory design or co-creation of learning and teaching (Bovill, 2020).

In exploring the concepts of co-teaching, co-learning and co-researching in tertiary education we found varied ways in which the literature referred to them. Co-teaching predominantly related to team teaching and the ways in which academics in a course teach together (Benjamin, 2000), or the team-teaching strategies that educators adopted in different contexts (Crawford & Jenkins, 2017). Co-learning focused on peer mentoring between students (Gucciardi, Mach & Mo, 2016), students as partners in the learning experience (Matthews, 2016), co-researching on project partnerships created during doctoral studies (Patricio & Santos, 2020), or ways that partnerships can be established between universities and industry (Walker et al., 2008). However, we did not find examples where coursework students and their teachers co-researched on student-led projects, reversing previously established roles of student and teacher.

In this chapter, the authors–two facilitators from a postgraduate diploma programme (educators C and T) and three students (P, E and R)–reflect on their experiences of co-teaching, what we learnt through the programme, and catalysts for our collaboration beyond the course which led to our co-researching together. We look back on our experiences and asked ourselves: What are the conditions needed to enable collaboration and how do these result in co-teaching and co-researching?

Methodology

The authors first met in 2016 during a postgraduate diploma course on educational technology at the University of Cape Town, continued working together virtually and since then published four papers together (Bagarukayo et al., 2016; Bagarukayo et al., 2017; Baguma et al., 2019; Namubiru-Ssentamu et al., 2020). We adopted a collaborative reflection on self-narrative approach to our research (Mendez, 2013; Roy & Uekusa, 2020). Using stimulus questions each of the authors wrote a personal narrative which focused on aspects of identity, self-conceptualisation and motivation. Narrative research, as explained by Kyratzis and Green (1997, p. 17), "entails a double narrative process, one that includes the narratives generated by those participating in the research, and one that represents the voice of the researcher as narrator of those narratives". We endeavoured to approach the research as an analytic autoethnography, given that our purpose was objective writing on and analysis of our particular group. Like other scholars reflecting on their practice (Romero-Hall et. al, 2018) we have used autoethnography to systematically enhance our understanding of "people situation and context" (p.21) As researchers we are members of the community which we were writing about, "visible in published texts and committed to developing theoretical understandings of broader social phenomena" (Mendez, 2013, p. 281). Educator C posed questions to the other four authors about their backgrounds, experiences in the course, what made them decide to return to study, tools and technologies they used, and the skills they either drew on or developed. Students P, E and R then reflected on collaboration during and after the course, and how they moved from their individual assignments into co-authoring research and co-publishing. Educators C and T reflected on their role in developing authentic learning experiences for students, how feedback helped develop learning, and how they engaged with students as colleagues.

In making sense of the data, educator C and student P then read through the reflections (some 15 000 words), noting key themes and commonalities. This was drafted for input and comments from the wider group, which operated as member checking. The themes which emerged arose from our collective understanding of the conditions and context of our collaboration. When, how and why we might collaborate was not something we had explicitly planned or discussed together before. The co-research was implicit to our collaboration, and just happened. However, in reflecting back on our experiences and making the invisible visible, we gained a greater understanding of the conditions and enablers for our interactions. We hope this can encourage and facilitate other fruitful and meaningful virtual research collaborations among facilitators and postgraduate students.

Although the analysis was thematic, on inspection of the emergent themes the authors were interested to see how this might align with theories around collaboration. Clearly, notions of a community of practice (Wenger, 2010) had resonance with the data, as did social learning theories such as Canadian-American psychologist Albert Bandura's (1977) view of learning as a process that occurs in interpersonal contexts. However, in looking for something more specific to collaboration, we found resonance with Colbry, Hurwitz, and Adair's (2014) six causal themes of collaboration, as they had followed a grounded coding process to explore the interpersonal level of collaboration. While this was not used as an analytical framework, we have drawn on it as a way of interpreting our findings.

The framework has two clusters, namely Individual First and Team First. In analysing our reflections, we definitely observed both individual motivations and group benefits, and have thus organised our findings by drawing on Colbry et al.'s (2014) collaboration theory as a framework. Individual First relates to the individual's perceived influence either upon the team or themselves, and includes turn-taking, observing or doing, and status-seeking. Team First collects the themes of building group cohesion, influencing others and organising work, and is characterised by the team's influence on the individual.

Findings

Co-teaching/co-learning

The programme was facilitated by a team of teachers with backgrounds in education, information systems, and e-learning, and included a diverse group of students (all professionals in their own disciplines and fields) from across Africa. Teaching and assessment in the course was underpinned by an authentic learning framework which positions learning and assessment tasks in students' real-life contexts (Reeves, Herrington & Oliver, 2002). Given that students were drawn from higher education institutions, quality assurance bodies, and the learning design industry across Africa, this approach was an appropriate strategy. It encouraged us to "formulate learning outcomes in terms of authentic practices of formulating and solving realistic problems" (Mayes & de Freitas, 2004, p.13). The course was designed to be a blended learning experience. Students undertook individual online tasks before joining an intensive block session on campus. The face- to-face sessions were a time for students to work together in groups, collaborate and learn from the facilitators and each other. Scaffolding was provided for the individual projects, which students would continue to complete online after the block.

The cohesion of the group began in the early days of the course, which shows that the cluster of Team First was present right at the start of the collaboration: "We stayed in the same residence which gave us a chance to consult each other in the evenings" (student R). However, beyond academic support, group cohesion was built during block sessions through "walking, shopping, cooking and eating together as well as sharing with each other about social life" (student P). In some ways this was part of the conscious design of the course, as the students note that the course itself was set up to encourage and value collaborative ways of working through interactions. This enabled the identification of each other's "strengths and support areas, including discussing the assignments and approaches to use, sharing resources and technical skills, as well as moral support for the times we were studying away from home and also back home" (student P). The co-teaching approach was part of the course ethos. As student P noted:

> I appreciated the way the PgDip EdTech course was structured, the quality and content of the modules, the quality of reading reference materials, the practical approach used to teach the modules, the co-facilitation mode, as well as the individual and group work assignments.

Two authors, educators C and T, had worked together before and each led a different module within the programme. During 2016 they co-taught on two modules, alternating the leadership role. This approach provides evidence of the individual's influence on the team as it foregrounded turn-taking.

The summative assessment in the two modules which we drew on in this collaboration consisted of an academic paper, in the form of a literature review about how technology could potentially mediate learning in students' respective contexts, and a design-based research project researching implementation of a particular tool or practice to address an educational opportunity or challenge. The assessment was constructed to create some check-in points, that would allow facilitators to provide timely feedback to students on smaller pieces of work. According to Hanesworth, Bracken and Elkington (2019), in the assessment context, 'timely' does not merely mean "just in time but [rather] best timed for the student learning journey" (p. 104). To facilitate the timely feedback, students were required to submit an abstract and a concept map of their papers and a one-page design-based research summary plan for their project. We used tools such as CMaps for concept mapping the initial proposal and then Dropbox,[1] Google Docs, and track changes in Microsoft Word to share documents and provide feedback. Online tools were necessary as students and educators were not co-located, as they lived in different countries.

'Preliminary' marks were assigned to drafts using the assessment rubrics, to give students an opportunity to incorporate feedback into their assessment. From the facilitators' perspective, this feedback provided a springboard for improvement. Sadler (2010, p. 538) emphasises that feedback should be constructive and supportive, and incorporate 'feedforward' principles, such as

> ... telling students about the strengths of their works; telling them (gently) about deficiencies, where they occurred, and their nature; telling students what would have improved their works; and pointing them to what could be done next time they complete a related type of response.

How the facilitators communicated the constructive feedback was crucial. The facilitators also had to bear in mind that most students were academic colleagues–in other words, peers. As facilitators, we also had to appreciate the different contexts and disciplinary expertise that our students brought with them. Being fully aware that assessors may still be subjective, irrespective of the rubric, each lecturer marked all of the students' assignments and used the Microsoft Word 'track changes' function or Google Docs (with comments) feature for elaborated input. As a postgraduate course, this was marked on a grading scale (facilitators moderated the marks and sent all the work to an external examiner). Given that assessment tasks were constructed authentically to have real-world significance, and afford opportunities for collaboration and reflection, students were provided with feedback even on completion of marking (through shared online documents e.g. Google Docs, video-conferencing and/or voice notes), so that they could continue to develop their ideas beyond completion of the course. In this sense, the feedback process was focused on influencing others through providing input to help students develop and grow their scholarship.

There were some interesting commonalities among students P, E and R. They all had extensive experience as lecturers themselves, and the intrinsic motivation to learn and move outside of their comfort zone. Some were also in leadership

---

[1] The Dropbox tool was used to create a folder for each student in the course. Students are only able to access their own folder. Students and instructors can both place files in the Dropbox folders. See https://longsight.screenstepslive.com/s/4586/m/59830/l/6101 73-what-is-the-drop-box-tool

positions in their own institutions, where they recognised the strategic imperative of educational technology. Others were "passionate about using technology in the classroom and studying its impact" (student E). All three sought to develop their own capabilities in this area.

As individuals, the students valued the community of practice in which they were learning, and actively sought group cohesion with each other, both during and after the course:

> ... the five of us from Uganda met for an evening ... the intention was to discuss and support each other in interpreting and enriching our learning, at the end of module one. (Student P)

Whilst they were African women from the same country, they did not all work in the same discipline or institution. Two students did work in close physical proximity, but did not realise they were embarking on the same learning journey until they travelled for the first block course. The students came from different disciplines and reflected back on how they each brought different strengths to their learning. Student P "comprehended faster theories and principles of learning", and student E "helped elaborate further eLearning theories and principles", while student R "supported the team on general technology aspects such as installation and configuration of ETs ... and on human computer interaction". This demonstrates what Colbry, Hurwitz, and Adair (2014, p. 69) refer to as turn-taking, or what might also be familiar as the notion of shared interest or practice (Wenger, 2010). The students acknowledged their different contributions and made a personal choice to both participate in the collaboration and provide leadership through their contribution to the collective.

In terms of the Individual First cluster, observing and doing are two ends of a passive-active dimension in group dynamics (Colbry et al., 2014). Relevant here is not just the process of interaction of the group, but how the three student authors had to move between their work-life role as a lecturer and learner role as a student shifted the experiences of the group.

The process of being a student again "was intense ... I did not expect it to be that demanding after having completed the PhD" (student E), and as student R notes, "being a blended learning student made me realise that in our era of technology ubiquity, learning for our students does not need to be limited to the classroom". Student P told how "being a blended learning student changed my own view about my students in various ways". They could not control the learning design and process of the course, as they might choose to in their work roles as lecturers. Even in relation to content the students described themselves as "still far away from being an ET practitioner, steward and leader" (student R) and valuing the "opportunity to interface with new technology and learn new methods of learning with technology" (student E).

Building group cohesion through collegiality was a value held by the group, who were not in any way obliged to collaborate with their facilitators. They reflected that initially they drew the facilitators in "because they facilitated the module. We felt that it would be unfair to publish this work without them" (student E), "given that we had worked on the assignments under their guidance" (student R). However, while the students led the publication, the facilitators "further input and guidance made the quality of the papers even better" (student R).

Co-researching

All three students were committed to using the course to "build our knowledge and competences in using educational technologies in teaching and learning" (student P). Each student chose a focus for their assessment that was grounded in an issue they faced as lecturer in their own institution. Examples included:

- Modelling online design with real-time feedback between learners and the educator, to motivate learners to learn individually and in groups to achieve the intended learning outcomes through the use of video, online reflection, and discussion. (Student P)

- Encouraging creativity and collaboration among students using a social media platform they were familiar with and could share either publicly or semi-publicly with a wider community of practice in order to develop Higher-Order Cognitive Skills (HOCS) such as decision making, critical thinking, problem-solving, and analysis. (Student E)

- Engaging learners' Higher-Order Thinking Skills (HOTS) for example, problem solving, raising complex questions, developing consistent arguments, and expressing their opinions from critical perspectives through use of an easily accessible and well adopted instant messaging technology. (Student R)

However, the group soon realised that there were strategic advantages to taking the collaboration further. In terms of Colbry et al.'s (2014) theme of status-seeking, this was shared by the group not just in terms of their careers but in maximising the outcomes of the time they were spending in their studies:

We realised this was authentic research and would impact academia, policy makers and practitioners. Besides, we were putting in a lot of effort and did not want the efforts of these long hours to go to waste. (Student E)

In addition, as academics, publications were needed "to apply for promotion within our respective institutions" (student P), so the collaborators were united in this shared goal. The collaborative endeavours had a shared impact in terms of status-seeking outside of the team. However, this dynamic from student to researcher shifted when the course facilitators, who were used to their role in providing feedback that was a "springboard for improvement" and "incorporated feedforward principles" (educator T), had to step back as the students took the lead over publications. Given the shared interest, and co-teaching/co-learning practices that had been part of the course, this wasn't a difficult shift. This may also have been helped by the lack of an egotistical agenda among the five women in the group. While this may have helped the continuous collaboration of these authors, there were other research collaborations with one of the male facilitators from the course (Bagarukayo et al., 2017).

It was at this point that more conscious decisions were made at a Team First level, such as how to organise work together. After the block course sessions, the students continued to maintain a connection and "immediately started a WhatsApp group and used it to collaborate" (student E). Initially, this was to support their coursework, but over time a friendship was forged and the WhatsApp group "the ET-UCT girls, as we call ourselves" (student E) "met physically to organise and attend a wedding for one of us and for a housewarming party for another" (student P).

Early on, the student group agreed on some rules around turn-taking, such as "each of us had to work on their respective assignment as lead author, and co-opt others as authors if they participated in the review process" (student P). This way of organising work provided a structure to the collaboration, although this did not always work out, and the group needed to be adaptable. Online collaboration is clearly an enabler of learning (Werker & Ooms, 2020), particularly if it has originated through temporary geographical proximity–spending time in the same spatial location/geographical proximity to others for a limited amount of time. This establishes a basis for trust and knowledge sharing. Social media, in particular, has been seen to facilitate collaboration among students and researchers (Al-Rahmi, Othman & Yusaf, 2015). Interestingly though, in exploring collaborations among academics in a European university context, Werker and Ooms (2020) noted that modern communication tools were used, and these were predominantly email, video-conferencing and audio calls. No mention was made of collaborative documents for co-creation of knowledge in online spaces. In our collaboration we predominantly used Google Docs, and communicated largely by email, and sometimes instant messenger and video conferencing.

Student E "was quick to act and sent us her first manuscript" (student P), and she noted "I guess I am the one who was most serious about this", as some "of the ladies were slow at responding" (student E). Student E was clearly a driver of the process and influenced others with her enthusiasm to draw in the rest of the team and inspire us. Additionally, "the line-up of the co-authors was a little tricky, since co-author contribution could not easily be measured, especially in cases where all co-authors made significant contributions to the paper" (student P), and whoever did not provide input was unfortunately not included.

Transparency was important, and on two papers the facilitators felt the students had led the authorship and negotiated the order of their authorship according to who was the lead for the course from where the collaboration had originated (Bagarukayo et al., 2016; Baguma, et al., 2019). However, the group chose to "collaborate to strengthen the quality of our publication" (student P) and valued different forms of influence and contribution, for example "we had supported each other during the course, acted as critical reviewers and therefore knew each other's assignments to at least some extent" (student P). The student authors valued the influence which the course facilitators had provided during the teaching of the programme, and drew educators C and T into the partnership because of that initial role. The facilitators were integral to the teaching and learning approaches used in the postgraduate diploma course, and in modelling examples and strategies for collaboration using online tools in their blended teaching and learning practice. However, when it came to co-researching together, the students took the lead and the facilitators took a backseat, providing input when requested and assisting in navigation and interpretation of research publication processes (e.g. reviewers' comments and changes). This seamlessness may have been easier because we had already engaged intellectually around the core aspects of the research, with iterations of feedback and input from the facilitators, as part of the course and assessment process. This meant we already had a cohesion of ideas as a foundation.

Conclusion

What interested us when we started the process of reflection for this chapter were the conditions that enabled collaboration. While it is a recognised practice for supervisors to co-publish with their students, it is more unusual for this to occur in a coursework context. The structure of the course was set up to model collaboration and socially situated learning and assignments were authentic. However, most students did not publish scholarly articles as a result of the course, and among those who did, it was a solo accomplishment. So what made our collaboration work when we didn't set out to collaborate in this way?

Using Colbry et al.'s (2014) collaboration theory as a way of examining these conditions, we can see that the Team First ethos was clearly present at the start, through the group cohesion that was established by the course design, co-teaching/co-learning approach and block format, which provided a solid basis for the collaboration. As the group interacted with each other, there were shared individual goals, including that of career advancement (status seeking). The glue that has kept the network active to date appears to be a combination of the values held by the group, that learning was enhanced by others (and the way they took turns to share this), how we learnt from each other (observing and doing), and the team motivation role that individual members took on at different times (influencing others). The enabling collaborative opportunities that simple technologies like Google Docs and WhatsApp provided a platform for us to organise the collaboration and continue to work together across three countries. In addition, the shared labour of co-researching and publishing together enhanced our collaboration.

In reflecting on our experience, we noted the common themes described below.

Appreciating both complementary and diverse contexts: We come from different disciplines, institutional contexts and cultures, so needed to appreciate our differences and be versatile. However, the fact that group members were from a range of disciplines helped us produce better-quality research papers than we would have done individually.

Building networks: Working together to improve and publish some of the assignments of the postgraduate programme has kept the team in Uganda in touch with each other, as well as educators C and T who live in different countries. It has provided continuous new opportunities for partnership even, for example, when educator C moved continents.

Lifelong learning: Through the continued collaboration among ourselves we have continued mentoring and receiving mentorship from each other through the virtual connection. This has also involved exposure to new technologies and pedagogies through our collaboration. However, we have challenges in terms of synchronising our different schedules to meet deadlines. Given the different locations (across a country and continents) and work/life imperatives of the team, synchronising schedules to meet the timelines of chosen publishers was (and is) challenging.

Friendship: As a result of the course and later the collaboration, we have become friends and do things together outside the research collaboration, such as supporting and attending each other's social events and keeping in touch online.

Shared success: Co-authorship has enabled us to publish more publications together than each one of us would have been able to do individually. It has enriched the quality not just of our research, but of our application of theory in practice. It has helped us to organise work, as each person's existing commitments and priorities differ over time.

We believe that while the co-teaching/co-learning pedagogy that framed this programme provided a foundation for collaborations beyond the course, it was the opportunity for the group to establish a bond and connect on both a professional and personal level that was the foundation for the research collaboration. This was enhanced through shared goals, an approach of learning from and with each other and taking turns in distributing workload, and having different members of the group take on the role of championship at different times.

References

Al-Rahmi, W., Othman, M. S. & Yusuf, L. M. (2015). The role of social media for collaborative learning to improve academic performance of students and researchers in Malaysian higher education. *International Review of Research in Open and Distributed Learning, 16*(4), pp. 177-204.

Bagarukayo, E., Ng'ambi, D., Baguma, R. & Namubiru-Ssentamu, P. (2017). Using Facebook to transfer knowledge into practice and aid student, lecturer and content interaction: A case of Bachelor of Information Technology undergraduate students at Makerere University. In P. Escudeiro, G. Costagliola, S. Zwacek, J. Uhomoibhi & B.M. McLaren (Eds.). *Proceedings of the 9th International Conference on Computer Supported Education,* 21-23 April 2017,.Cham: Springer, (pp. 402-410). doi: 10.5220/0006329104020410

Bagarukayo, E., Namubiru-Ssentamu, P., Mayisela, T. & Brown, C. (2016). Activity Theory as a lens to understand how Facebook develops knowledge application skills. *International Journal of Education and Development using Information and Communication Technology, 12*(3), pp. 128-140.

Baguma, R., Bagarukayo, E., Namubiru-Ssentamu, P., Brown, C. & Mayisela, T. (2019). Using WhatsApp in teaching to develop higher order thinking skills-a literature review using the Activity Theory lens. *International Journal of Education and Development using Information and Communication Technology, 15*(2), pp. 98-116.

Bandura, A. (1977). *Social Learning Theory.* New York: General Learning Press.

Benjamin J. (2000) The scholarship of teaching in teams: What does it look like in practice? *Higher Education Research & Development, 19*(2), pp. 191-204.

Brown, C., Davis, N. & Eulatth-Vidal, W. (2019). Student engagement in flexible and distance learning in Aotearoa New Zealand. In A. Kamp (Ed.), *Education Studies in Aotearoa: Key disciplines and emerging directions.* Wellington: NZCER.

Bovill, C. (2020) Co-creation in learning and teaching: the case for a whole-class approach in higher education. *Higher Education, 79,* pp. 1023-1037.

Colbry, S., Hurwitz, M. & Adair, R. (2014). Collaboration theory. *Journal of Leadership Education, 13*(14), pp. 63-75.

Crawford, R. & Jenkins, L. (2017). Blended learning and team teaching: Adapting pedagogy in response to the changing digital tertiary environment. *Australasian Journal of Educational Technology, 33*(2), pp. 51-72.

Gucciardi, E., Mach, C. & Mo, S. (2016) Student-faculty team teaching–A learning approach, *Mentoring & Tutoring: Partnership in Learning, 24*(5), pp. 441-455.

Hanesworth, P., Bracken, S. & Elkington, S. (2019). A typology for a social justice approach to assessment: Learning from universal design and culturally sustaining pedagogy. *Teaching in Higher Education, 24*(1), pp. 98-114.

Kelly, A. (2018). Co-teaching in higher education: Reflections from an early career academic. *Journal of Learning and Teaching in Higher Education, 1,* pp. 181-188.

Kyratzis, A. & Green, J. (1997). Jointly constructed narratives in classrooms: Co-construction of friendship and community through language. *Teaching and Teacher Education, 13,* pp. 17-37.

Lava, V. F. (2012). Inquiry into co-teaching in an inclusive classroom. *Inquiry in Education, 3*(2), pp. 1-28. http://digitalcommons.nl.edu/ie/vol3/iss2/5

Matthews, K. (2016) Students as partners as the future of student engagement. *Student Engagement in Higher Education Journal, 1*(1), pp. 1-5. https://sehej. raise-network.com/raise/article/view/380/338

Mayes, T. & de Freitas, S. (2004). *Review of e-learning theories, frameworks and models.* London: Joint Information Systems Committee. http://www.jisc.ac.uk/ whatwedo/programmes/elearningpedagogy/outcomes.aspx

Mendez, M. (2013). Autoethnography as a research method: Advantages, limitations and criticisms. *Colombian Applied Linguistics Journal, 15*(2), pp. 279-287.

Namubiru-Ssentamu, P., Ng'ambi, D., Bagarukayo, E., Baguma, R. Nabushawo, M. H. & Nalubowa, C. (2020). Enhancing student interactions in online learning: A case of using YouTube in a distance learning module in a Higher Education institution in Uganda. *Higher Education Research, 5*(4), pp. 103-116.

Patricio M.T. & Santos, P. (2020). Collaborative research projects in doctoral programs: A case study in Portugal. *Studies in Higher Education, 45*(11), pp. 2311-2323.

Reeves, T.C., Herrington, J. & and Oliver, R. (2002). Authentic activities and on-line learning. In A. Goody, J. Harrington, and M. Northcote (Eds.). *Quality conversations: Research and Development in Higher Education,* Vol. 25. Jamison, ACT:HERDSA, (pp. 562-567).

Romero-Hall, E., Aldemir, T., Colorado-Resa, J.T., Dickson-Deane, C., Watson, G.S., & Sadaf, A. (2018). Undisclosed stories of instructional design female scholars in academia. Women's Studies International Forum. 71, pp. 19-28.

Roy, R. & Uekusa, S. (2020). Collaborative autoethnography: "self-reflection" as a timely alternative research approach during the global pandemic. *Qualitative Research Journal, 20*(4), pp. 383-392.

Sadler, D. R. (2010). Beyond feedback: Developing student capability in complex appraisal. *Assessment & Evaluation in Higher Education, 35*(5), pp. 535–550.

Veletsianos, G. (2010). A definition of emerging technologies for education. In G. Veletsianos (Ed.), *Emerging Technologies in Distance Education.* Edmonton: Athabasca University Press. http://www.aupress.ca/index.php/books/120177

Walker, D. H. T., Anbari, F. T., Bredillet, C., Söderlund, J., Cicmil, S. & Thomas, J. (2008). Collaborative academic/practitioner research in project management: Examples and applications. *International Journal of Managing Projects in Business, 1*(2), pp. 168-192.

Wenger, E. (2010). Communities of practice and social learning systems: The career of a concept. In C. Blackmore (Ed.), *Social Learning Systems and communities of practice.* London: Springer Verlag and the Open University.

Werker C. & Ooms, W. (2020). Substituting face-to-face contacts in academics' collaborations: Modern communication tools, proximity, and brokerage. *Studies in Higher Education, 45*(7), pp. 1431-1447.

Chapter 4

Looking back, moving forward: University-industry collaboration for architectural education, innovation and transformation

Jolanda Morkel

STADIO Higher Education, South Africa

Eunice Ndeto Ivala

Cape Peninsula University of Technology, South Africa

Lone Poulsen

Open Architecture, South Africa

Rodney Harber

Open Architecture, South Africa

Abstract

In the context of a rapidly changing higher education landscape, and an evolving world of work, no less so in the global South, universities and industry are looking for new ways to collaborate to achieve sustainable and relevant educational solutions. The case explored in this chapter is situated in architectural education in South Africa, where the aim of the collaboration was not to produce research, artefacts or profit. Instead, the university-industry collaboration (UIC) was motivated by the shared pursuit of demographic transformation of the architectural profession. Using a critical action research approach, the authors reflect on the collaboration of Cape Peninsula University of Technology with Open Architecture, a non-profit educational transformation unit linked to the South African Institute of Architects. The authors show that industry can play a catalytic role where university systems fall short, to implement educational innovation for transformation. This case revealed a different kind of bi-directional educational UIC–one that follows an organic process which relies on the informal social interactions between the organisations, and the unique contributions of the individuals and teams involved–producing results that would not be possible through the individual efforts of the respective collaborators.

Keywords: university-industry collaboration, architectural education, education innovation, blended learning, online learning, South Africa

***

Introduction

Higher education (HE) is under pressure–constrained by dwindling resources, threatened by public health concerns, challenged by a call for decolonised curricula, and the need for equity, inclusion and social justice (Czerniewicz, 2018; Czerniewicz, Trotter & Haupt, 2019; Harber, 2020; Morkel & Cronjé, 2019). Furthermore, the role of the university in society is changing–not only is it expected to contribute to the socio-political project, but it is increasingly having to rely on the support of external stakeholders to serve its communities (Nsanzumuhire & Groot, 2020). With reference to university-industry collaboration (UIC), Clauson and Sheth (2017, p. 105) suggested that "teaching and learning on campus is changing radically and rapidly as institutions seek their footing in a new paradigm".

More specific to the educational context of the case that this chapter is based on, the signature pedagogy (Shulman, 2005) of the architecture studio, also referred to as the legacy model (Salama & Crosbie, 2020), is in dire need of a rethink (Brown, 2020; Morkel & Cronjé, 2019). Problems associated with asymmetrical power relations between students and design tutors, ritualised practices, student diversity, access, and inclusion are widely acknowledged (Morkel & Cronjé, 2019; Morkel & Delport, 2020; Olweny, 2020) in this context. Furthermore, demographic transformation of the architectural profession in South Africa (SA) is still slow (Harber, 2018; Harber, 2020; Morkel, 2013, Poulsen & Morkel, 2016) and "(T)here is a pressing need to explore alternative models for architectural education" (Harber, 2018, p. 14).

The collaboration between the Cape Peninsula University of Technology (CPUT), the largest university in the Western Cape province of SA, and Open Architecture (OA), a non-profit entity linked to the South African Institute of Architects (SAIA), aimed to address these challenges. The CPUT-OA collaboration produced the first blended undergraduate programme in architecture in Southern Africa, namely the 2-year part-time Baccalaureus Technologiae (BTech) degree programme in Architectural Technology. The mode of delivery was blended, comprising online learning, occasional on-campus blocks, and office-based mentoring. The first intake was in January 2014 and the collaboration was concluded at the end of 2019 when BTech programmes were phased out nationally. At CPUT the BTech degree was replaced by the Advanced Diploma programme in 2020. The design of the new Advanced Diploma, which is offered in a blended part-time format in-house, was specifically informed by the part-time BTech programme (CPUT, 2020b).

The four authors of this chapter represent both the university and the profession. Although 'industry' is not a preferred term when used in the context of the architectural discipline, we use 'industry' here in the place of 'profession' to align with the terminology used in the literature. We were interested in exploring this case, which does not follow the path of a typical UIC, generally associated with technology transfer, research, and commercialisation (Plewa at al., 2013). We explore in response to Mozambiquean scholars' Zavale and Langa's (2018) call that "further and in-depth research is still needed to address and conceptualize the ways through which universities and firms collaborate" (p. 14). The latter authors made this conclusion after systematic literature review that focused on UICs in sub-Saharan African countries. Building on the literature, we explored this case, which was based on a different kind of UIC to those generally found in the literature.

The chapter describes the methodology, followed by the role of industry and the workplace in architectural education, in the context of UIC literature. Next, a reflection on the CPUT-OA collaboration as a UIC, referring to the mechanisms for and some of the barriers to implementation, is provided. The chapter concludes with a summary of main findings and suggestions for future research.

Methodology

Using a critical action research approach, the authors reflect on a UIC between CPUT and OA. Critical action research employs a similar process as action research, but instead of a rational focus and a concern for efficiencies, social inequalities and power relations are challenged (Carr & Kemmis, 1986). This research focus is aimed at liberating the architecture studio from its traditional 'legacy' model (Salama & Crombie, 2020). The authors reflect on this programme to explore the UIC as a bi-directional educational collaboration (Nsanzumuhire & Groot, 2020) situated in the global South. This work is done in response to literature pointing out the existence of a research coverage gap in developing countries compared to developed countries, and Nsanzumuhire and Groot's (2020) finding that educational and industry collaboration is neglected in research. The authors represent the university and industry collaborators: the first author was the CPUT coordinator for the programme; the second author is a professor in Learning and Teaching with Technology at CPUT, under whose mentorship the first author fulfilled her role; the third author was the Programme Director of OA; and the fourth author is a founder and Board Director of OA.

In this chapter, writers draw on literature that they authored and co-authored in respect of the UIC, to understand "the rationality and justice of (authors) own social (and) educational practices, as well as (authors) understanding of these practices and the situations in which these practices are carried out" (Kemmis, 2008, p. 1). The authors adopted Kemmis and McTaggart's (1988) definition of action research, which emphasises three focus areas, namely practices, understandings and situations. In respect of the four steps of the action research model formulated by Kemmis and McTaggart (1988), the first three steps in the self-reflective cycle, namely plan, action and observation, were covered in previously co-authored literature, allowing this chapter to focus on the fourth and final step: reflection.

To this end, the authors referred to recent and current reporting, websites and blog posts on the undergraduate programme that resulted from the collaboration, specifically with regard to past students' narratives ('back stories' published on a blog that promoted the new Advanced Diploma programme) and official reporting on the results of the BTech degree programme and the UIC. The authors considered the ethical risk of this study, in which they draw on their own experiences as well as online resources and other materials freely available in the public domain. Where needed, we obtained the relevant permissions.

The reflection focused on the three areas highlighted as under-researched in the global South (Zavale & Langa, 2018, p. 1) the modes or channels of interaction, 2) the kind of knowledge and resources that universities and firms exchange, and 3) the outcomes yielded from these processes. This work aims to add to the body of knowledge on UICs in the global South, to inform follow-up initiatives of the respective collaborators, and to guide future UICs in this context.

Role of industry and the workplace in architectural education

University and industry are "increasingly finding it mutually beneficial to collaborate" (Guimon, 2013. p. 2). Through collaboration with industry, the university can move their traditional role of teaching and research toward a 'third mission'–to contribute to economic growth and development–and industry, in turn, can access external sources of knowledge. Although UIC can support the promise of an "Africa rising" narrative (Mbataru, 2015, n.p.), there is limited literature on UIC in the global South (Nsanzumuhire & Groot, 2020). Furthermore, the existing literature almost exclusively focuses on research, technology transfer and commercialisation as the drivers for UIC (Arza & Carattoli, 2017; Clark & Wilson, 2017). Rajalo and Vadi (2017, p. 43) suggest that:

U-I collaboration has been characterised by a 'cultural divide' between partners in terms of goals, perspectives, motives, and routines; therefore, such collaboration is highly multifaceted.

Based on his observations during a visit to the Oxford Brookes University in the United Kingdom around 2010, founding member of OA Professor Rodney Harber started to conceptualise a distance-learning initiative for architectural education in SA (Harber, 2020). This was inspired by the initiative of the Royal Institute of British Architects based at Oxford Brookes University and operating across Europe. This model used office-based mentoring and asynchronous online support, mainly via email (p. 10). The programme was aimed at mature and working architectural practitioners, and it led to professional registration rather than a qualification.

As Rodney Harber dreamed of his initiative, colleagues at the Department of Architectural Technology and Interior Design at CPUT, with the help of central staff support centres such as the Centre for Higher Education Development, Fundani, and the Centre for Innovative Educational Technologies at CPUT, experimented with alternative modes of learning and teaching. They did so by expanding the onsite studio into the community, as well as online, as part of a full-time work-integrated undergraduate programme (Morkel, 2010; Morkel, 2011; Morkel & Voulgarelis, 2011a, 2011b; Ivala & Gachago, 2012; Gachago et al., 2013; Morkel, Ivala & Gachago, 2013). At the same event where the OA concept was publicly revealed (Harber, 2020), at the New Paradigms Conference in Durban in October 2012, the CPUT online studio methodology was also presented (Morkel, 2012).

Based on the vision of Professor Harber and drawing on the CPUT experience of implementing a blended learning and teaching model, as well as informal conversations between CPUT and OA that started early in 2012, CPUT management approved the part-time programme 18 months later. The collaboration between CPUT and OA was guided by a signed Memorandum of Agreement (MoA). This specified a service fee payable by CPUT to OA, to provide teaching, facilitation, and coordination, including travel and accommodation costs for out-of-town staff. Initially, OA provided an online platform, but over time the CPUT learning management system (LMS), namely Blackboard, was employed. To adhere to quality assurance requirements, CPUT took responsibility for assessment and moderation, and a dedicated full-time CPUT senior academic staff member taught on the programme and performed the role of the CPUT coordinator. Content for the programme was developed by both parties and the IP was shared equally. To ensure alignment with the full-time programme offered by CPUT, the subject outcomes were identical, and a shared team of external moderators was appointed across the full-time and part-time programmes.

Reflection on the CPUT-OA collaboration as a UIC

Here the authors reflect on this collaboration in terms of the three under-researched topics identified by Zavale and Langa (2018), namely the modes or channels of interaction; the kind of knowledge and resources that universities and firms exchange; and the outcomes yielded from these processes, in order to explore how a UIC might facilitate implementation of educational innovation for transformation.

The modes or channels of interaction

Considering the four channels of interaction posited by Arza (cited in Nsanzumuhire & Groot, 2020), namely traditional channels, service channels, commercial channels and bi-directional channels, this educational collaboration most closely fits the latter. Traditional bi-directional channels include publication, research and development of joint projects, contract research, patents, conferences and meetings, and consultancies. Although research and publication did not form part of the MoA and this was not the main objective of the UIC, the innovation associated with the UIC presented opportunities for pedagogical research outputs.

This UIC fits the categorisation of Kunntu and Takala (2017) as an educational collaboration for jointly organised courses. CPUT provided the accredited curriculum and one dedicated CPUT educator, who also handled the course coordination for CPUT. As a representative of the architectural profession, OA shared the coordination responsibilities. Contrary to what Kunntu and Takala (2017) warn against–namely that academic work is often overlooked in UICs–in this case, it was indeed the focus. The collaboration was initiated around the academic project, and academic work dominated the channels of interaction.

Bi-directional channels, including networking with firms, marketing, and recruitment of students, were present via active upkeep of the OA website and Facebook page, through which the programme was promoted to the public. This compensated for the delayed updating of the university website and the absence of active marketing of the programme by the university, due to resource constraints. As a non-profit organisation, OA was unlike the typical industry collaborator that could provide employment to students. Instead, it provided validity through its professional standing and strong links with the professional accreditation body. This, together with OA's active and wide marketing reach, meant that the programme attracted applicants from diverse geographical areas and workplace contexts. Because of the blended mode of delivery and the limited time students were required to spend on campus, these working applicants, recruited from all over SA and some neighbouring countries, could enrol on the course regardless of location.

Although there was an accredited CPUT curriculum for the undergraduate programme, and permission for the part-time offering had been granted by the university management, its implementation was hampered by complex change management challenges at the university. These originated from a merger process–"constrained by historically based cultural and institutional barriers, which take time to overcome" (Guimon, 2013, p. 3). These obstacles, together with the (pre-pandemic) resistance of architecture educators to accept a changing educational paradigm, hindered advancement of the necessary support and infrastructure in time to offer the part-time programme in a blended, flexible, and online mode in-house at CPUT (Morkel & Cronjé, 2019).

In turn, the SAIA had received a mandate from their membership to support OA, a non-profit entity, to promote transformation of the architectural profession through strategic collaboration with an accredited architectural learning site (ALS). Seed funding was secured by OA from a local member Institute, the KZNIA, and a brick manufacturer, Corobrik, to support the setting up of an online learning platform. All they needed was an accredited curriculum. Although their original intent was to concentrate their efforts at postgraduate level, they agreed to shift their focus to the CPUT undergraduate offering, because CPUT showed an interest and had the knowledge of the blended learning model; and so, a mutually beneficial collaboration was established. The CPUT part-time curriculum was executed through a blended learning design, with the organisational support of OA, and the endorsement of the profession that it represents.

The data revealed that this UIC was a unique kind of educational collaboration, where the industry collaborator made it possible for the university to implement a non-traditional learning design when it was not yet ready to do so in-house. A close comparison to this kind of bi-directional educational collaboration that we recently found in the literature dates from 1993, when an undergraduate distance Corporate Engineering Degree Program (CEDP) was developed for industry employees, to allow them to study part-time while continuing to work (Bengiamin et al., 1998). In addition to the prominent online component of the programme, as well as the blocked, hands-on laboratory, another similarity of the UIC with the CPUT-OA collaboration is the alignment of the CEDP programme delivery to the needs of non-traditional students who are mature and working, highly motivated and self-directed (Bengiamin et al., 1998, p. 277):

> This innovative program is a model for UIC in making engineering education accessible to a broad base of adult learners.

In this CEDP programme, the University of North Dakota collaborated with the CEDP Consortium, comprising Dupont, GE Plastics, and Hutchinson Technology

Inc., together with 3M. The programme accommodated approximately 300 students. In both the case of CPUT and the University of North Dakota, the universities saw their role extended to what is commonly referred to in the literature as the 'third mission' (Guimon, 2013; Dalmarco et al., cited in Nsanzumuhire & Groot, 2020, p. 1). This suggests not only the expectation that universities will share their knowledge and expertise with stakeholders and society, but that they will seek to contribute to solving socio-economic problems. In this case, CPUT, through its collaboration with OA, responded to the need of architectural practitioners who were unable to pursue full-time studies, and enabled them to study part-time, mainly remotely and online.

The challenges posed by the lack of suitable institutional systems to support alternative organisational and business models (Morkel & Cronjé, 2019), were recompensed by the commitment of individuals. This pointed to the complex "multi-layered ecosystem consisting of interconnected perspectives on individual, organisational and institutional levels" as suggested by Skute et al. (2017, p. 941). Reflecting on the six-year project, the authors identified trust, good relationships, and open communication between individuals as essential characteristics of the CPUT-OA UIC. This observation supports Rajalo and Vadi's (2017, p. 43) assertion that "in a collaboration, partners need to cross organisational boundaries to proceed, but in doing so, relationships on the individual level become crucial".

The small team meant that colleagues on both sides of the collaboration worked closely together. A WhatsApp group was used by the teaching and coordinating staff to make announcements, ask questions, share ideas, and send reminders. This led to "an open atmosphere with a high level of trust between the partners" as suggested by Bruneel et al., cited in Kunntu and Takala (2017, p. 5).

The kind of knowledge and resources that universities and firms exchange

The main sources of knowledge that the university contributed to the UIC were the accredited curriculum and the blended learning model, while the industry, through OA and the student employers, provided links with the profession, the appointment of teaching staff other than the CPUT coordinator, efficient systems, and workplace experience and support. The part-time programme was aligned with the equivalent full-time programme in terms of the admission criteria, fees, curriculum, assessment, selection, and moderation processes. The blended learning design employed office-based mentoring, online lectures, online project submissions and feedback, interactive online design studios, and on-campus block release interaction (Morkel, 2013; Poulsen & Morkel, 2016; Morkel & Cronjé, 2019). Although this blended model was formulated by and tested at CPUT on the full-time programme a few years prior to commencement of the UIC, the detailed implementation of the part-time programme was developed jointly by both collaborators. The Programme Director of OA taught on the programme, which meant there was a close link between on the ground realities and decision making. This speaks to Kunntu and Takala's (2017) identification of courses jointly organised by academia and industry as an effective way of gaining knowledge and skill.

The online and blended learning design interventions developed at CPUT since 2010 always included work-integrated or workplace-based learning components (Morkel, 2010, 2011; Morkel & Voulgarelis, 2011a, 2011b; Gachago et al., 2013; Morkel et al., 2013). At a university of technology the workplace is an important setting for authentic learning, and online and digital technology have proven to unlock this potential for a blended learning and teaching approach (Morkel, 2013, 2017; Morkel & Garraway, 2013; Morkel & Cronjé, 2019). Students who enrolled on the part-time blended programme were required to each assign a registered architectural professional as a workplace mentor, and those who received good support from their offices were generally more likely to succeed.

A female student who graduated in 2019 initially enrolled for the programme in the first (2014) cohort, but dropped out and returned a few years later, when she was better prepared to balance work and study commitments (CPUT AT & ID: Backstories AT, n.d.):

> I quickly had to learn that the programme could not be separated from work as it could only be successful if it was integrated along with it. At that time I struggled to do just that and decided to suspend my endeavours to obtain a BTech degree to pursue it at a later time. After a few years of [work] experience I decided to pursue the programme again in 2017. But this time I was prepared. I knew that it was important to build a relationship with your employers to be able to successfully integrate the programme within the work place (sic). I have built a support system out of family, friends, an amazing mentor and fellow employees. During the two years of studying part-time I had to learn to ask for help.

Another example of a case which demonstrates a student's success as dependent on the workplace is a 2017 graduate who since obtained his master's degree full-time at another institution (CPUT AT & ID: Backstories AT, n.d.):

> Though I lost my first job, comfort and dropped out of school in my first year 2015, l recoiled with a new employer who happens to be my friend now ...

Although workplace mentorship was required, it was not graded as part of a formal work- integrated module (Samuel, Donovan & Lee, 2018). Work placements were not made by the university nor the industry collaborator, and the MoA with the employer acted more like a guide than a contract. Differences in the nature of the respective architectural offices, and their potential to provide the students with exposure to work of a certain scale and complexity, made it problematic for the students' office work to be graded, in lieu of university projects. The MoA that set out the student and employer roles and responsibilities prescribed that the employer should provide mentorship, and allow the student time to attend three one-week block release programmes on campus: in February, July and November. It also explained that one afternoon per week should be set aside for synchronous online engagements, and that, ideally, a working student should be able to dedicate a minimum of two days per week towards their studies.

Internet provision and access to printing facilities at the office were not prescribed either, but individually negotiated. Most working students lacked the skills to conduct these difficult negotiation conversations with their employers. For this reason, a one-day Step Up workshop conducted by an external facilitator, covering self-awareness, time management and other important skills and mindsets, was introduced (Morkel & Pearce, 2013). In most cases, employers understood their signing of the MoA to simply mean that they would 'allow' their student employees to enrol in the programme. Many did not feel obliged to contribute time for mentoring or to allow office time towards the students' studies. Ironically, the strength that the practices brought through the provision of workplace contexts for the working students also provided the main obstacle to some of the students' success.

The collaborators realised that better communication and building relationships with the employers was necessary. Towards this end, they formulated quarterly newsletters, conducted online surveys, and offered continuing professional development (CPD) credits in return for short learning interventions that would allow them to engage with the students around the demands of the programme. However, these sessions were not well attended. The reason for the low participation rate might be because either employers were not timeously informed, the timing was not convenient, or the CPD allocation was not attractive.

Although a handful of employers showed their interest and provided good support to their student employees, this aspect of the programme presented the most significant challenge (Poulsen & Morkel, 2016). Even students who received good workplace support found it difficult to keep up with the programme workload (CPUT AT & ID: Backstories AT, n.d.):

I found myself really struggling to come to terms with this immense workload. My personal life (socializing, sports, family etc) became non-existent.

The blended part-time programme closely followed the structure of the full-time programme. This meant that there were some inevitable compromises in the learning design, to adapt the existing model to a part-time blended offering. Considering that the part-time students might have exceeded the relevant notional hours in the part-time BTech programme, CPUT lecturers carefully considered the notional hours linked to the credits of each subject in the learning design process of the new Advanced Diploma that replaced the BTech programme. The notional hours are the total number of hours that a student is expected to work to successfully complete the programme. At the time of writing, the first Advanced Diploma cohort had not yet graduated, so it is not possible to report on the effectiveness or ineffectiveness of this strategy.

Outcomes yielded from these processes

The CPUT-OA collaboration came about in response to the slow demographic transformation of the architectural profession in SA, and the shared objective to support prospective architectural professionals from historically disadvantaged groups (HDGs) (Republic of SA, 2019), who had been unable to complete their studies full-time due to financial and other constraints (Morkel, 2013; Poulsen & Morkel, 2016). Although this group [students] did not exclusively comprise South African citizens, the historically disadvantaged individuals (HDIs) referred to here are from communities who "suffered a considerable degree of marginalization by virtue of being black, originating from poor families, and who graduated from relatively under resourced schools" (Cross & Atinde, 2015, p. 308).

The architectural profession in SA is regulated by the South African Council for the Architectural Profession. The Council registers architectural professionals at the levels of draughtspersons, architectural technologists, senior architectural technologists, and architects. Despite various attempts by universities to support HDIs, most of whom were compelled by financial constraints, family or health reasons to exit the education system early, (e.g. at the diploma or other undergraduate levels), the demographic transformation of the profession has remained slow. This means that most architectural professionals from HDGs are registered at the 'lower levels', i.e. as draughtspersons or technologists, and consequently effectively excluded from taking up senior positions in the architectural profession. Also, individuals who wish to complete studies whilst raising children, persons who need to be mobile for work or family reasons, students with chronic illness or other health issues, and those located in rural and remote areas away from campuses, needed an alternative to full-time campus-based study (OA, n.d.). These students were targeted by the blended undergraduate programme, to act as a bridge to more advanced study (Poulsen & Morkel, 2016; Poulsen, 2020).

The main outcome from the UIC was the graduation of 79 students in five cohorts from 2015 to 2019. These graduates, of whom 60% were HDIs, would not otherwise have had the opportunity to upgrade their qualifications in Southern Africa (OA, 2015, 2019). However, approximately 30% of the students who enrolled, dropped out—most in the first quarter, and mostly students from HDGs. Of those who graduated, 75% did so in the minimum time of two years, but the rest took longer (OA, 2019a; CPUT, 2016). This showed the collaborators that students were not unsuccessful due to academic challenges, but rather because they struggled to cope with the workload and juggling studies and work.

Another important outcome of this UIC was the testing and development of a successful blended learning and teaching model as an alternative for undergraduate education in Architecture in SA, responding to Prof. Harber's (2018, p. 15) lament:

> It should now be apparent that all our schools of architecture are too similar in every respect and that as long as a baseline of accreditation is retained there is great potential to offer various levels of course emphasis, financial models and ownership.

By the time the mandatory replacement of BTech degrees nationally came into effect at the end of 2019, CPUT had developed systems and capacity to implement the replacement curriculum independently. Furthermore, based on the good results and positive feedback from students, moderators and industry, the blended model was expanded to the offering of the Advanced Diploma programme in Interior Design. Also, OA had built a reputation and track record, based on which it could approach other HE institutions to negotiate future collaborations.

When the new Advanced Diploma qualification in Architecture was designed, there was no full-time option to align to, and therefore the design addressed the challenges that the BTech pilot highlighted. For example, rather than spreading the main subjects of Design and Technology over two years, in the new programme the first year focuses on the building of foundational skills and the second year on studio application. This allows students to adapt to the new study environment and helps them to establish a work-study balance. At the time of writing, the students of the first cohort had not yet completed the second year of the two-year part-time programme, and therefore it was not possible to report on the impact of these design decisions.

To allow a degree of flexibility, the new curriculum was designed to allow students to advance to the second year of study, repeating a maximum of two of the year one subjects that they might have failed the first time. To address the time constraints, it was decided to allow students to submit work produced at the office for assessment. However, due to differences in workplace focuses, expertise, and support, it was difficult to establish a significant overlap between work that students produced at the office and the assessable outcomes required to fulfil the curriculum requirements. This challenge remains unresolved.

Approximately 10% of the students accessed the part-time programme without having obtained the prerequisite diploma qualification, but qualified for access via Recognition of Prior Learning (RPL) achieved through their extensive work experience. Two of the RPL students graduated *cum laude*. Furthermore, two of the 79 students have since graduated with professional master's qualifications, through full-time studies at other universities in SA, and two are under way. Many of the remaining graduates are awaiting a similar blended part-time option to obtain their professional master's qualification, which would enable them to register as Professional Architects. The CPUT Postgraduate Diploma and Master's of Architecture programmes that were designed based on this blended model have been submitted for statutory approval.

An unintended outcome of the part-time programme is the students' ability to practice architecture online, in the same way that they studied (CPUT AT & ID: Backstories AT, n.d.):

> Inspired by this new approach to studying architecture, I wanted to know if it was possible for an architect to work completely online. ... I had a deep desire to travel internationally with my partner for an extended period of time ... So, from July 2019, I spent 9 months traveling South East Asia while still working full-time. The experience was a success, and not only helped us understand new ways of working together but also put our team at an advantage when we were required to work from home as a result of the COVID-19 pandemic.

Furthermore, through this UIC, the Cape Institute for Architecture started offering blended CPD events to practitioners spread across the country, thereby allowing those in remote areas also to obtain CPD credits through them. Their experience with this methodology prepared them well for the restrictions that came with the outbreak of the pandemic. Additionally, through the UIC, CPUT became a member of the Global Studio project with member institutions from America, Canada, SA, Uganda, and Australia, among others.

The above outcomes, including an increase in graduates from HDGs, and the knowledge to design and offer blended programmes and CPD events, were facilitated by this educational innovation. As claimed by Rajalo and Vadi (2017), collaborators who come from different domains can produce innovative solutions together, motivated by the need to create new knowledge, methods, and approaches. Innovation was employed to achieve the transformation goal shared by the university and the industry collaborators. As suggested by Mbataru (2015), it is not that innovation is not present in Africa, but often the systems are lacking, and university bureaucracy and timelines delay progress (par.16). With the necessary industry support and employing technology, he argues, university education can help the continent to catch up with the rest of the world, which is important at a time when the 'Africa rising' narrative is gaining momentum. This argument is supported by the World Economic Forum (2017, par. 5): "A collaboration between the public and private sectors can help to foster an environment that promotes an innovative mindset and encourages and nurtures our brain potential".

Conclusion

Guided by Zavale and Langa's (2018) model which addresses the modes or channels of interaction, the kind of knowledge and resources that universities and firms exchange, and the outcomes yielded from these processes, this case revealed a different kind of bi-directional educational UIC. The authors argue that an industry collaborator can play a catalytic role where university systems fall short. The primary knowledge and resources that the university and industry exchanged in this UIC included the accredited curriculum, office-based learning contexts, professional endorsement, links to practitioner networks, varying degrees of mentorship, and the implementation of robust and sustainable processes. The outcomes yielded from this UIC include a notable contribution to the demographic transformation of the architectural profession, and a blended learning design on which subsequent programmes were built, and which prepared students for more blended and online workplace practices.

The new knowledge that was created "that neither of the collaborators have previously possessed" (Ankrah & Al-Rabbaa, 2015, pp. 396-397) enabled this bi-directional educational innovation. Considering that the knowledge creation was located more in the "informal social interactions between the organisations, than focusing on planned resource and knowledge transfer" (Ankrah & Al-Rabbaa, 2015, p. 399), points to the categorisation of the process as organic ('irrational' according to the literature). Moreover, what arose was not through the combination of what the respective collaborators provided alone, but rather it was developed through and inspired by their association. More than that, the outcomes that were yielded through the channels of interaction, drawing on knowledge and resources, relied on what Rajalo and Vadi (2017, p. 53) refer to as "the specific characteristics of acting individuals and teams" when they claim that:

Organisations create the context for the collaboration, while motivation and maturity for that depends rather on the specific characteristics of acting individuals and teams than on the general organisational processes.

This work is timeous, considering the global post-pandemic economic reality and the need for alternative and humanised models of educational delivery. Such alternative models may include interdisciplinary approaches, flexible, blended, hybrid flexible (hyflex) and online interventions, and strategic collaboration with industry partners. The findings presented in this chapter are relevant not only for architectural education, but professional education more broadly, and specifically in the context of Southern Africa. Future research might explore the new CPUT Advanced Diploma results, as well as consider the intersection of two bodies of literature which, to date, have not been integrated, namely literature on the UIC and HE innovation facilitation, specifically situated in the global South.

References

Ankrah, S. N. & Al-Tabbaa, O. (2015). Universities-Industry Collaboration: A Systematic Review. *Scandinavian Journal of Management*, 31(3), pp. 287–408.

Arza, V. & Carattoli, M. (2017). Personal ties in university-industry linkages: A case-study from Argentina. *The Journal of Technology Transfer*, 42(4), 814-840. doi: 10.1007/s10961-016-9544-x]

Bengiamin, N. N., Johnson, A., Zidon, M., Moen, D. & Ludlow, D. K. (1998). The development of an undergraduate distance learning engineering degree for industry—a university/industry collaboration. *Journal of Engineering Education*, 87(3), p. 277.

Brown, J.B. (2020). *From denial to acceptance: a turning point for design studio in architecture education*. https://distancedesigneducation.com/2020/05/11/from-denial-to-acceptance-a-turning-point-for-design-studio-in-architecture-education/

Carr, W. & Kemmis, S. (1986). *Becoming critical: Knowing through action research*. Geelong: Deakin University.

Clark, C. H. & Wilson, B. P. (2017). The potential for university collaboration and online learning to internationalise Geography education. *Journal of Geography in Higher Education*, 41(4), pp. 488-505.

Clauson, C. & Sheth, R. (2017). University-Industry Collaborations are driving creation of next-generation learning spaces. *Planning for Higher Education*, 45(4), pp. 105-117.

Cape Peninsula University of Technology. (2016). Report to Senate: Part-time BTech Architectural Technology Programme April 2016. Unpublished Report.

Cape Peninsula University of Technology AT & ID. (2020a). Advanced Diplomas in Architectural Technology and Interior Design. https://sites.google.com/view/cput-at-id-ad/home

Cape Peninsula University of Technology AT & ID. (2020b). Backstories AT. https://sites.google.com/view/cput-at-id-ad/backstories/backstories-at?authuser=0

Cross, M. & Atinde, V. (2015). The pedagogy of the marginalized: Understanding how historically disadvantaged students negotiate their epistemic access in a diverse university environment. *Review of Education, Pedagogy, and Cultural Studies*, 37(4), pp. 308-325.

Czerniewicz, L. (2018). Inequality as higher education goes online. In N.B. Dohn, S. Cranmer, J. Sime, M. De Laat & T. Ryberg (Eds.), *Networked Learning Research in Networked Learning*, pp. 95-106. Cham: Springer. doi: 10.1007/978-3-319-74857-3_6

Czerniewicz, L., Trotter, H. & Haupt, G. (2019). Online teaching in response to student protests and campus shutdowns: Academics' perspectives. *International Journal of Educational Technology in Higher Education*, 16(1), pp. 1-22.

Gachago, D., Ivala, E., Felix-Minnaar, J., Morkel, J. & Vajat, N. (2013). Towards the development of digital storytelling practices for use in resource-poor environments, across disciplines and with students from diverse backgrounds. *South African Journal for Higher Education*, 28(3), pp. 961-982.

Guimón, J. (2013). Promoting university-industry collaboration in developing countries. *World Bank*, 3, pp. 12-48.

Harber, R. (2018). Time for other models for teaching architecture? *Journal of the South African Institute of Architects*, 78, pp. 13-15.

Harber, R. (2020). From the Conventional to Open Architecture and E-Learning. *Journal of the KwaZulu-Natal Region of the South African Institute of Architects*, 45(2), pp. 10-12.

Ivala, E. & Gachago, D. (2012). Social media for enhancing student engagement: The use of Facebook and blogs at a University of Technology. *South African Journal for Higher Education*, 26(1), pp. 152-167.

Kemmis, S. (2008). Critical theory and participatory action research. In P. Reason & H. Bradbury (eds), *The SAGE Handbook of Action Research: Participative Inquiry and Practice* (2nd ed., pp. 121-138). London: SAGE.

Kemmis, S. & McTaggart, R. (1988). *The action research planner* (3rd ed.). Geelong: Deakin University Press.

Kunttu, L. & Takala, J. (2017). Facilitating Role of Educational Involvement in University-Industry Collaboration. *Paper presented at The XXVIII ISPIM Innovation Conference – Composing the Innovation Symphony*, Austria, Vienna, 18-21 June 2017 (pp. 1-11).

Mbataru, P. (2015). Enhancing university-industry linkages for 'rising Africa'. *University World News*. https://www.universityworldnews.com/post.php?story=20150523091500358

Morkel, J. (2010). Architecture goes online. The online architecture studio, towards an instructional design framework for design learning by distance education. *Poster presentation at the IDEA conference*, Faculty of Informatics and Design, CPUT, Cape Town.

Morkel, J. (2011). The use of educational technology for Work Integrated Learning. *Presentation delivered at the National Seminar on Work Integrated Learning*, University of the Western Cape, 3 November 2011.

Morkel, J. (2012). Design learning goes online: The role of ICT in architecture education. *New Paradigms Conference*, Durban, 26-27 October 2012.

Morkel, J. (2013). Designing authentic architectural education for the future: A case for Open Architecture. *Journal of the South African Institute of Architects*, 64, pp. 19-20.

Morkel, J. (2017). An exploration of Socratic learning in a webinar setting. In J. Anderson (Ed.), *Architecture Connects. Association of Architectural Educators 4th International Conference*, pp. 336-344. Oxford: Brookes University.

Morkel, J. & Cronjé, J. (2019). Flexible Learning Provision for Architecture in South Africa: Lessons Learnt from an Industry-University Collaboration. In C. L. Scott & E. N. Ivala (Eds.), *Faculty Perspectives on Vocational Training in South Africa*, pp. 19-33. New York: Routledge.

Morkel, J., Delport, H., Burton, L. O., Olweny, M., & Feast, S. (2021). Towards an Ecosystem-of-Learning for Architectural Education: Reflecting on a network of six pedagogical clusters. *Charrette, 7*(1), 15-40.

Morkel, J. & Garraway, J. (2013). Community, Work and Architectural Education. *Paper presented at the Authentic Learning Colloquium*, Bellville, 22 March 2013.

Morkel, J., Ivala E. & Gachago, D. (2013). Cognitive apprenticeship and work integrated learning: Design-based research for improving an undergraduate program in architectural technology. *HELTASA Conference 2013*, Pretoria, 27-29 November.

Morkel, J. & Pearce, C. (2013). CPUT step up and onwards in Architecture. *Paper presented at the Innovative Pedagogical Practices in Extended Curriculum Programmes (ECPs) Regional Conference*, Cape Town, 29 August 2013.

Morkel, J. & Voulgarelis, H. (2011a). Online and onsite: architecture studio goes virtual... and virtually real. *Paper presented at the Current Trends in Design Education Symposium, CPUT*, Cape Town, 4 August 2011.

Morkel J. & Voulgarelis H. (2011b). Extending the Studio with Facebook. *Paper presented at the E-learning update at The River Club*, Cape Town, 20-21 September 2011.

Nsanzumuhire, S. U. & Groot, W. (2020). Context perspective on University-Industry Collaboration processes: A systematic review of literature. *Journal of Cleaner Production*, 258, pp. 1-24.

Open Architecture. (2015). *OA Progress Report to SAIA*. Unpublished Report.

Open Architecture. (2019a). *SAIA AGM Report*. Unpublished Report.

Open Architecture. (2019b). *Part-time BTech Architectural Technology: CPUT-OA collaboration. Close-out report in respect of the students that went through the system and the students currently in the system*. Unpublished Report.

Open Architecture. (n.d.) Architecture Collaborations. http://openarchitecture.co.za/collaborations

Olweny, M. R. (2020). Architectural education in sub-Saharan Africa: An investigation into pedagogical positions and knowledge frameworks. *The Journal of Architecture*, 25(6), pp. 717-735.

Plewa, C., Korff, N., Johnson, C., Macpherson, G., Baaken, T. & Rampersad, G. C. (2013). The evolution of university–industry linkages—A framework. *Journal of Engineering and Technology Management*, 30(1), pp. 21-44.

Poulsen, L. (2020). Perspective 5, Post-COVID-19 Perspectives. https://www.youtube.com/watch?v=Bp9DQrDmvIY

Poulsen, L. & Morkel, J. (2016). Open architecture: a blended learning model for architectural education, Architecture South Africa. *Journal of the South African Institute of Architects*, 78(3), pp 28-30.

Rajalo, S. & Vadi, M. (2017). University-industry innovation collaboration: Reconceptualization. *Technovation*, 62, pp. 42-54.

Republic of South Africa. 2019. Inquiry and Equity Ownership by Historically Disadvantaged Groups and the Application of the ICT Sector Code in the ICT Sector. *Government Gazette* No. 42234, 15 February 2019.

Salama, A. M. & Crosbie. M.J. (2020). Educating architects in a post-pandemic world. https://commonedge.org/educating-architects-in-a-post-pandemic-world/

Samuel, D., Donovan C. & Lee, J. (2018). University-industry teaching collaborations: A case study of the MSc in Structural Integrity co-produced by Brunel University London and The Welding Institute. *Studies in Higher Education*, 43 (4), pp. 769-785.

Shulman, L.S. 2005. Signature pedagogies in the professions. *Daedalus*, 134(3), pp. 52-59.

Skute, I., Zalewska-Kurek, K., Hatak, I. & de Weerd-Nederhof, P. 2017. Mapping the field: a bibliometric analysis of the literature on university-industry collaborations. *The Journal of Technology Transfer*, 44(3), pp. 916-947. doi: 10.1007/s10961-017-9637-1

World Economic Forum. (2017). It's time for an innovation revolution in Africa. https://www.weforum.org/agenda/2017/01/its-time-for-an-innovation-revolution-in-africa/

Zavale, N. & Langa, P. (2018). University-industry linkages' literature on Sub-Saharan Africa: Systematic literature review and bibliometric account. *Scientometrics*, 116(1), pp. 1-49. doi: 10.1007/s11192-018-2760-4

Chapter 5

Co-researching and technology use in higher education: Benefits,implications, and challenges

Nokukhanya Noqiniselo Jili

University of Zululand, South Africa

Mfundo Mandla Masuku

University of KwaZulu Natal, South Africa

Dina Mashiyane

University of the Free State, South Africa

Abstract

Researchers, particularly in higher learning institutions, should be involved in diverse collaborations to remain relevant, increase productivity, and be globally competitive. Co-researching enhances interdisciplinary networks and partnerships across various institutions, and can increase the research outputs of researchers. The fourth Industrial Revolution effects a change in the research landscape, where innovative ways are introduced and implemented to enhance co-researching. This chapter examines the benefits, implications, and challenges of co-researching and using technology in higher education in the twenty-first century. The extant literature on the impact of co-researching and using technology in higher education was reviewed. It contends that co-researching is a vital process where researchers with distinctive characteristics, skills, and knowledge can collaborate and identify a common research niche area. However, the challenge is that while there are technological tools that are freely available and accessible to everyone, researchers are not aware of their existence or are struggling to understand the potential of these tools and how beneficial they can be, especially for enhancing co-researching attempts. Moreover, a lack of skills, awareness, advocacy, and resources, and insufficient budgets hinder a digitally transformed research landscape. Improved technology used in research can enhance both local and global research collaboration. This would increase research output by further attracting more research partners globally. Determined researchers will therefore be prepared to pursue research, collaborate and contribute to a particular field of study.

Keywords: co-researching, graduate attributes, higher education, South Africa, technology

***

Introduction

Institutions of higher learning are significant determinants of information and knowledge systems. They are the dominant producers of new knowledge, they critique information and seek new local ideas and global applications for existing knowledge. Co-researching is not a new concept, and it is regarded as the key to producing new knowledge and enhancing research productivity (Graham et al., 2019). Co-researching allows researchers to share their different capabilities and diverse insights into the same issues. This is widely regarded as valuable to navigating the complexities of research (Chubb et al., 2021).

However, in South Africa challenges such as the digital divide, access to funding, breakdown of communication, lack of skills and awareness, and insufficient resources hinder researchers' efficiency. Hence, to overcome these challenges, co-researching and the use of technology could assist researchers in learning from colleagues across disciplines and institutions. Researchers could also learn from researchers with diverse research experience, knowledge, and perspectives (Katz & Martin, 1997; Viale, 2010; Chubb et al., 2021).

Research is a core pillar of higher education; it provides innovative knowledge in diverse fields of study. This includes, but is not limited to, the sciences, technology, arts, humanities, and social sciences. Co-researching and using technology are vital for connecting knowledge and competencies to innovative ideas and research settings.

Therefore, this chapter contends that technology is a valuable device that researchers can employ to support collaboration. Various technological platforms and tools exist to support co-researching attempts. Elements of the digital divide, such as a lack of awareness, advocacy, insufficient skills, availability, and budget implications, contribute to lack of their use within the South African context. Co-researching without adequate resources and tools can hinder research productivity and output. In contrast, employing technological tools for enhancing co-research attempts can only be beneficial to institutions.

Cloud-based computing platforms, such as virtual research environments (VREs), reference management tools, academic and social media platforms, institutional and data repositories, all enable the sharing of content, ideas, documents, and data, and concurrent collaboration on documents (Barker et al., 2019). Using technology allows researchers to share experiences with nearby peers, which includes knowledge sharing with remote experts (Ens et al., 2019).

However, some scholars contend that using technology in higher education institutions focuses mainly on teaching and e-learning; therefore, there is a dearth of literature focusing on managing co-researching using technologies (Daud & Zakaria, 2017). Co-researching is increasingly recognised as a technique enhancing the depth and influence of research in higher education, while delivering benefits for both researchers and institutions (Hampton & Parker, 2011; Potter et al., 2020). This practice applies to researchers from the same discipline, in South Africa and globally.

Co-researching enables researchers to produce better knowledge through their collective intellect by providing a broader and more informed perspective than sole researching. Co-researching is observed as a strategic effort towards team building, and sharing knowledge and resources through technology. This promotes the efficiency of knowledge exchange, while reducing the time taken to access these resources (Hara et al., 2003; Zhang & Tang, 2017). Technology facilitates collaboration and enhances communication among researchers from various geographical areas with diverse expertise in the knowledge structuring and production process (Kumazawa et al., 2017). Institutions should offer technological support by providing information and communication technology (ICT) facilities. This would include strategic planning to encourage co-researching and setting goals worthy for research collaboration.

Students are also showing interest in adopting active and participatory functions. These roles allow them to collaborate with their supervisors to conduct research and disseminate their findings through publications (Bozeman et al., 2013; Leahey & Reikowsky, 2008). Institutions of higher learning must embrace those who believe in collaboration. They should create an enabling environment to increase their productivity and contribute to the body of knowledge.

This chapter provides a short overview of the literature on co-research in higher education, followed by a discussion of the different tools to support co-research, such as the internet, Skype, document-sharing programs, and co-editing software. There are advantages of using technology in co-research, such as the blurring of geographic boundaries despite increased specialisation (Hunter & Leahey, 2008), and access to innovative data through technology, particularly in the context of the open access movement. Technology supports co-researching, facilitates communication, and enhances local and global research collaboration to increase research output by attracting more research partners globally, while grooming students to pursue research in a particular field. This study also offers insights into the challenges of co-research and how to mitigate them.

Literature review

Conceptualising co-researching in higher education

Weir et al. (2011) and Eikey et al. (2015) described co-researching as planned engagements among researchers or a research team. This may indicate in-person engagement or engagement mediated by technology, where information is exchanged to produce written scientific knowledge in the form of publications. Previously in South Africa, traditional institutions of higher learning were predominately teaching entities; however, there was a refocus since 2005 to further a prioritised research agenda (Cloete et al., 2015; Chiware & Becker, 2018).

Institutions of higher learning are investing considerable resources into institutionalising and mainstreaming co-researching by developing frameworks supporting research, technology and innovation interventions and recruitment strategies. These include the employment of highly skilled researchers to play a mentoring role to emerging researchers. It also includes the exploration of co-research across and beyond local institutions, to access and transfer much needed research expertise. Nason and Pillutla (1998) reiterated the need for the institutionalisation of co-researching, because not all higher education institutions have the same set of goals and prioritise a collaborative research agenda.

Some scholars indicate that co-researching is usually based on the social structure of relations. This can be either at a personal level, through personal interactions and connections, or by tapping into existing collaboration networks (Kretschmer, 2004; Guan & Liu, 2016). Co-research across different contexts, disciplines and access to resources is not always easy and needs a shared vision guiding the collaboration. Co-researching should be inspired by an idea compelling enough to acquire the support of each collaborator with their institutions. They should establish a sense of the commonalities permeating them, while adhering to the diverse activities in their research project. Co-researchers should be committed, connected, and bound by common research aspirations. Co-researching is recognised as a learning journey which provides the focus and energy to learn from one another and uplift collaborators' research aspirations, particularly in publishing (Chubb et al., 2021).

This chapter contends that co-researching is an important process where researchers with distinct characteristics, skills, and knowledge can collaborate and identify a common research niche area. The chapter further acknowledges that although co-researching is a learning process; it is susceptible to challenges emanating from diverse ways of thinking, and personal and institutional shortcomings. Policy leaders and academic managers also encourage co-researching across disciplines, institutions, and national boundaries by employing cooperation strategies. Brandenburger and Nalebuff (1996, p. 637) observed that "cooperation between competitors" improves the competitive advantage of research units, and stimulates economic growth (Sonnenwald, 2007). It is advanced that co-researching improves research output. It also capacitates researchers to acquire the diverse research skills needed in the twenty-first century. Through co-researching, researchers can advance knowledge from various epistemic positions. Most importantly, it improves the reach and impact of research, as discussed in detail in the next section.

Implications of co-researching with various researchers

Co-researching enhances the exposure of authors, because such research is published in respective journals in each author's field. That research therefore receives more citations than single-authored articles (Suárez-Balseiro et al., 2009). Co-researching also enhances an individual scholar's reputation. The scholar may become known in a field because of collaborative research. Co-researching therefore provides a chance for researchers to enhance their visibility, which participating researchers and their affiliated institutions benefit from.

When researchers collaborate, they invite experts, often well-known and research-productive peers, to work together. Most collaborative researchers are research scholars who are active in their fields of study (Kronegger et al., 2012). This is observed when researchers invite their peers from other countries to collaborate (Abramo & D'Angelo, 2014). Global collaboration outperforms domestic collaboration, both in quality and quantity (Aldieri et al., 2019). Furthermore, Aldieri et al. (2019) established that global collaboration has a positive effect on the impact of a publication. Global co-researched publications have an increased chance of being cited by co-authors and other researchers. For example, Kwiek (2020) demonstrated that articles co-authored with global peers are cited more often than domestically co-authored publications. Co-researching contributes to an author's affiliated institution and publication and citation data, all of which contribute to university rankings.

Most global rankings pay little attention to whether a report is produced by a single author or multiple authors. Publication credits are shared equally for each affiliated institution when a report is produced by authors from various institutions. Researchers in South Africa and other developing countries indicate a preference for publication in foreign journals, as these provide greater visibility.

There is high competition for publication in established and high-influence journals, such as those listed by the Institute of Scientific Information (ISI), the

International Bibliography of the Social Sciences (IBSS), Scopus and the Social Sciences Index. These journals are viewed as having high significance, and authors from developing countries need to compete with established researchers from developed countries.

Pouris and Ho (2014) indicated that global co-researching by African researchers increased by 66% over a recent five-year period, mainly in the areas of medicine and natural resources. Dozier et al. (2014) revealed that South Africa has a collaboration rate of 80%, with a high percentage of global co-authorship. A critical factor for the dramatic increase is access to global resources through technology. Various authors argue that co-researching among regional countries in Africa is minimal compared to other countries (Onyancha & Maluleka, 2011; Martin & Umubyeyi, 2019). In South Africa, research funding is structured to encourage publication, but not necessarily co-authorship with authors outside the institution; authors must share the funds allocated for the publication with local collaborators (Dozier et al., 2014).

Researchers can interact faster with one another because of the ease of access to information precipitated by the internet, and its potential to support communication and collaboration among dispersed academics. This rapid interaction enhances research skills, learning and communication, and can at times occur online. Table 5.1 illustrates the differences between information flow before and after introducing information and communications technology (ICT), especially in Asia and Africa. This alteration in the mode of information exchange through internet technology favours contemporary researchers, while enhancing their research skills.

Table 5.1: Comparison of information flows before and after introducing internet technology

Before	**Currently**
Outdated references in the library	Recent literature accessible online
Manually accessible library collections	Libraries or databases accessible online
Slow exchange of information	Fast exchange of information
Publication of scientific articles takes years	Publication takes a few months
Paid subscription journals	Open access journals; creative commons (CC)

Source: Regoniel (2015).

Researchers' access to ICT tools plays a positive role through enhancement outside the institution and for global collaboration. Using ICT facilities bridges the divergence created by the physical distance among collaborators. These divergences harm the levels of co-researching and productivity (Chiware & Becker, 2018). Many developing countries are still lagging behind in the adaption, adoption, access, and application of ICTs, which is a scenario counterproductive to knowledge creation (Mukherjee, 2011). Research team members participate in research initiatives by using freely available tools such as Google Apps, and other research collaboration technologies (DeFranco & Laplante, 2018). This was previously impossible because of lack of funding or mobility.

Improvements in ICTs have enabled collaboration among geographically dispersed research units and have increased the incidence of more successful research (Kouzes et al., 1996; Finholt, 2002; Atkins et al., 2003; Hara et al., 2003; Nentwich, 2003).

Daud and Zakaria (2017) contended that the inadequate use of collaborative technologies is caused by the non-availability of technology, a lack of institutional support, and not having a culture of co-researching. This suggests that institutions of higher learning should promote technological tools, such as virtual research environments, academic social networking sites (ASNS), online reference management tools, virtual meeting and conferencing and others, with comprehensive technology platforms to support research tasks for virtual collaborations (Daud & Zakaria, 2017). There are various technological platforms available to enhance research endeavours. Some of these platforms are freely accessible, whereas others are available on a subscription basis. The following section discusses some of the popular tools and technologies in co-research projects/practices.

Virtual research environments

Virtual research environments (VREs) or collaborative research environments are hubs or platforms created for research projects (Lokers, 2020). These are often developed by a community of researchers embarking on a research project. Various universities and research institutions employ these platforms to foster collaboration research attempts (Van Wyk, Bothma & Holmner, 2020). Features are customised according to the needs of the research project, and data, documents, references, and other resources can be embedded and shared on the platform. These tools apply to various scientific domains, ranging from high-energy physics and astrophysics, to humanities and the social sciences (Barker et al., 2019). VREs are exceptionally valuable for enhancing the collaboration, management, and preservation of knowledge that can be shared to satisfy the information needs of a community of practice. This is evident in many countries.

A study on the enablers and barriers of knowledge management practices in South Africa and Mauritius reported the use of VREs in facilitating engagement and collaboration among South African researchers (Ramjeawon & Rowley, 2020).

In the United States of America, the Regenstrief Center for Healthcare Engineering at Purdue University implemented the Regenstrief National Center for Medical Device Informatics (REMEDI) model. This is an example of a VRE adopted by over 140 hospitals, where health professionals can collaborate in sharing data related to infusion pumps (Zentner & Zink, 2017).

As a measure to assemble various stakeholders, the Research Data Alliance facilitates a Virtual Research Environment Interest Group. This group aims to support researchers and institutions planning to implement these research gateways (Barker et al., 2019).

More affordable VREs could be established on cloud-based collaboration platforms, such as Google Drive and Microsoft OneDrive, which allow collaborative writing, commenting, and sharing of documents and resources.

Academic social networking sites

Social media has developed exceptionally within the last 10 years, offering online spaces where individuals from various levels of society can engage in discussion of diverse topics, be it on a personal or professional level. ASNS are not only beneficial for enhancing access, visibility, and effect of the research output, they can also construct collaborative networks. Researchers can join communities of practices based on their fields of expertise and research interests, find collaborators, and share work in progress, including published content (Yan & Zhang, 2018). Developing platforms, such as Mendeley, Academia.edu, and ResearchGate, enable information creation and distribution among researchers, with no location or time barriers (He & Jeng, 2016).

The user base of these platforms continues to expand exponentially. Since its inception in 2008, ResearchGate reported over 19 million registered members (ResearchGate, 2020). Boudry, and Durand-Barthez (2020) report over 145 million users (Academia.edu, 2020). Mendeley, as both an ASNS and reference management tool, boasts over 6 million users (Mendeley, 2020). The following graph reflects the annual growth in sign-up on Academi.edu.

Figure 5.1: Academia.edu annual user base

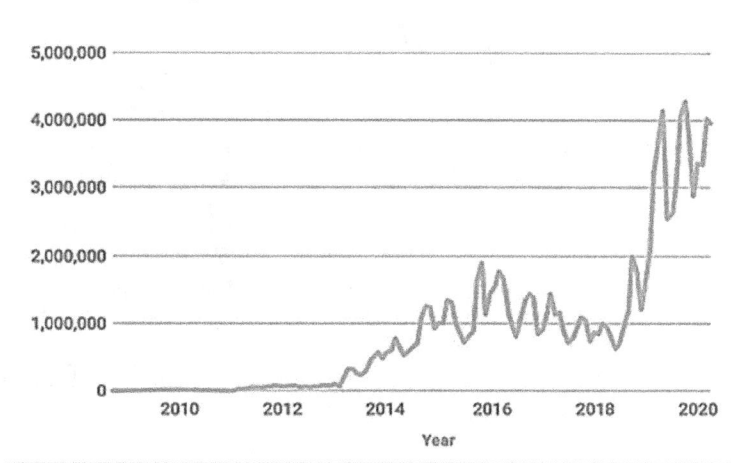

Source: Academia.edu (2020)

Results from a study by Elsayed (2016) indicated that 70% of researchers joined these platforms to interact with other researchers, whereas 24% indicated that they are likely to join for collaborative attempts. El-Berry (2015) reported an exceptional level of awareness and usage of these platforms for constructing networks. Conversely, Meishar-Tal and Pieterse (2017) established that researchers rarely interact or collaborate on these platforms. Interestingly, case studies conducted by various research institutions (Carnegie Mellon University, Hong Kong Baptist University, ETH Zurich and ETH-Bibliothek, Institut Pasteur, Technical University of Denmark, International Food Policy Research Institute and Stanford University) published on the Mendeley platform reported positively on the tool's effectiveness for enhancing engagement and collaboration among researchers and librarians (Mendeley, 2020).

Online reference management tools

Researchers using reference management platforms can share and collaborate to support referencing attempts. These tools are available either as open-source or proprietary software. They can surpass manual referencing and enhance collaboration in terms of sharing references (Ebrahim, 2017). Researchers can establish relevant literature, collect and organise references, and cite automatically with a built-in citation plug-in embedded in Microsoft Word.

Concerning co-researching, individuals can share a list of collected references with collaborators. A reference management tool, such as Mendeley, has a variety of functionalities beyond managing references. This platform enables networking with like-minded individuals to collaborate on research projects through various interest groups. Various citation styles and formats are supported. Additional styles can be installed directly in the programs. For example, as a proprietary software EndNote supports over 6000 journal styles that can be installed in the program. EndNote has a feature to match manuscripts to journals (Muthuraj et al., 2018), whereby researchers can identify potential journals to submit their manuscripts to. The platform also recommends high-influence journals indexed on the Web of Science.

Tools with desktop and online versions allow for synchronisation to enable cloud data storage. Various academic information search databases support proprietary reference management tools, including Ebscohost, ScienceDirect, Emerald Insight, Google Scholar, and Jstor. These tools have built-in citation features (Zaugg et al., 2011). Opportunities for collaboration and managing references are endless with Paperpile and Papers, examples of proprietary tools featuring use of Google Docs. Most of these tools allow migration from one reference management platform to another; for example, researchers can export their Mendeley library to the EndNote platform.

However, ironically, with all these benefits, researchers are barely using these tools. This is confirmed by a study conducted by the University of Iowa, which aimed to ascertain the usage patterns of EndNote for research collaboration. The results indicated that researchers use EndNote for references, but not for collaboration (Regan et al., 2017). Tables 5.2 and 5.3 provide examples of online reference management tools and their access modes.

Table 5.2: Free/Open sources online reference management tools

Open source/free	Desktop Version	Online/cloud version	Browser extension/web importer
Cite this for me		✔	✔
Zotero	✔	✔	✔
JabRef	✔	✔	✔
Mendeley	✔	✔	✔
Citationsy		✔	✔

Table 5.3: Proprietary online reference management tools

Proprietary tools	Desktop version	Online/cloud version	Browser extension/web importer
EndNote	✔	✔	
Refworks	✔	✔	
Citavi	✔	✔	✔
Paperpile	✔	✔	✔
Papers	✔	✔	✔

Virtual conferencing and meeting platforms

ICT facilities are crucial strategic resources in higher education, as they provide researchers with opportunities to expand their choices through knowing what works best in their various fields of study (Jamian et al., 2012). For example, computer conferencing systems typically include not only e-mail and bulletin boards, but also 'many-to-many' communications. Although some of the online referencing platforms offer the benefits of enhancing communication, there are virtual platforms which have made it possible for researchers to share ideas, knowledge and work, and to meet virtually without any location barriers. These include Zoom, Skype, Microsoft Teams, Google Meet and TeamViewer, as indicated in Table 5.4. They are available on free/basic plans and subscription plans where users get additional benefits. This model of access is also referred to as Freemium.

Table 5.4 gives examples of the most popular virtual meeting and conferencing platforms and their modes of accessibility.

Table 5.4: Examples of popular virtual conferencing and meeting platforms

Platform	Desktop version	Online/cloud version	Mobile application	Freemium
Zoom	✓	✔	✔	✔
Microsoft Teams	✔	✔	✔	✔
Skype	✔	✔	✔	✔
Cisco Webex	✔	✔	✔	✔
Google Meet	✔	✔	✔	✔

There is evidence in the literature noting the benefits of these platforms for enhancing co-researching (Sá, 2019; Rubinger, 2020). Researchers from across the globe can attend and participate in virtual conferences, and have the opportunity to share their knowledge, and to network and build communities of practice. In addition to this, these platforms provide endless conferencing opportunities. Some of the conferences are now available to researchers free of charge, whereas others are available for a fee–but still cheaper than a face-to-face conference. Furthermore, these tools have the benefit of improving virtual research processes such as data collection, particularly for qualitative research.

A study conducted by Archibald et al. (2019) on the feasibility of Zoom as a tool for conducting qualitative interviews yielded more positive results than challenges indicated by both the participants and researchers. Platforms such as Wonder are now trying to recreate the serendipitous 'mingling' or networking that happens in between conference presentations or at cocktail receptions.

Challenges in co-researching

The challenges presented here do not encompass all of the difficulties that can arise in co-researching. This chapter focuses on those which are frequently raised, through experience and the literature, as real or perceived barriers to the co-creation of knowledge through partnerships.

Co-researching among seasoned and emerging researchers

There are difficulties for a single researcher to conduct holistic and pluralistic research. Researchers have different perspectives, possess different knowledge resources and are from different parts of the world. Co-researching is therefore a significant part of the emerging research communities for creating a more effective knowledge-sharing space (Charlotte et al., 2014). By 2016, 60% of all scientific publications were globally co-authored (NSB, 2016; Kozma & Calero-Medina, 2019). Encouraging co-researching is an effective way to increase research output. Co-researching is a developmental process and a strategy which can be initiated by either emerging or experienced researchers. This exercise requires collaborators with high morale and a clear strategic direction towards achieving their research agendas. Integrating technology in research can advance and sustain research collaboration among emerging researchers and contribute to attainment of their research agendas (Oguguo et al., 2020). Co-researching using technology creates linkages between experienced and emerging researchers, to combine research ideas from diverse disciplines and contexts.

Some emerging researchers expect experienced researchers to produce strategic planning on collaboration techniques. Steinmacher et al. (2013) contended that without regard to seniority, research collaboration involves the formulation of rules of engagement and a shared understanding, which decrees how researchers collaborate on shared platforms. This approach was conceived as being 'top-down', where experienced researchers impose their research ideas on emerging researchers who are perceived as receivers of information and instructions. This approach poses some challenges among collaborators, such as low participation from emerging researchers because it is assumed that knowledge is required from seasoned researchers.

Sutherland and Naidoo (2016) attested that collaborative research activities are sometimes filled with conflict, which may hinder decisions in attaining a research agenda. Furthermore, power lies with the senior researchers–and they hold full authority and base their decisions on their own views and experiences, not those of emerging researchers. Sometimes this leaves emerging researchers with the perception that their views and inputs do not add value in the collaboration. This indicates that conflicts could possibly undermine the productivity of research collaboration. Ideally, senior researchers are not the only sources of knowledge, and emerging researchers are not the only ones who receive knowledge and information, with senior researchers also learning from emerging researchers.

Experienced researchers are not restricted from sharing their subjective experiences where emerging researchers might learn from them. It may transpire that emerging researchers have less power, and may therefore resent others in the team. This suggests that emerging researchers should be able to express their ideas freely as well as listening to experienced researchers, which would lead to new insights.

Zhang and Tang (2017) expounded that integrating technology in research among researchers positively moderates the relationship between collaboration breadth and innovation performance. However, Nason and Pillutla (1998) averred that conflict in collaborative research is sometimes caused by limited resources from less prestigious higher education institutions. Despite the power dynamics inherent in collaboration, Howard et al. (2016) attested that co-researching through use of technology enhances innovative performance and helps to expand the researcher's network. In terms of research collaboration power dynamics and conflicts, trust among researchers in a team is fundamental to positive research collaboration.

Scholars such as Dirks and Ferrin (2001) and Charlotte et al. (2014) have suggested that employing interpersonal trust would result in positive expectations among emerging and senior researchers about their actions, and could yield positive research output. By improving the collaborative process, trust and respect are key to promoting and managing interdependencies between researchers in the team in their respective expertise spaces. Co-researching requires openness and willingness from both emerging and seasoned researchers to be part of the process, to avoid any manipulative behaviour that is destructive toward attainment of a research agenda.

Bittner and Heidemeier (2013) stated that individuals in a collaborative environment develop diverse concepts, resulting in high-quality research output. Senior researchers are mandated to reinforce clarity, enthusiasm, communication, and commitment to drive a research agenda. Co-researching can therefore create a space for more democratic and reflexive research in process-oriented sustainability science, where all parties will benefit equally (Miller, 2013; Kumazawa et al., 2017).

Barriers to using technological tools for co-researching

Technologically innovative initiatives were and still are compromised by the digital divide. This disruption has existed for years, and is more prevalent in developing countries. The research landscape cannot be digitally transformed due to concerns about a lack of skills, awareness, advocacy and resources, and insufficient budgets (Van Wyk, Bothma & Holmner, 2020). A lack of awareness of the potential benefits of these tools hinders their usage. Most of the tools listed above are freely available and accessible to everyone, but some researchers are not aware of their existence and how beneficial they can be, particularly for enhancing co-researching attempts. Interestingly, barriers to using academic social media platforms non-related to the digital divide are also emphasised in the literature. A study conducted among 24 physicians globally indicated that researchers were sceptical of using these platforms. This was attributable to a lack of maintaining confidentiality, and of active participation, time, and trust, workplace acceptance and support, and information anarchy (Panahi et al., 2016).

Online data sets are provided on various data repositories for access by research communities. Numerous studies proved that the anonymity of participants' information can easily be de-anonymised when paired with other datasets (Malin & Sweeney, 2004; Ohm, 2009; Vitak et al., 2016).

Communication breakdown

Most research conducted by a team of researchers is likely to have encountered challenges, particularly those associated with communication breakdown and teamwork dynamics. Such difficulties are exacerbated when the researchers come from dissimilar disciplinary backgrounds (Freshwater et al., 2006; Melber, 2015). Researchers from diverse disciplines are likely to use dissimilar notions and frameworks, and this is the case even when the disciplines of participating researchers seem closely related. It is therefore important to ensure a mutual understanding and common use of jargon throughout the research process.

Establishment of a functional communication system is essential to successful co-researching. Ideally, co-researching is a mechanism to promote greater collegiality among researchers, departments, and institutions. A functional system of communication can promote and maintain an open dialogue between researchers throughout a research project. A system of communication should provide transparent feedback up and down the chain of command. It can also prioritise open discussion and strategically attempt to identify and discuss threats to research.

Co-researchers may fail to implement a well-conceived research plan if they are unable or unwilling to share resources, exchange information, or behave in a collegial manner. A communication breakdown represents a major hurdle in the dissolution of collaborative research relationships. It can lead to initiation of a host of threats to the responsible conduct of research (Charlotte et al., 2014).

There are several strategies to discuss the breakdown of communication in twenty-first century research. Advances in technology are incorporated to improve communication efficacy. Besides existing technologies such as the internet, telephone and fax services, technological advancements include the increasing reliance on e-mail, teleconferencing, videoconferencing, access to project-specific websites, and using numerous electronic chats. Despite these advancements, the concern remains that an over-reliance on technology to promote communication cannot be a substitute for a shared commitment to accountability in following through on all assigned tasks. Individuals may still prefer to be non-communicative with new or old technology. Any impediment to communication, technological or otherwise, may be reflected in the research quality.

Conclusion

Co-researching and technology use in institutions of higher learning has received little attention so far in the literature, both globally and locally. This chapter revealed that co-researching through technology has the potential to improve research output. It can reach greater numbers of collaborators, with more innovative forms of research. It can be contended that partnership and co-researching are needed to maximise the benefits increasingly evidenced by these collaborative attempts. Based on the analysis conducted, it is concluded that co-researching through technology is essential to promoting and expanding intercontinental collaborations.

The underlying challenges of using technology for co-researching are lack of awareness, knowledge, skills, and availability of resources. Research-intensive institutions can strategise in developing research policies, and fostering the implementation of various technological tools and platforms to enhance collaboration. As some authors emphasise, for the future of African research, a balanced partnership with researchers and institutions needs to be established with researchers and institutions in Africa and abroad. This is required to ensure that the quantity and quality of involvement are discussed and agreed upon on an equal basis to enhance scientific research.

Co-researching involves sharing power and an openness to innovative ways of working and learning together as researchers by using technology.

References

Abramo, G. & D'Angelo, C. A. (2014). How do you define and measure research productivity? *Scientometrics*, *101*(2), pp. 1129-1144.

Academia.edu (2021). Our mission is to accelerate the world's research. https://www.academia.edu/about

Aldieri, L., Guida, G., Kotsemir, M. & Vinci, C. P. (2019). An investigation of the impact of research collaboration on academic performance in Italy. *Quality & Quantity, 53*(4), pp. 2003-2040.

Archibald, M. M., Ambagtsheer, R. C., Casey, M. G. & Lawless, M. (2019). Using zoom video conferencing for qualitative data collection: perceptions and experiences of researchers and participants. *International Journal of Qualitative Methods, 18*, 1609406919874596. doi: 10.1177/1609406919874596

Barker, M., Olabarriaga, S. D., Wilkins-Diehr, N., Gesing, S., Katz, D. S., Shahand, S. & Treloar, A. (2019). The global impact of science gateways, virtual research environments and virtual laboratories. *Future Generation Computer Systems, 95*, pp. 240-248.

Bittner, J. V. & Heidemeier, H. (2013). Competitive mindsets, creativity, and the role of regulatory focus. *Thinking skills and creativity, 9*, 59-68.

Bozeman, B., Fay, D. & Slade, C. P. (2013). Research collaboration in universities and academic entrepreneurship: the-state-of-the-art. *Journal of Technology Transfer, 38*(1), pp. 1-67.

Brandenburger, A. M. & Nalebuff, B. J. (1996). *Co-opetition.* New York: Crown Business.

Boudry, C. & Durand-Barthez, M., (2020). Use of author identifier services (ORCID, ResearcherID) and academic social networks (Academia. edu, ResearchGate) by the researchers of the University of Caen Normandy (France): A case study. *Plos one, 15*(9), p.e0238583.

Charlotte, J., Jan, N. & Jakob, L. (2014). Faculty trust, conflict and the use of knowledge in an international higher education context. *Journal of Educational Sciences & Psychology, 4*(2), pp. 1-14.

Chiware, E. R. & Becker, D. A. (2018). Research trends and collaborations by applied science researchers in South African universities of technology: 2007–2017. *The Journal of Academic Librarianship, 44*(4), pp. 468-476.

Chubb, L.A., Fouché, C.B. & Kengah, K.S., (2021). Co-researching complexities: Learning strategies for edge walking in community–university research partnerships. *Research for All, 5*(1), pp. 157-173.

Cloete, N., Maassen, P. & Bailey, T. (2015). *Knowledge production and contradictory functions in African higher education.* Cape Town: African Minds.

Daud, N. M. & Zakaria, H. (2017). Impact of antecedent factors on collaborative technologies usage among academic researchers in Malaysian research universities. *International Journal of Information and Learning Technology, 34*(3), pp. 189-209.

DeFranco, J. F. & Laplante, P. (2018). A software engineering team research mapping study. *Team Performance Management: An International Journal, 24*(3/4), pp. 203-248.

Dirks, K. T. & Ferrin, D. L. (2001). The role of trust in organizational settings. *Organization Science, 12*(4), pp. 450-467.

Dozier, A. M., Martina, C. A., O'Dell, N. L., Fogg, T. T., Lurie, S. J., Rubinstein, E. P. & Pearson, T. A. (2014). Identifying emerging research collaborations and networks: Method development. *Evaluation & the Health Professions, 37*(1), pp. 19-32.

Ebrahim, N. A. (2017). Online Reference Management Tools for Improving Research Visibility and Impact. https://www.researchgate.net/publication/

320096984_Online_Reference_Management_Tools_for_Improving_Research
_Visibility_and_Impact

Eikey, E. V., Reddy, M. C. & Kuziemsky, C. E. (2015). Examining the role of collaboration in studies of health information technologies in biomedical informatics: A systematic review of 25 years of research. *Journal of Biomedical Informatics, 57*, pp. 263-277.

El-Berry, D. K. (2015). Awareness and use of academic social networking sites by the academic staff at the South Valley University in Egypt. *Journal of Library and Information Sciences, 3*(2), pp. 115-132.

Elsayed, A. M. (2016). The use of academic social networks among Arab researchers: A survey. *Social Science Computer Review, 34*(3), pp. 378-391.

Ens, B., Lanir, J., Tang, A., Bateman, S., Lee, G., Piumsomboon, T. & Billinghurst, M. (2019). Revisiting collaboration through mixed reality: The evolution of groupware. *International Journal of Human-Computer Studies, 131*, pp. 81-98.

Freshwater, D., Sherwood, G. & Drury, V. (2006). International research collaboration: Issues, benefits and challenges of the global network. *Journal of Research in Nursing, 11*(4), pp. 295-303.

Graham, I.D., McCutcheon, C. & Kothari, A. (2019). Exploring the frontiers of research co-production: the Integrated Knowledge Translation Research Network concept papers. *Health Research Policy Systems, 17*, p. 88. doi: 10.1186/s12961-019-0501-7

Guan, J. & Liu, N. (2016). Exploitative and exploratory innovations in knowledge network and collaboration network: A patent analysis in the technological field of nano-energy. *Research Policy, 45*(1), pp. 97-112.

Hampton, S. E. & Parker, J. N. (2011). Collaboration and productivity in scientific synthesis. *BioScience, 61*, pp. 900-910.

Hara, N., Solomon, P., Kim, S. L. & Sonnenwald, D. H. (2003). An emerging view of scientific collaboration: Scientists' perspectives on collaboration and factors that impact collaboration. *Journal of the American Society for Information science and Technology, 54*(10), pp. 952-965.

He, D. & Jeng, W. (2016). Scholarly collaboration on the academic social web. *Synthesis Lectures on Information Concepts, Retrieval, and Services, 8*(1), pp. 1-106.

Howard, M., Steensma, H. K., Lyles, M. & Dhanaraj, C. (2016). Learning to collaborate through collaboration: How allying with expert firms influences collaborative innovation within novice firms. *Strategic Management Journal, 37*(10), pp. 2092-2103.

Hunter, L. & Leahey, E. (2008). Collaborative research in sociology: Trends and contributing factors. *The American Sociologist, 39*(4), pp. 290-306.

Jamian, M., Ab Jalil, H., & Krauss, S. E. (2012). Malaysian public university learning environments: Assessing conduciveness through ICT affordances. *Procedia-Social and Behavioral Sciences, 35*, pp. 154-161.

Katz, J. S. & Martin, B. R. (1997). What is research collaboration? *Research Policy, 26*(1), pp. 1-18.

Kozma, C. & Calero-Medina, C. (2019). The role of South African researchers in intercontinental collaboration. *Scientometrics, 121*(3), pp. 1293-1321.

Kretschmer, H. (2004). Author productivity and geodesic distance in bibliographic co-authorship networks, and visibility on the Web. *Scientometrics, 60*(3), pp. 409-420.

Kronegger, L., Mali, F., Ferligoj, A. & Doreian, P. (2012). Collaboration structures in Slovenian scientific communities. *Scientometrics, 90*(2), pp. 631-647.

Kumazawa, T., Hara, K., Endo, A. & Taniguchi, M. (2017). Supporting collaboration in interdisciplinary research of water–energy–food nexus by means of ontology engineering. *Journal of Hydrology: Regional Studies, 11*, pp. 31-43.

Kwiek, M. (2020). Internationalists and locals: international research collaboration in a resource-poor system. *Scientometrics, 124*(1), pp. 57-105.

Leahey, E. & Reikowsky, R. C. (2008). Research specialization and collaboration patterns in sociology. *Social Studies of Science, 38*(3), pp. 425-440.

Lokers, R. M., Knapen, M. R., Candela, L., Hoek, S. & Meijninger, W. (2020). Using Virtual Research Environments in Agro-Environmental Research. *International Symposium on Environmental Software Systems* (pp. 115-121). Cham, Switzerland: Springer.

Malin, B. & Sweeney, L. (2004). How (not) to protect genomic data privacy in a distributed network: Using trail re-identification to evaluate and design anonymity protection systems. *Journal of Biomedical Informatics, 37*(3), pp. 179-192.

Martin, S. B. & Umubyeyi, V. L. (2019). What works in education in emergencies: Co-researching and co-authoring. *NSI* 02, NORRAG Special Issue, Data collection and Evidence Building to Support Education in Emergencies.

Meishar-Tal, H. & Pieterse, E. (2017). Why do academics use academic social networking sites? *International Review of Research in Open and Distributed Learning, 18*(1), pp. 1-22.

Melber, H. (2015). Knowledge is power and power affects knowledge: Challenges for research collaboration in and with Africa. *Africa Development, 40*(4), pp. 21-42.

Mendeley. (2020). *Our users.* https://www.elsevier.com/solutions/mendeley/who-uses

Miller, T. R. (2013). Constructing sustainability science: emerging perspectives and research trajectories. *Sustainability Science, 8*(2), pp. 279-293.

Mukherjee, S. (2011). Application of ICT in rural development: Opportunities and challenges. *Global Media Journal, 2*(2), pp. 1-8.

Muthuraj, A., Rajkumar, T. & Arputharaj, J. I. (2018). *EndNote: Reference Management Tool for Managing Research.* https://www.researchgate.net/publication/3225 39617_EndNote_Reference_Management_Tool_for_Managing_Research

Nason, S. W. & Pillutla, M. M. (1998). Towards a model of international research teams. *Journal of Managerial Psychology, 13*(3/4), pp. 156-166.

National Science Board. (2016). *Science and engineering indicators 2016.* Alexandria, Virginia: National Science Board.

Oguguo, P. C., Freitas, I. M. B., & Genet, C. (2020). Multilevel institutional analyses of firm benefits from R&D collaboration. *Technological Forecasting and Social Change, 151*, pp. 119-841.

Ohm, P. (2009). Broken promises of privacy: Responding to the surprising failure of anonymization. *UCLA Law Review, 57*, p. 1701.

Onyancha, O. B. & Maluleka, J. R. (2011). Knowledge production through collaborative research in sub-Saharan Africa: How much do countries contribute to each other's knowledge output and citation impact? *Scientometrics, 87*(2), 315-336.

Panahi, S., Watson, J., & Partridge, H. (2016). Social media and physicians: exploring the benefits and challenges. *Health Informatics Journal, 22*(2), pp. 99-112.

Potter, R.W., Szomszor, M. & Adams, J. (2020). Interpreting CNCIs on a country-scale: The effect of domestic and international collaboration type. *Journal of Informetrics, 14*(4), 101075.

Pouris, A. & Ho, Y. S. (2014). Research emphasis and collaboration in Africa. *Scientometrics, 98*(3), 2169-2184.

Ramjeawon, P. & Rowley, J. (2020). Enablers and barriers to knowledge management in universities: Perspectives from South Africa and Mauritius. *Aslib Journal of Information Management, 72*(5), pp. 745-764

Regan, M., Healy, H. & DeBerg, J. (2017). *Pure Collaboration: Supporting EndNote Sharing Options.* Midwest Chapter of the Medical Library Association Annual Meeting. https://ir.uiowa.edu/cgi/viewcontent.cgi?article=1307&context=lib_pubs

Regoniel, P. (2015). The Role of Internet Technology in Enhancing Research Skills [Blog Post]. *SimplyEducate.Me.* https://simplyeducate.me/2015/10/17/internet-technology-research-skills/

ResearchGate (2020). *About.* https://www.researchgate.net/about

Rubinger, L., Gazendam, A., Ekhtiari, S., Nucci, N., Payne, A., Johal, H., Khanduja, V. & Bhandari, M. (2020). Maximizing virtual meetings and conferences: A review of best practices. *International Orthopaedics, 44*, pp. 1461-1466.

Sá, M. J., Ferreira, C. M. & Serpa, S. (2019). Virtual and face-to-face academic conferences: comparison and potentials. *Journal of Educational and Social Research, 9*(2), pp. 35-35.

Sonnenwald, D. H. (2007). Scientific collaboration. *Annual Review of Information Science and Technology, 41*(1), pp. 643-681.

Steinmacher, I., Chaves, A. P. & Gerosa, M. A. (2013). Awareness support in distributed software development: A systematic review and mapping of the literature. *Computer Supported Cooperative Work, 22*(2-3), pp. 113-158.

Suárez-Balseiro, C., García-Zorita, C. & Sanz-Casado, E. (2009). Multi-authorship and its impact on the visibility of research from Puerto Rico. *Information Processing & Management, 45*(4), pp. 469-476.

Sutherland, M. & Naidoo, S. (2016). A management dilemma: Positioning employees for internal competition versus internal collaboration. Is coopetition possible? *South African Journal of Business Management, 47*(1), pp. 75-87.

Van Wyk, J., Bothma, T. & Holmner, M. (2020). A conceptual virtual research environment model for the management of research data, a South African perspective. *Library Management, 41*(6/7), pp. 417-446. doi: 10.1108/LM-02-2020-0037

Viale, R. (2010). Knowledge-driven capitalization of knowledge. In R. Viale & H. Etzkowitz (Eds.), *The capitalization of knowledge.* Cheltenham: Edward Elgar.

Vitak, J., Shilton, K. & Ashktorab, Z. (2016). Beyond the Belmont principles: Ethical challenges, practices, and beliefs in the online data research community. *Proceedings of the 19th ACM Conference on Computer-Supported Cooperative Work & Social Computing* (pp. 941-953). doi: 10.1145/2818048.282007

Weir, C. R., Hammond, K. W., Embi, P. J., Efthimiadis, E. N., Thielke, S. M. & Hedeen, A. N. (2011). An exploration of the impact of computerized patient documentation on clinical collaboration. *International Journal of Medical Informatics, 80*(8), pp. e62-e71.

Yan, W. & Zhang, Y. (2018). Research universities on the ResearchGate social networking site: An examination of institutional differences, research activity level, and social networks formed. *Journal of Informetrics, 12*(1), pp. 385-400.

Zaugg, H., West, R. E., Tateishi, I. & Randall, D. L. (2011). Mendeley: Creating communities of scholarly inquiry through research collaboration. *TechTrends, 55*(1), pp. 32-36.

Zentner, M. & Zink, R. (2017). HUBzero and CatalyzeCare: A community driven platform for data sharing and collaboration in medical informatics research. *PeerJ Preprints.*

Zhang, G. & Tang, C. (2017). How could firm's internal R&D collaboration bring more innovation? *Technological Forecasting and Social Change, 125*, pp. 299-308.

Chapter 6

Exploiting technologies in networked designing, training and research engagement in African universities: A case of the Partnership for African Social and Governance Research

Pauline Ngimwa

Partnership for African Social and Governance Research, Kenya

Proscovia Namubiru Ssentamu

Uganda Management Institute, Uganda

Connie Nshemereirwe

Actualise Africa, Uganda

Abstract

The conglomeration and affordances of modern digital technologies empower scholars and researchers, including those in remote and technologically underserved regions, to engage in networked projects and course design, training, and research. This not only introduces flexibility in the way scholarship is conducted, but also enriches the scholarship of course design, training, research and engagement through sharing competences in more effective ways. The need to network online has become greater in the COVID-19 dispensation, as the world adopts restrictions around closer physical interactions. In this chapter we use the experiences of the Partnership for African Social and Governance Research (PASGR), a Pan-African organisation based in Nairobi, Kenya as the platform for our reflection.

For over a decade now, PASGR has collaborated with research institutions, researchers and scholars in universities in 16 African countries. We showcase how PASGR has provided spaces that support co-designing of projects and courses, co-training, and co-researching activities. We reflect on the technologies and skills used to link African and international scholars in public policy and research capacity building. Specifically, we examine how various technologies enable facilitators in Kenya, Nigeria, Uganda, Ethiopia, South Africa and Australia to co-design and co-teach short professional development research courses for participants across the continent. We also share experiences on how researchers in Nigeria, Kenya and the United Kingdom (UK) are able to meet virtually and design research projects. Finally, we discuss challenges of connecting virtually on various designing, training and research projects across different contexts, cultures and technological capacities, and the strategies utilised in mitigating the attendant intricacies.

The chapter presents some lessons on how the affordances of networked technologies can be exploited to empower scholars and researchers from Africa and beyond to collaborate and actively engage in various development projects in multicultural settings. Policy makers and leaders in charge of creating supportive environments for international collaborations may also find this useful.

Keywords: technologies, affordances, co-designing, co-training, co-researching, virtual communities, COVID-19, Pan-Africa, East Africa

***

Introduction

Modern technologies have increasingly enabled scholars and researchers to search for and share new knowledge and skills in the contemporary world, where mass movement is on the rise. Such movement can be individually, institutionally, physically and/or virtually initiated through various forms of networks and collaborations. It is against this background that the authors reflect on their experiences in harnessing technologies in networked course design, training and research engagement.

For over a decade the Partnership for African Social and Governance Research (PASGR) has collaborated with universities and individual researchers and scholars in 16 African countries. We showcase how PASGR has exploited the virtual space to support collaborative project and course design, training and research. In the ensuing sections, we provide a brief historical, contextual and conceptual background plus the methodology used. We then provide detailed reflections on the scope and nature of the virtual networks harnessed by PASGR and her partners, and the technologies used to enable networking and their affordances. We conclude by discussing the challenges of connecting virtually using various technologies, the mitigation strategies, and lessons learnt.

Background

PASGR was founded to respond to the declining capacity of social science for effective and high-quality training and research in governance and public policy in Africa. As an independent Pan-African organisation located in Nairobi, Kenya, PASGR partners with individual scholars and researchers, universities, research think tanks, civil society organisations, business and policy communities, to produce and disseminate policy-relevant research; design and deliver short professional development courses for researchers and policy actors; and facilitate the development of collaborative higher education programmes.

PASGR implements its mission through a three-pillar approach. The first is the higher education programme, which through formal partnerships with African universities delivers a collaborative Master of Research and Public Policy to 14 universities, a PhD in Public Policy, and a transformative pedagogy training through the Partnership for Pedagogical Leadership in Africa (PedaL). The second pillar is the Professional Development and Training programme, which delivers experiential professional development aimed at building policy actors' and researchers' skills and competencies in policy-engaged research. The third pillar is the Research programme, which works with African social scientists to produce high-quality governance research aimed at improving institutions, and ultimately transforming the living conditions of people in the countries where the research is conducted. The Research programme also implements PASGR's policy uptake strategy through the *Utafiti Sera* series–a Kiswahili phrase for research policy community.

Conceptual review

Conceptually, the authors are guided by six questions–*Why?*, *What?*, *How?*, *Who?*, *Where?* and *When?*–as analytical lenses to reflect on various technologies used in collaborative project design, implementation, and evaluation activities. The question 'Why?' is perhaps the most significant in selecting particular technologies. It is important to reflect on the goal and intended outcome of using the technologies, because this provides the rationale for the engagement, its robustness and project sustainability. The key stakeholders should agree on the relevance of networking, and why particular technologies should be used.

The 'What?' question focuses on the actual technologies used in the various project activities. According to the University of Victoria Center for Youth and Research (n.d.), training institutions should consider whose knowledge and ways of knowing are given priority. Similarly, in selecting technologies to use, it is crucial to reflect on what technologies and whose technologies they are relative to specific project activities.

The 'How?' question focuses on the strategies used to link the project activities to the technology during collaborative design, implementation, and evaluation to facilitate the achievement of the intended outputs and outcomes. The digital age has enabled various ways in which knowledge and skills can be shared, and the need to virtually connect has become even more critical due to the global COVID-19 pandemic.

The 'Who?' question focuses on the agents that use the technologies. Understanding the profiles of the various agents and their roles guides customisation of the project activities and technologies to their needs, abilities, interests, and learning context. According to the University of Victoria Center for Youth and Research (n.d., slide 1):

> ... Education should not occur in a vacuum, and these [community] links are essential for contextualizing knowledge, deepening understanding, encouraging community involvement, and reconnecting students with a vital support system.

Projects and technologies anchored in the values, belief systems and skill sets of the 'community' enable such a 'community' to profit from and share knowledge and skills through various support networks.

The 'Where?' question focuses on the locale or spaces where the technologies are being used. Again, the digital age has ushered in a variety of ways in which knowledge and skills can be prepared, stored, and shared. Unlike the traditional face-to-face method, and depending on the mediating circumstances, the flipped spaces provide a variety of flexible, innovative, and exciting approaches, ranging from blended to purely online engagements.

The 'When?' question focuses on the time at which the technologies are used in the project lifecycle. The above six questions aim at providing the agents with more engagement options, allowing them to connect virtually through reflection and sharing, thereby transforming themselves as well as the communities they interact with.

Methodology

In writing this chapter, we engaged in critical reflection on our experiences through various lenses. We adapted educational technologist scholars Matt Bower's (2008) affordance analysis e-learning design methodology, and Mike Sharples et al.'s (2009) generative framework for new modes of learning, to match various project activities to various technologies based on their inherent utility value [affordances]. Guided by the two frameworks and the six questions, we were able to collaboratively reflect on and provide first-person accounts of our lived experiences, thereby contributing to alternative ways of knowing (Morley, 2008).

Drawing on Bower's (2008) conceptualisation of 'affordances', which according to Gibson (1997) are the action possibilities provided to the actor by the environment, the functionality of the technologies used by PASGR are carefully analysed and selected to ensure a right match between them and the selected PASGR activities. Although Bower (2008) originally conceived affordance analysis as a design methodology for matching learning tasks with learning technologies, we adapted it as a design methodology.

Our reflections were made through the lenses of the Programme Manager of PASGR's Professional Development and Training Programme that offers research training to African researchers, an alumnus of this training programme, and a trainer in the programme. We critically reflected on our deeper and more complex understanding of practice experience (Fook, 2011), by focusing on what we considered good practices and challenges from various viewpoints. As noted by Fook (2011), critical reflection is used in professional learning settings to assist practitioners to improve practice by learning from experience.

The writing process was in three stages. Firstly, after agreeing on the topic and themes to reflect on, each team member approached the themes from their viewpoint. Secondly, we documented and shared our reflections through email; and finally, we agreed on and harmonised our reflections into a chapter following a very iterative process. The reflections were enriched with a review of relevant literature.

Scope of virtual networking in project design, training and research by PASGR

By its very nature, and as ingrained in its name, PASGR operates under the principle of partnership and therefore has multiple partners widely distributed across the African continent and other parts of the world. While face-to-face interaction with PASGR's partners has been the preferred mode of engagement, virtual interactions have become increasingly popular due to their efficiency, cost- effectiveness, ability to enable communities to remain connected, particularly relevant in the face of COVID-19.

We focus on four key activities where PASGR uses various technologies to network with her virtual communities: virtual meetings for course design; selection of facilitators and participants; co-training; and co-researching.

Project design virtual meetings

PASGR employs a range of technologies to connect with its virtual communities of training facilitators and researchers in course design of projects. Some of the meetings are either held spontaneously in response to emerging issues, or as a follow-up on agreed actions. Others are scheduled to last 2–4 hours, with time moderation and built-in breaks to allow participants to refresh, read and consult sources, just as would have proved useful in physical meetings. The importance of such breaks has become more obvious during COVID-19 with long hours of interactions, in order to counter 'Zoom fatigue'.

The technologies used in virtual meetings range from phone calls, WhatsApp calls and messages, Google Hangouts and Skype calls to more advanced video and conference facilities, such as Microsoft Teams, Zoom, GoToMeeting and video conferencing. Guided by the six questions, Bower's (2008) affordance analysis and Sharples et al.'s (2009) generative framework, we matched the virtual meetings for project design with technologies (Table 6.1).

Table 6.1: Matching virtual meetings for project design with selected technologies

Mediating circumstance: Pure online					
Conceptual lenses					
What technologies are used?	**Why are these technologies used? (Affordances)**	**How are the technologies used? (Strategy in activity)**	**Who uses the technologies? (Agent)**	**Where are the technologies used? (Locale)**	**When are the technologies used? (Timing)**
Polycom video conferencing unit, computers, laptops, smartphones	Examples are media, technical, portability, viewability, accessibility, intractability, manipulability, and compatibility affordances	Online meetings for project co-designing	Course designers, facilitators, researchers PASGR Secretariat	Dispersed/ virtual	Continuously from project inception to conclusion
Voice over Internet Protocol (Zoom, GoToMeeting, Skype, Video Conferencing)	Examples are media, spatial, temporary, navigation, synthesis, technical, usability, and aesthetic affordances	As above			
Email	Examples are share-ability, Recording ability, and interactability affordances	Providing feedback on peer reviews and editing			

Sources: Adopted and modified from Bower (2008) and Sharples et al. (2009)

The interactive technologies highlighted in Table 6.1 are selected because of various media, spatial, temporal, synthesis, technical, and aesthetic affordances (Ssentamu et al., 2020; Bower, 2008). A combination of these affordances allows for various abilities, such as viewability, watchability recordability, save-ability, accessibility, retrievability and flexibility. In addition, these technologies provide space for the incorporation of media such as PowerPoint slides and Prezi, blog posts, and podcasts, and give access to various platforms, including the virtual learning environment. Most importantly, multiple participation is also enabled, thus encouraging inclusivity. Sharples et al. (2009) describe interactive technologies as enabling integration, embeddedness and accessibility; providing rich feedback; learning community trails and gaming to learn in instances where learning is the target. A combination of affordances renders such technologies versatile and interesting to use in both synchronous and asynchronous spaces to enhance interactivity.

Since PASGR's notion of partnership extends to designing learning materials, a lot of work is achieved remotely. This has been afforded through the creation of dynamic virtual communities of practice (CoPs) comprising course designers, facilitators and researchers. These communities work together virtually with facilitation from the PASGR Secretariat. Below we describe two examples of projects that have been achieved while working remotely, and some of the approaches that have been employed to support this.

Converting face-to-face modules into blended learning mode

The blended learning project focused on converting existing short course modules into a blended learning mode that combines online and face-to-face formats. After an initial face-to-face meeting aimed at orientation, training and planning by course developers located in Kenya, Uganda, South Africa, Nigeria, Ethiopia, Tanzania, UK, United States of America (USA) and Australia, the team worked with an instructional design expert via email, phone calls, and Zoom to prepare the modules, which were finally uploaded onto the learning management system (LMS) on the Moodle platform. This was an iterative process that required peer review until materials were in good enough shape to be uploaded to the Moodle.

In hindsight, this blended learning project set the foundation for later work that would see these course modules converted into purely online courses, as has become necessary in delivering training in a COVID-19 environment. For instance, some of these modules have been delivered online to students in PASGR's PhD in Public Policy programme during the pandemic, in place of a planned physical academic seminar. This process revealed a major capacity gap among university lecturers in designing online courses and online facilitation, and provided an opportunity to address these gaps through an online course— that has also been developed and delivered online during the COVID pandemic period. The course comprises three core modules: Online Course Design, Online Facilitation and Innovative Assessment, and is implemented under PASGR's PedaL project. So far, this new online course has been delivered to over 350 participants in partner institutions from Eastern, Western and Southern Africa.

Co-designing e-cases

The second example is designing PASGR's multimedia learning materials, referred to as e-cases. Following the same approach, the course developers had an initial face-to-face workshop for training and planning. Thereafter, the teams dispersed to work remotely, with support from trainers based in Kenya and the USA. The PASGR technical team provided technical support through virtual meetings. A second face-to-face workshop helped fill capacity gaps in refining the resources.

Technologies in selection processes

Selection and mentorship of facilitators

One of the important aspects in heightening African ownership and sustainability of the PASGR training programme is the way in which potential facilitators are identified and mentored. After each training, facilitators normally have email and phone conversations about participants who can be mentored to become facilitators. The mentorship process follows virtually using email and Skype. These mentees shadow the more experienced facilitators for about a year, after which they are gradually given more facilitation responsibility, until they can stand on their own and mentor others. The model of identifying participants who show promise and/or express interest in furthering the mission of PASGR expands the pool of facilitators to select from.

The importance of this gradual process was evident in the recent transition from a blended to purely online offering of the programme. The need for this transition was in response to recurring difficulties with participants being unable to afford to travel to a central location, and the attendant costs of accommodating, transporting and maintaining the facilitators. High costs meant that this valuable training opportunity was inaccessible to many willing and qualified participants across the continent, making a purely online approach necessary.

After five years of building the facilitators' capacity, testing and refining the blended offering, it was possible to assemble an all-African team to work with a professional online education specialist to convert the courses into online format. COVID-19 only speeded up this transition.

Selection of course participants

The PASGR Secretariat advertises the programme across the continent through an e-newsletter and social media (Facebook, Twitter and WhatsApp) targeting academics and policy makers. Applications are submitted via a dedicated online portal, which requires applicants to briefly outline their motivation for applying for the course, as well as the context in which they intend to apply their learning. Over the years, the number of applicants has outstripped the available capacity, necessitating tighter selection according to set criteria. The course facilitators, supported by the PASGR office, are usually called upon to score the applicants remotely, and the final selection is made in this way. In Table 6.2 we adapt Bower's affordance analysis and Sharples et al.'s (2009) generative framework, guided by our conceptual lenses to match selection of facilitators and their capacity building, and selection of participants with the selected technologies.

Table 6.2: Matching selection of facilitators and participants with selected technologies

Mediating circumstances: Blended					
Conceptual Lenses					
What technologies are used?	**Why are these technologies used? (Affordances)**	**How are the technologies used? (Strategy in activity)**	**Who uses the technologies? (Agent)**	**Where are the technologies used? (Locale)**	**When are the technologies used? (Timing)**
Computers/laptops/ smartphones	As in Table 6.1	Selection of facilitators. Inform Secretariat of selected facilitators	Facilitators, PASGR Secretariat	Dispersed/ virtual	3 months before programme starts
Internet	Examples are media, spatial, temporary, navigation, synthesis, technical, usability, and aesthetic affordances				
Computers/laptops/ smartphones	As in Table 6.1	Capacity building of facilitators –mentoring new facilitators	Old facilitators, PASGR Secretariat		After selection
Internet, e-newsletter, Twitter, Facebook, online selection tool (bespoke application)	As above	Selection of Participants: advertising, remote scoring of applicants, selection of participants	Facilitators, applicants, PASGR Secretariat		3 months before programme starts

Sources: Adopted and modified from Bower (2008) and Sharples et al. (2009)

Co-training and co-learning

Co-training is hailed by proponents of social constructivist learning as an effective way of enhancing faculty collaboration in joint intellectual and practical endeavours (Lewis & Sincan, 2009), and providing students with multiple perspectives and feedback (Scribner-MacLean & Miller, 2011). PASGR leverages these benefits by encouraging co-training in all of the programmes, which is enabled through Moodle and face-to-face interactions. Course facilitators are trained on the use of the Moodle platform for course delivery, after which they can upload learning materials onto it. Each course is allocated a coordinator, who leads the course teams in online facilitation and ensures that participants are adequately engaged and supported. The coordinator works closely with PASGR staff to ensure seamless facilitation. Such support includes orienting participants to the various technologies during the learning process. Participants are encouraged to have a computer and Internet connectivity as basic learning technologies.

Since participants are normally busy professionals, academics and researchers with limited time for face-to-face training, PASGR has adopted a blended learning approach that combines four weeks of pre-training online-facilitated engagement and 10 days of face-to-face training. While face-to-face engagement is easier to manage and to keep the participants active, the pre-training engagement requires extra effort to keep participants focused and motivated to achieve the set learning outcomes. Therefore, PASGR adopted the notion of redundancy commonly used in the media and communications (Hii & Fong, 2012). Redundancy is a reiterative process aimed at guarding against loss of information, by employing mutually reinforcing, sometimes redundant but certainly overlapping media of communication. For example, a facilitator can communicate something during a face-to-face engagement and share it again through an email and again through the WhatsApp group. Although this results in redundancy, it ensures that adult learners who have multiple roles receive the message. Redundancy is also practical when participants are either uncomfortable or have no exposure in working with certain technologies.

Since PASGR's interest is inclusiveness, scaffolding ensures that all participants achieve the expected learning outcomes. This pedagogical approach has enabled the facilitators to assume the role of 'shepherds', who spot the 'virtually lost' participants and bring them back to the fold. One of the course facilitators introduced the approach after noticing that only a handful of participants initially engaged on the Moodle platform, as noted below:

> Why I added WhatsApp: poor response on Moodle; instantaneity of IMs; ability to share both messages and files; instant personal touch ... How do we respond to these categories of adults ... [Participant A] made his first post on WhatsApp before I even introduced the group? [Participant B] made his a few hours before we finally closed ... How do we help those arriving here hurried and harassed ... torn between teaching/working, raising family and doing online work? (Facilitator's self-evaluation, 2019)

Once an activity is shared on Moodle, there is follow-up in the WhatsApp groups and by email. Email and WhatsApp allow posting of tasks and files; however, interactive engagement is limited, and therefore the facilitator quickly shifts from the role of the 'shepherd' to an encourager. Figure 6.1 shows an online engagement on Moodle.

Figure 6.1: Online engagement on Moodle (facilitator's posting, 2018)

Reading and Discussion VII: Ethics in research

by .̣.,̣.......̣ ̣.̣.̣.̣.̣a - Tuesday, 6 March 2018, 11:59 PM

In their attempts to conduct ground-breaking and award-winning research, researchers sometimes run foul of the principles of ethics. These violations are sometimes major, leading to pains of different kinds for research participants and even loss of lives. Other times, they are minor or little noticed. Read the attached document on research ethics, paying careful attention to pages 6 - 15. Briefly state how you would practically observe the three principles of ethics stated in the document when you finally conduct the research proposed in your concept note.

Deadline for submission: Wednesday 7 March, 2018; 12 midnight, GMT. (I hope this time is ethical!)

This brings us to the end of the online engagement for Advanced Research Design. From now on, we will be dealing with the electives... Stay tuned.

Figure 6.2: WhatsApp message encouraging participants to move to Moodle

Today's assignment is on Moodle. Please read and send your comments to Moodle. We have up to mid day tomorrow to submit our responses. As we know, this is the last assignment on ARD. Please remember to turn in the outstanding assignments if you have not done that yet.

4:34 PM

Source: Programme Manager and Head of Professional Development and Training, Moodle Post, 2019

From a participant's perspective, the use of multimedia technologies during training is crucial for reminding students about current and upcoming tasks, as well as providing alternative fora through which the same and various information can be accessed.

Guided by the conceptual lenses and frameworks elaborated earlier on, Table 6.3 provides a summary of the matching of the co-training/learning activities, and the mediating circumstances with the technologies used.

Table 6.3: Matching the co-training and co-learning activities with selected technologies

Mediating circumstances: Blended					
Conceptual lenses					
What technologies are used?	Why are these technologies used? (Affordances)	How are the technologies used? (Strategy in activity)	Who uses the technologies? (Agent)	Where are the technologies used? (Locale)	When are the technologies used? (Timing)
Computers/ laptops, smartphones	As in Table 6.1	During pre-programme online engagement: Engage participants in the theory aspects + peer learning For providing readings followed by forum discussions	Facilitators Participants	Dispersed/ virtual	4 weeks prior to face-to-face start
Moodle, email, WhatsApp	Examples are media, spatial, temporary, navigation, synthesis, technical usability, and aesthetic affordances	Co-facilitation Individualised/peer/ group learning Flexibility Instantaneity Create redundancy to get message across			
Computers/ laptops	As in Table 6.1	Face-to-face engagement between facilitators and participants, and among participants; moderated application to own context; peer learning		Virtual: various sites across the continent, e.g., Nairobi, Lagos, Bulawayo, Ibadan, etc.	10-day period at selected intervals
PowerPoint/ YouTube videos	Examples are media, spatial, temporary, navigation, synthesis, and technical usability, and aesthetic/ sensory appeal affordances	In presenting concepts in alternative formats (images, video and text), project prompts for discussion, and allow for real-time adjustment of content to be presented in response to changing circumstances in learning environment; co-facilitation; peer learning		Face-to-face at programme site	

Sources: Adopted and modified from Bower (2008) and Sharples et al., (2009)

The interactive technologies have a variety of affordances, including but not limited to those highlighted in Tables 6.1, 6.2 and 6.3. In addition, these technologies can be structured and re-designed to fit users' needs (Ssentamu et al., 2020).

Co-researching

Although country teams undertake several research projects, coordination of these teams from conceptualisation to execution happens remotely, with support from the PASGR Secretariat. Online engagement of project teams is usually intense during the design stage. This allows ideas to be discussed virtually and refined before face-to-face meetings, consequently saving time and related costs. An example of co-researching is presented in Chapter 5 of this book (Brown et al.). Adapting Bower's (2008) affordance analysis and Sharples et al.'s (2009) generative framework, and guided by our conceptual lenses, we match co-researching activities and mediating circumstances with the selected technologies, as summarised in Table 6.4.

Table 6.4: Matching the co-researching activities with selected technologies

Mediating circumstance: Blended					
Conceptual lenses					
What technologies are used?	**Why are these technologies used? (Affordances)**	**How are the technologies used? (Strategy in activity)**	**Who uses the technologies? (Agent)**	**Where are the technologies used? (Locale)**	**When are the technologies used? (Timing)**
Computers/ laptops/ smartphones, Voice over Internet Protocol (Zoom, GoToMeeting, Skype, video conferencing)	As in Table 6.1	For conceptuali-sation, designing, executing and dissemina-ting	PASGR Secretariat, Research partners, Researchers	Dispersed/ virtual Face-to-face at program-me site	During conceptualisa-tion, designing, executing and disseminating
Emails, WhatsApp	As in Table 6.1				

Sources: Adopted and modified from Bower (2008) and Sharples et al. (2009)

Challenges in connecting virtually using technologies

Despite the technological affordances highlighted in Tables 6.1–6.4 above, applying the six questions in our conceptual framework, Bower's (2008) affordance analysis and Sharples et al.'s (2009) generative framework revealed challenges in virtually connecting various PASGR activities across contexts, cultures and technological capacities. Some of these challenges are outlined below.

Affordability

Use of any technology comes with a cost to PASGR and her partners. In a 2018 Pew Research Center survey, sub-Saharan Africa had the lowest rate of smartphone ownership worldwide. The same study reported people with more education, higher incomes, those aged 18–29 years, and men as more likely to own smartphones. This has pedagogical and other implications in terms of access, equality and use of technologies. COVID-19 has exposed an even wider digital divide in the delivery of digital learning in Africa (Nyerere, 2020; Nganga, Waruru & Nakweya, 2020).

Further, data bundles are expensive, with some countries levying a higher tax on internet useage (Sarpong, 2018). This is limiting to individuals who have to meet the cost themselves. Some universities that PASGR collaborates with do not provide an internet connection for lecturers or students. Technologies such as video-conferencing units are expensive to buy and maintain, while accompanying applications are proprietary-based and thus require periodic renewal of licences. Some partners cannot afford such technology-related costs.

Capacity

Before the COVID-19 pandemic, PASGR's partners projected inadequate capacity and unwillingness to work virtually using modern technologies. Most of them were accustomed to face-to-face collaborative projects and therefore resisted working virtually. Some lacked familiarity with LMSs, and had trouble knowing where to post their responses or how to access the learning resources. However, the inevitable shift to online engagement due to the COVID-19 pandemic is helping participants to improve this capacity, but other limitations such competing demands, including full-time teaching and research workloads, and exercising the discipline to dedicate time to remote working are becoming more evident. Furthermore, the COVID-19 pandemic has exposed additional capacity gaps among university academics, like the ability to convert existing face-to-face courses to e-learning, as well as online facilitation.

Connectivity

Most African countries, especially where PASGR has operations, experience poor internet connectivity. The 2018 Pew Research Center survey noted that sub-Saharan Africa has the lowest level of internet use worldwide, ranging from 59% in South Africa to 25% in Tanzania, compared to 89% in the United States of America (USA). Virtual technologies depend on good internet bandwidth, and much time is wasted trying to get participants connected, and to capture, record and share their contributions. Additionally, some of the physical locations experience frequent power outages, which affects access, reliability and quality.

Motivation

There is a lack of motivation for adoption of technologies by some of the facilitators and participants of PASGR's training programme, since some universities do not either require or encourage teaching staff and students to use technologies. This is partly as a result of the existing policy gaps in the recognition of e-learning during staff promotions. Some universities even question related quality assurance mechanisms. These are encumbrances to the development of digital-savvy competences.

Fast-paced digital technological growth

Although the fast-paced growth of digital technologies transforms a growing number of daily interactions throughout all spheres of life, it also presents challenges (Sharples et al., 2009, p. 28), especially in low-resourced sub-Saharan Africa. Training and research organisations such as PASGR have to work round the clock to ensure a digital-savvy environment, not only to survive but thrive in the twenty-first century in terms of the training packages, how they are taught, the research carried out, the technologies used and their capabilities, and adaptability and innovativeness of human resources such as organisational leaders, programme managers, facilitators, participants and support staff.

Collaborating across diverse teams

While collaborating across different teams enriches outputs through cross-fertilisation of ideas, it also introduces into the group certain dynamics, such as delays and managing divergent and sometimes conflicting ideas. There is also the challenge of managing different time zones. Setting ground rules at the beginning and identifying suitable times when everyone is available are some of the methods deployed to deal with such challenges.

Mitigation strategies

While internet connection remains a key challenge, mobile phone penetration in Africa is encouraging (Pew Research Center, 2018). Mobile phones are currently used for a multitude of innovative applications. PASGR has taken advantage of this, by creating a capability of being hosted on a mobile app. For example, Moodle has a mobile phone interface. Technologies such as Zoom, GoToMeeting, Skype and WhatsApp can be accessed through a cell phone. Therefore, most tasks are accomplished using mobile data as opposed to internet bandwidth.

Capacity development and strengthening is key to successful online engagement. PASGR has adopted an approach of commencing major projects with face-to-face or virtual inception workshops. These forums also provide a platform for training, project planning and team bonding. Partners disperse to their locations with a clear sense of the expected outputs, skills and motivation to connect virtually. This fosters the creation of robust virtual CoPs that move on to more collaborative projects outside of PASGR work, such as the writing of this chapter. PASGR incorporates online training and support sessions, and continuous monitoring on how to use technology to facilitate joint virtual activities. Much of this is achieved via the LMS. Further, the COVID-19 pandemic opened an opportunity for PASGR and its partners to provide training on how to design and deliver online courses.

In order to overcome cost challenges, PASGR has deliberately chosen to use the open-source Moodle application. This is informed by affordability and familiarity to partner universities, where over 90% of them use the platform. PASGR also considered interoperability, which ensures that the technology is available for a variety of devices and platforms, such as mobile phones and laptops, as well as Windows, Android and iOS. In addition, Moodle has a responsive design, which ensures that webpages render well on a variety of devices and screen sizes. Furthermore, where possible and explicitly requested, PASGR considers compensation for bandwidth.

Lessons learnt

PASGR is one of the cases that verify that technology has the potential to support continental and international partnerships among universities and research institutions, facilitated by networked technologies. Technology has propelled close networking among participants and facilitators from widely differing backgrounds, cultures and locations, to combine global perspectives and local relevance (Stewart & Gachago, 2016). However, there is a need for context-sensitive use of technology, guided by what can be availed at minimum cost, but with maximum outputs and outcomes. Course designers and implementers should ask themselves the following question: 'What technologies are currently in the hands of the learners and the teachers that can be harnessed?'.

Further, adoption of networked technologies requires capacity building. While online technologies are useful and desirable, they cannot succeed without capacity building of the users. In most cases user guides are insufficient, and dedicated hands-on training is needed to address users' immediate needs. Participants like to see meaning in what they are being trained on (asking the key question: "What will I use this knowledge for?"). If this is not taken into consideration, motivation for technological adoption and use, and capacity building efforts are less fruitful. It is also important to do user-profiling and match this with available technologies, in order to develop appropriate strategies that support effective use of these technologies. This became most apparent when technology was applied in order to remain virtually connected in the face of COVID-19.

Mobile technologies are critical in virtual connections. While not optimum, mobile penetration in Africa is still the best option, with many people in Africa able to connect via mobile phones (Pew Research Center, 2018). Therefore, designing online technologies to support virtual collaborations should integrate apps into systems as plug-ins or extensions. Integrating social media apps such as WhatsApp, Telegram, Facebook, YouTube and Twitter has proved effective in developing a system that attracts widespread use.

Online CoPs are effective for online collaboration. Projects designed to support growth of robust CoPs thrive where there are incentives, which do not necessarily have to be monetary. Although honoraria are good incentives, PASGR discovered that training opportunities, staff exchange and mobility opportunities are powerful motivators in supporting growth and developing a sense of ownership among CoPs.

Research increasingly relies on technology; therefore, in addition to ongoing capacity building, organisations such as PASGR and universities must ring-fence budgets to invest in technologies and quality infrastructure that support research. This requires analysing the affordances of the technologies before purchasing them. When users are knowledgeable of the affordances of technologies, they have the ability to use such technologies and harness them in more creative ways. Although originally Bower (2008) conceived affordance analysis as a design methodology for matching learning tasks with learning technologies, it can also be creatively used in any endeavour requiring use of interactive technologies. We recommend a follow-up study to interrogate how PASGR partner universities in the 16 African countries consider the nature of collaboration using networked spaces.

References

Bower, M. (2008). Affordance analysis–matching learning tasks with learning technologies. *Educational Media International, 45*(1), pp. 3-15.

Brown, C., Ssentamu, N. P., Bagarukayo, E., Baguma, R. & Mayisela, T. (2021) Translating learning into collaborative research: Reflections from a Postgraduate cohort. In D. Gachago, P. Shangase, & N. E. Ivala (Eds.), *Co-teaching/researching in an Unequal World: Using Virtual Classrooms to Connect Africa, and Africa and the World*. (Chapter 5). Wilmington, DE: Vernon Press.

Fook J. (2011). Developing critical reflection as a research method. In J. Higgs, A. Titchen, D. Horsfall. & D. Bridges (Eds.), *Creative Spaces for Qualitative Researching. Practice, Education, Work and Society*, pp. 55-64. Rotterdam, The Netherlands: Sense Publishers.

Gibson, J. J. (1997). *The Ecological Approach to Visual Perception*. Boston: Houghton Mifflin Harcourt (HMH).

Hii, S. C. & Fong, S. F. (2012). Effects of multimedia redundancy in history learning. In: N. M. Seel (Ed.), *Encyclopedia of the Sciences of Learning*. Boston, MA: Springer.

Lewis, K. O. & Sincan, M. (2009). International co-teaching of medical informatics for training-the-trainers in content and distance education. *Journal of Asynchronous Learning Networks, 13*(2), pp. 33-47.

Morley, C. (2008). Critical reflection as a research methodology. In P. Liamputtong & J. Rumbold (Eds.), *Knowing differently: Arts-based and collaborative research methods*, pp. 265-280. New York, NY: Nova Science Publishers.

Ssentamu, N. P., Ng'ambi, D., Bagarukayo, E., Baguma, R., Nabushawo, M. H. & Nalubowa, C. (2020). Enhancing student interactions in online learning: A case of using YouTube in a distance learning module in a higher education institution in Uganda. *Higher Education Research, 5*(4), pp. 103-116. doi: 10.11648/j.her.20200504.11

Pew Research Center (2018). *Internet connectivity seen as having positive impact on life in Sub-Saharan Africa, but digital divides persist*. https://www.pewresearch. org/global/wp-content/uploads/sites/2/2018/10/Pew-Research-Center_ Technology-use-in-Sub-Saharan-Africa_2018-10-09.pdf

Nganga, G., Waruru, M. & Nakweya, G. (2020) Universities Face Multiple Challenges in Wake of COVID-19 Closures. *University World News*. https://www.university worldnews.com/post.php?story=20200407162549396.

Nyerere, J. (2020). Moving Online Huge Challenge for Kenya's Higher Education. *Social Science Space*. https://www.socialsciencespace.com/2020/05/moving -online-huge-challenge-for-kenyas-higher-education/

Scribner-MacLean, M. & Miller, H. (2011) Strategies for Success for Online for Online Co-Teaching. *Journal of Online Learning and Teaching, 7*(3), pp. 419-425.

Sharples, M., Crook, C., Ian, J., Kay, D., Chowcat, I., Balmer, K. & Stokes, E. (2009). *New Modes of Technology-enhanced Learning: Opportunities and challenges*. http://www.becta.org.uk on 18-02-16.

Sarpong, E. (2018). *How some African governments are keeping millions of citizens offline*. https://a4ai.org/why-is-africa-taxing-online-services.

Stewart, K. & Gachago, D. (2016). Being Human Today: A Digital Storytelling Pedagogy for Transcontinental Border Crossing. *British Journal for Educational Technology, 47*(3), pp. 528-542.

University of Victoria Center for Youth & Research. (n.d). *Decolonisation in an Educational Context*. https://www.uvic.ca/research/centres/youthsociety/ assets/docs/briefs/decolonizing-education-research-brief.pdf

Chapter 7

Co-research and co-teaching in community-based adult education: Promoting information technology and nutrition in rural Limpopo, South Africa

Busisiwe Alant

University of KwaZulu-Natal, South Africa

Rowan Thompson

STADIO School of Education, South Africa

Abstract

Little has been written about how the needs that single, unemployed, rural mothers (SURMs) express for extramural learning with information technology (IT) and for improved nutrition could be used to develop a context-based course through co-researching and co-teaching. This chapter explores the affordances of co-research and co-teaching to develop and implement a context-based intervention in Limpopo Province, South Africa. The intervention consisted of a combination of a tailor-made IT and nutrition skills training course, which was adapted for a cohort of out-of-school SURMs. The course was delivered by two facilitators, supported *in situ*, through a workshop, and virtually by a remote researcher from the University of KwaZulu-Natal. The chapter contributes to discussions around incorporating a community of practice approach, as part of the scaffolding within the community-based participatory action research framework (CBPAR), to understand affordances as possibilities for action that can be both enabling and constraining. Co-researching and co-teaching illustrate that it is not only access to a basic IT and nutrition course, but also economic, social, and cultural dynamics that play a decisive role in our ability to fully grasp the concept of 'affordance' in this context.

Keywords: affordances, Information Technologies (IT) and basic adult education nutrition course, community-based participatory action research, co-research and co-teaching, possibilities of action, single unemployed rural mothers, South Africa

***

Introduction

In line with the theme of this book, the purpose of this chapter is to raise and discuss many of the issues and concerns that could guide the thinking and practice of researchers as they strive to design and implement responsive, community-based co-research and co-teaching programmes aimed at out-of-school youth. In this regard, we explore the affordances that co-research and co-teaching provide to support the development and implementation of a context-based information technology (IT) and basic adult education (BAE) nutrition intervention aimed at single, unemployed rural mothers (SURMs). The role that Information and Communication Technology[1] (ICT) plays in out-of-school programmes or adult literacy and numeracy provision has long been established (Organisation for Economic Co-operation and Development [OECD], 2006). We inquire into the capabilities generated by collaborative research and teaching to address SURMs' IT and nutritional education needs, and afford them the opportunity to improve their own nutrition (as well as that of their children), and prospects for securing employment.

Smith and Turpin (2017) write at length about the challenges that ICT for development intervention projects in rural communities face in order to come to successful execution. The primary challenge is the development of an intervention that is "suited to the needs of a specific community" (Smith & Turpin, 2017, p. 345). A Human Sciences Research Council (HSRC) audit, conducted in eight different rural development sites, sums up the challenges faced by those seeking to implement technological innovations in rural areas of South Africa as follows:

- Lack of community consultation, resulting in conflict.
- Employment of inappropriate models.
- Poor conceptualisation of development interventions.
- Questionable sustainability of activities.
- Lack of project level monitoring and evaluation (HSRC, 2013).

---

[1] The chapter uses ICT in a broad sense: the term here refers to a range of technologies that includes computers; digital broadcasting; telecommunication technologies (such as mobile phones affording access to e-mail and other forms of computer-mediated communication); and electronic information resources such as the worldwide web and CD-ROMs (OECD, 2006, p. 14).

Given all these barriers to progress and the implementation of collaboration, and noting particularly Smith and Turpin's advice regarding the importance of contextual needs for effective rural interventions, we asked the following research question: How do co-research and co-teaching support the development and implementation of a context-based IT and BAE nutrition intervention aimed at single, unemployed, rural mothers?

To examine this question, we adopted a conceptual lens inspired by the theory of affordances (Strong et al., 2014). Strong et al.'s model of technology affordance stems from trying to understand IT-associated organisational change. Their contention with current theorising is that it does not pay sufficient attention to the objectives of change, the role of IT in organisational change, and the multilevel nature of change processes. They seek to develop a theory about change that "acknowledges the impact of individual practices without losing the IT artifact itself and that simultaneously accommodates individual level actions and the effects of organizational structures on the change process" (Strong et al., 2014, p. 57). Thus, affordances are conceptualised as the opportunities or enablers (as well as constraints) related to technology that stem from goal-oriented intentional behaviour, which result in concrete actions (Bobsin, Petrini & Pozzebon, 2017).

Background to the study

The marginality of the context

We consider 'affordances' against the background of South Africa's history and context of inequality, where the overall "contours of civic participation continue to be sculpted and truncated by economic forces" (Donner & Walton, 2013, p. 350). Indeed, the issue of participation and access is a concern in South Africa, particularly because it affects low-income and rural areas disproportionately, fuelling the gap between the 'haves' and 'have-nots'.

Our co-researching and co-teaching community project was undertaken in the small rural village of Mulamula (22°58'16"S 30°40'25"E). Amenities are limited and include a resource-constrained preschool/crèche, two primary schools, one high school, one general store, one butcher shop, and a bottle store. The village is administered by the Traditional Council's tribal office. Recreational opportunities are few. Besides a dusty football field, there is a hall used for meetings and women's craft groups. SURMs have little or no opportunity for any form of community-based education or recreational learning beyond traditional dancing, basic needlecrafts, and beadwork. Thus, alcohol and sexual activity become 'easy escapes' (Fihlani, 2018)–unfortunate features that are common to rural areas across South Africa.

The research project was designed to enable different stakeholders–IT trainers/facilitators, the Mulamula Education Centre Project (MECP) members, SURMs and University of KwaZulu-Natal (UKZN) researchers–to work together through a distributed and co-located community of practice (CoP) (Wenger, 1998), to establish a relevant, context-based IT and BAE nutrition course, and to focus on the co-researching and co-teaching of IT skills and nutrition to SURMs in a community-based education setting. The offering of IT training to SURMs arose through community-level discussions driven by the MECP Director, Professor Tivani Mashamba-Thompson, on the need to include skills training on IT, nutrition, and childcare in their programme.

The marginality of out-of-school youth in South Africa

Within the broader context of rural developmental needs, it is useful to look at the question of the marginality of out-of-school youth in more detail. Out-of-school youth and adults are a crucial target population in a world increasingly concerned about literacy, employability and lifelong learning (OECD, 2006, p. 10). The SURMs in this study represent a population that is identified by the United Nations as a priority group for human development, as well as the eradication of poverty and disease.

Studies on educational performance show a disturbing pattern of students dropping out from school as they move from primary to secondary school (De Witte et al., 2013; Spaull, 2015; Hartnack, 2017). Hartnack (2017, p. 1) notes that most school dropout in South Africa occurs in grades 10 and 11, which results in 50% of learners in any one cohort dropping out before reaching grade 12. In other words, if around 1,155, 629 million learners are registered for Grade 1 in any particular year, only 629,155 (54%) odd will make it to Grade 12.

However, these statistics do not project the reality of school drop-out, as teenage pregnancies are not included. It is estimated that 182 000 South African teenagers become pregnant each year, many of whom are still at school. In Limpopo Province alone, 1638 children were born to teenagers between April 2017 and March 2018 (Fihlani, 2018). Teenage pregnancy has a "negative impact on young mothers and their children, by placing limits on the mother's educational achievement and economic stability" (Modisaotsile, 2012, p. 5). This situation often ends schooling and disrupts the leap from education to employment, with negative consequences for young women (Bhana et al., 2010).

In South Africa progressive policies exist which are designed to keep pregnant teenagers in schools, and to allow and keep teenage mothers in schools, as well as to permit their re-entry as young mothers after giving birth (Bhana et al., 2010). However, less than a third return to complete their studies (Modisaotsile, 2012) due to the lack of school, home, and community support (Livingstone, 2019). Access to alternative forms of education will no doubt increase their chances of getting an education and progressing to gainful employment.

The 54% matric completion rate, mentioned above, indicates a huge untapped market for post-school learners wishing to complete their formal education or to acquire skills/knowledge to gain employment. This is effectively the niche that the SURMs in this study occupy. Although most did not complete matric (85%), they yearn for further education. They had been out of school for more than 10 years, and were still unemployed.

Methodology

Community-based participatory action research (CBPAR)

The methodological framework (Figure 7.1) adopted in this study (developed by one of the authors, Thompson, 2016) builds on the CBPAR model "where traditional researchers and community members are jointly involved at each step" (Balazs & Morello-Frosch, 2013, p. 11). It places the community at the heart of the research and indicates that the 'relevance, rigour and reach' (the 3Rs) of the study are applicable at key stages in the cycle. An understanding of relevance is necessary when setting out the goals/objectives and designing the study so that it will benefit the participants. It also applies to the handling and processing of data, and maintaining focus on what is relevant to the research questions. Rigour is vital to maintain a recognised standard and quality as a piece of social knowledge. Reach relates to the value of the research for the community involved, as well as for the wider community who should also benefit from the research.

Additional key practical elements of the CBPAR process include the recognition of local knowledge and perspectives in the research process, and in the planning of interventions, thereby involving the community in all of the stages (Cornwall & Jewkes, 1995). Although not necessarily understanding all of the medical and nutritional needs of their child, the SURMs' own life experiences have exposed them to a wealth of social, practical, and physical challenges, influencing their earlier perceptions. As mothers, they bring an inherent critical perspective to the class through their heightened need to feed, clothe, shelter, and protect their child. By incorporating these critical perspectives, it was hoped that certain 'hidden issues' would be brought to the fore, increasing the value of the course.

Figure 7.1. Cyclical process of CBPAR with emphasis on the 3Rs (adapted from Balazs & Morello-Frosch, 2013)

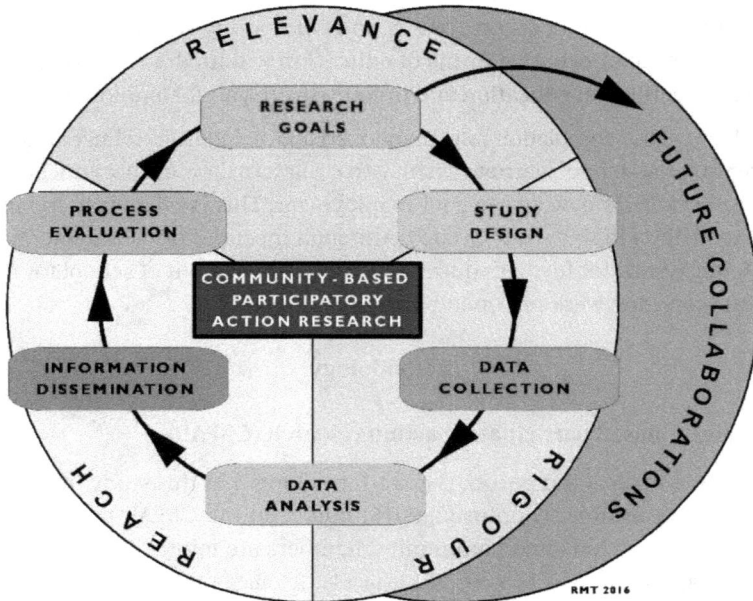

(Thompson, 2016, p. 53)

Within the CBPAR approach, it was also necessary to consider the issues affecting the participation of individuals and local organisations in collaboratives, whether co-located or distributed. This was part of the "relational dynamics" necessary to construct "relations, realities and outcomes" in the village (Kevany & MacMichael, 2014, p. 38). We needed to consider factors such as:

- Varying literacy levels of educators, students, and local project stakeholders;

- Varying social backgrounds and education levels of *all* participants;

- Strong cultural and other local influences; and

- Tribal hierarchy and established state school and village management systems.

Furthermore, access and entry protocols were followed, in accordance with UKZN's ethical clearance (number HSS/0573/015M) and the local tribal office. The latter was also informed of all activities in advance, and a list of participants and their personal details was provided for village records. These steps acknowledged their role in the process and promoted community ownership of the intervention.

Recruitment process

The actual course recruitment process yielded 20 SURMs. The collaborative community-based recruitment process unfolded as follows:

- Invitation letters were sent to the Mulamula Traditional Council Office, to be handed out to SURMs collecting month-end welfare grants–done via word-of-mouth and cell phone message texting.

- Older mothers (>25 years) in the village were contacted telephonically through the MECP Director, to establish a communication network with SURMs via older 'matriarch' figures.

- Workshop course posters/flyers were sent to the Traditional Council offices and the two course facilitators, Boikie Maluleke and Sacha Lenz, to distribute to the community.

- An informal briefing session was held the evening before the workshop, to brief SURMs and course facilitators about its content, and to promote the event.

Research participants

The single, unemployed, rural mothers (SURMs)

Figure 7.2. SURMs' ages

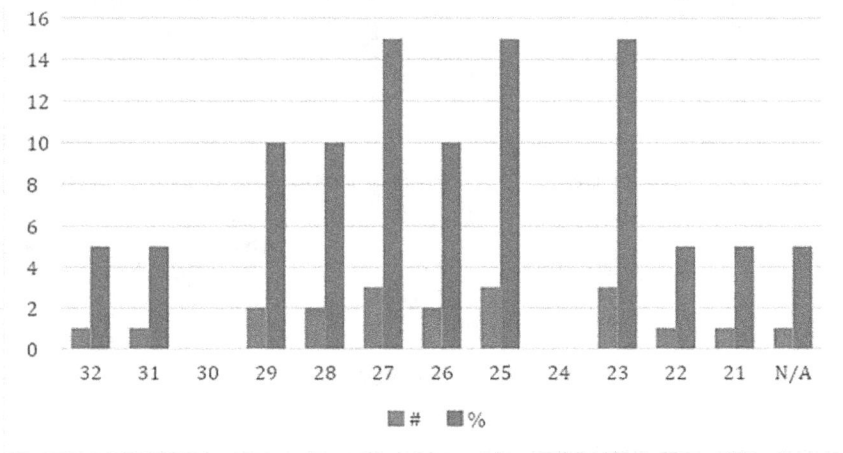

Single Unemployed Rural Mothers' Age

The study involved 20 out-of-school SURMs, a group identified by the community as in need of support. The exclusion criteria of 'SURMs older than 18 years and younger than 25 with at least one child under the age of 5' could not be applied. As indicated in Figure 7.2, the participants' ages ranged from 21 to 32 years. Overall, only seven (35%) met the exclusion criteria; one (5%) SURM who met the age criterion had a child older than 5; the 26+ category included 11 (55%) of the SURMs; one (5%) did not divulge her age (hence N/A); the 21–25- year age category comprised eight (40%) SURMs. However, 60% did not volunteer information regarding the age of their children, while nine SURMs (45%) freely shared how many children they had: seven (35%) reported having one child, and two (10%) reported having two children.

The co-facilitators

The *drivers* of the intervention were the two young males who trained and facilitated the course–Boikie Maluleke (BM) and Sascha Lenz (SL). BM, aged 22, matriculated from Shingwedzi High School in Malamulele in 2011, and graduated from an ICT course in Polokwane at the beginning of 2015. He had been involved with MECP events as a volunteer since the first United Kingdom school exchange programme[2] in August 2013. He speaks English and XiTsonga fluently and shows natural talent as a researcher and facilitator. SL, a 27-year-old German volunteer, started teaching ICT courses with the help of BM in May 2015 as part of a 'social volunteering' (the term he uses) sabbatical. He has a degree in Engineering Design and Computer Technology. He left his health systems computer programming job in Germany to volunteer in Mulamula and help establish the MECP ICT facility following an invitation by the MECP Director. It is through SL that donations of laptop computers and other software and hardware were secured from German sponsors. During the study, BM and SL shared a house in the village for better collaboration on how best to deliver the course.

The MECP

In addition, there were MECP members and other older local mothers. Everybody collaborated in a distributed CoP (Wenger, 1998). This is illustrated in Figure 7.3 below.

---

[2] Sevenoaks School, Sevenoaks, Kent, UK, has supported the Mulamula project since its inception in August 2011. See: http://www.sevenoaksschool.org/news/article/news/mulamula-trip-2013)

Figure 7.3. Participants in the study (Thompson, 2016, p. 53)

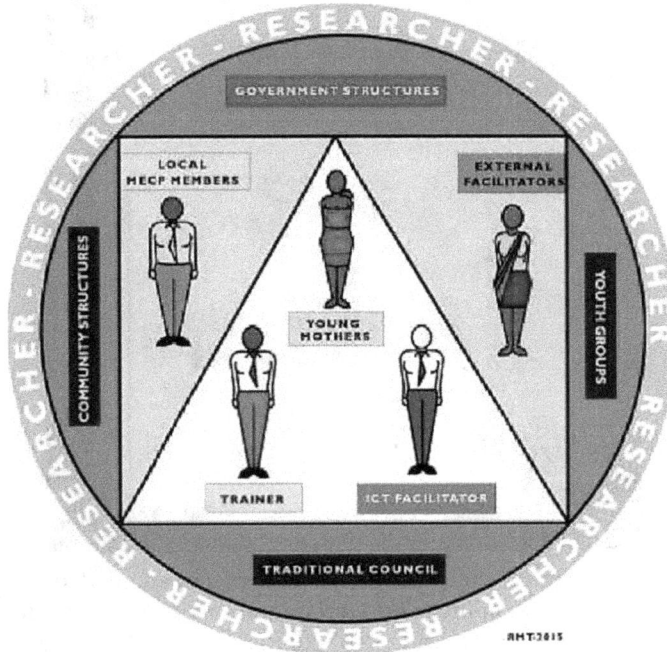

Figure 7.3 places the SURMs inside a triangle of shared experience with BM and SL (forming the actual classroom), supported by the immediate external personalities (MECP members and village facilitators) contained within the wider community and its structures. Incorporating a distributed CoP approach, as part of the scaffolding with the CBPAR intervention, enabled the traditional hierarchies (such as tribal institutions) to be merged into the dialogue as peripheral contributors (Lave, 1991), without the implementation being seen as a challenge to traditional structures.

Co-development and design of the IT and BAE nutrition skills training course

The IT basics and BAE nutrition skills training course was designed following consultation with all stakeholders during a workshop a month prior to implementation. No 'off the shelf' ICT basics and BAE nutrition course existed prior to this, and it was therefore necessary to produce original material to meet the SURMs' needs.

The SURMs negotiated the best days and time slots for delivery of the course. Figure 7.4 illustrates the process.

Figure 7.4. Voting for 'best day' time schedule

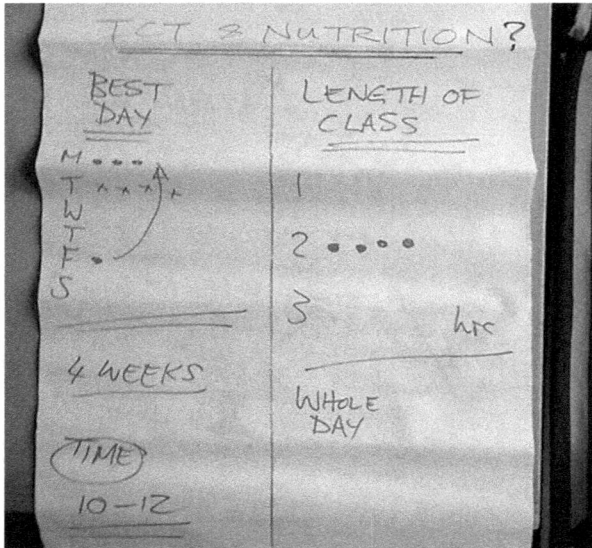

The course was written in collaboration with the co-researchers/co-facilitators, in order to offer it at the appropriate level for the cohort. The IT content of the course was agreed upon following two months of trials of the two basic ICT courses developed: one for Grade 11, one for Grade 12 high school students, and the other for local primary school and high school teachers. The BAE Nutrition content of the course was written in consultation with the researchers at UKZN and further discussed with the MECPs, BM, SL, and SURMs.

Development of the IT basics and BAE nutrition course entailed the following:

- First literature review–to locate sources relevant for development of the IT course, including ICDL/ECDL (International Computer Literacy Licence/European Computer Driving Licence); Microsoft (MS) Office resources; and books/manuals on computer basics.

- Explicating the initial IT basics course.

- Trialling the initial IT basics course with selected community members– SL trialled the course with various groups at the village location. He was also encouraged to expand the course to include specific software training in the use of: MS Word, MS Excel, and MS PowerPoint. This was done in discussion with the local facilitator, BM, in order to gain consensus on what was achievable with the course for the SURMs.

- Trialling the initial IT basics course with Grade 12 high school students and teachers from the local high school, and then combining it with nutrition content to create the SURMs course.

- Second literature review–to locate nutrition content for the refined IT basics and BAE Nutrition combined course. Sources included the World Health Organization (WHO), United Nations International Children's Emergency Fund (UNICEF), and World Food Programme.

Thereafter, discussions commenced on the IT basics and BAE nutrition combined course. The outcome was a 12-point worksheet course (Table 7.1). During the above processes, virtual dialogues were maintained with the MECP, BM, SL and SURMs via email, text messaging, Skype, and WhatsApp.

Table 7.1: Questions on the 12 worksheet course schedule

Worksheet	Question posed
Worksheet 1	What is nutrition and why is it important?
Worksheet 2	What are the common food groups?
Worksheet 3	How much of these food groups do I need to eat each day?
Worksheet 4	What are vitamins and minerals needed for?
Worksheet 5	Explaining the importance of nutrition to others.
Worksheet 6	What is a calorie? How many calories are there in … ?
Worksheet 7	What nutrition is best for my baby before birth?
Worksheet 8	What locally sourced nutrition is best for my baby after birth?
Worksheet 9	Why are fluids important for young mothers?
Worksheet 10	How can I afford the best nutrition for my child as he/she grows?
Worksheet 11	How can locally produced foods help in a nutritious diet?
Worksheet 12	Why does pregnancy affect how much you should eat as a young mother?

Co-teaching the IT and BAE nutrition combined course

Implementation of the intervention took place in July–August 2015, over the course of six weeks. The SURMs attended two classes per week on Mondays and Tuesdays at Mahlefunye Primary School in Mulamula village. Classes commenced after regular school hours. The ICT laboratory was used, although no fixed computers were in place. Instead, 14 donated laptops were supplied by MECP donors. Classes were taught using a digital data projector. BM and SL set up a numbered folder system, so that the SURMs could save their work on the laptops for review without the need for expensive printing. Resource worksheets and nutrition resource datasheets were shared and discussed with BM and SL prior to commencement of the course. These were preloaded onto the laptops, so that the SURMs could access them during lessons. This reduced the need for an expensive network connection. The advantage of using online/cloud storage is that any files you move or copy into a OneDrive folder in File Explorer automatically sync (or back up) to your OneDrive storage in the cloud, and vice versa. Any folder you create in OneDrive in File Explorer also appears in your cloud OneDrive.

The record of examples of students' work was organised as a method of retaining evidence for verification of the course–through UKZN or ICDL–and as a method of assessing the ability level and progress of SURMs as they progressed through the activities. Table 7.2 provides an example (Worksheet 7) of the content of one of the 12 worksheets that was designed. It shows the type of activity, topic, resources, and instructions that were given to the SURMs in order to address the question: What nutrition is best for my baby before birth? The exploration of this task began in Worksheet 5, where the SURMs explored the question: How would you explain the importance of nutrition to others? For this reason, the numbering begins at (f) in the Table.

Table 7.2: Worksheet : What nutrition is best for my baby before birth?

ICT activity	Using imported graphics and text	Software	MS Word
BAE activity	Prenatal nutrition	Topic	Criteria for a balanced diet for young mothers
Instructions	f. Import the image 'Pregnant Young Mother' (or a scanned image) from your desktop to create the central image for a poster below. g. Use the 'Insert' text box feature to add boxes around the image to show the main food types you have been studying. h. Use 'Insert' Shapes features to add arrows and other features to link the text boxes to the central image. i. Save your poster file as 'Nutrition guide for pregnant young mothers' poster' j. Extension: Add extra notes in the text boxes to explain/reinforce your headings.		

Most of the SURMs could construct convincing arguments in both English and XiTshonga about the importance of good nutrition. Responses ranged from:

"To have a strong system and have a normal life; To give you energy and your child to have a health[y] life; To heve [have] a health[y] baby *kuniva na matimba* (To have strength …)"

to

"Kuvanarihanyuabyi lerinene mavaabyi mafambela kulena wen (Healthy living keeps sickness/disease at bay)".

Figure 7.5 is an illustration of how one of the SURMs responded to the question: What nutrition is best for my baby before birth? (Worksheet 7). All SURMs were able to identify the two key micronutrients–vitamin A and iron–essential for pregnant women. This knowledge is critical, because micronutrient deficiencies are mentioned in a report by the National Department of Health (2019) as major contributors to childhood morbidity and mortality.

Figure 7.5: Illustration of a SURM's work

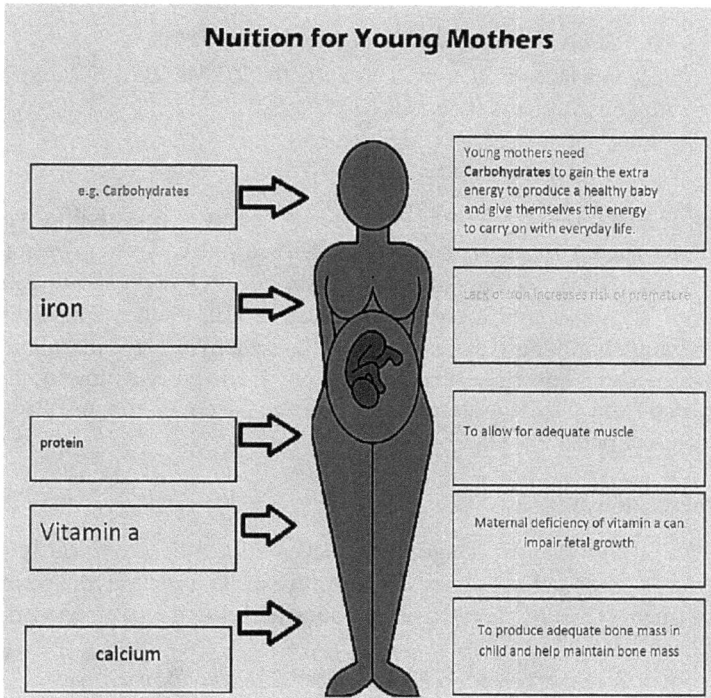

Collaborative evaluation and monitoring of the course

The initial workshop, discussions, and feedback from the lessons produced by the SURMs, BM, and SL were used to evaluate and monitor the course. During and after the workshop, evaluation forms were issued to gather feedback from all stakeholders. The monitoring was conducted in different ways in order to get an overview of the course's impact on the stakeholders.

Recorded informal interviews were done with BM and SL via Skype to monitor implementation of the course (following initial dialogues via WhatsApp and SMS). Monitoring was also carried out as follows:

- Logging of student classwork. This was achieved by saving it to student desktop folders on numbered laptops (students used the same laptops throughout) to avoid having to buy an expensive cable network server for the laptops.
- Video recording of lessons.
- Informal discussion of the course in the classroom with BM and SL present.

The following key tools were used to obtain feedback on the actual course:

- Completion of course evaluation forms by SURMs.
- Recorded face-to-face interviews with SURMs, BM, SL, and MECP using an interview schedule.

Results

A thematic grounded approach was used to analyse the qualitative data (Fraenkel & Wallen, 1993; Glaser & Strauss, 2009). Relevant codes were organised in MS Excel, and NVivo 10. Qualitative analysis software was used to establish patterns of responses and highlight key features and themes. The data were further arranged under the themes which emerged, in order to maintain focus on the key research question: How do co-research and co-teaching support the development and implementation of a context-based IT and BAE Nutrition intervention aimed at SURMs?

Pre-intervention stage

During the pre-intervention stage, three moves were critical to the affordances provided by co-researching: (i) the collaborative development of the course; (ii) the recruitment of SURMs; and (iii) organisation and attendance of the workshop.

Collaborative development of an IT basics and BAE nutrition course

As stated earlier, no 'off the shelf' IT basics and BAE nutrition course existed prior to this course. It therefore became a necessity to produce original material. The development of contextualised teaching approaches was recognised as a valuable way to enhance learning, by "presenting information in familiar contexts, contexts in which the information is useful" (Harwell, 2003, p. 5).

Collaborative recruitment of SURMs

The snowballing recruiting technique employed word of mouth and cell phone texting and showcased the affordances of collaborative research. We saw the numbers jump from a mere six SURMs who attended the workshop to a total of 20 SURMs who enrolled for and attended the course. The maintenance of regular attendance of the course by SURMs foregrounded the issue of the taken-for-granted support–'hidden support'–offered by the community. Mothers, grandmothers, extended family members and friends volunteered to look after the SURMs' children while they attended the course. The results point to the precarious nature of this 'hidden support'.

Establishment of CoPs through the workshop

To set the scene for the course to be provided, a digital projector was used to project from a laptop onto the wall of the meeting hall. The equipment was explained in simple terms, in order to introduce the huge potential of computers and their associated hardware to the participants. Table 7.3 lists what was discussed:

Table 7.3: What was discussed at the workshop and why

Slide/Screen	Reason
Start-up screen/Screen saver	• Use of images (*to personalize computer*) • Date and Time (*evidence of a computer working passively*) • Security/Password screen (*user security features*)
Desktop view	• Icons (*similar to a smart phone's*) • Folders (*to store files in an organised way – like a virtual office*) • Background images (*to personalize computer*)
Powerpoint Slideshow	• Slideshow format was explained as a good teaching aid (pictures and images combined) • The deeper purpose of the study was explained through 6-8 slides which summarized: aims, objectives, research methods, data to be collected and methods of analysis etc. • The use of hand drawn (scanned) and internet source images in the slideshow was explained. • The motivation to explore a combined ICT and nutrition course was discussed using the slideshow as an example. (vulnerability of hardware, methods of communicating messages regarding access to good diet supplements etc.)
Hardware	• The key parts of the laptop and projector were explained: keyboard, screen, inputs/outputs, light source, lens adjustment/focus etc. in order to communicate the complexity but user friendliness of modern computers. • Cost of hardware was mentioned (without specific costs being assigned to items being used)

The workshop was attended by 12 participants who represented the following stakeholder groupings: SURMs, Traditional Council representatives, IT facilitators, MECP representatives.

Evaluation of the initial workshop shows that the SURMs believed that their needs and expectations would be met by the course. The interest and motivations expressed were used not only as the basis of designing and structuring the SURMs' course evaluations, but to establish better understanding of what was required in the IT and BAE nutrition course. As can be seen from the excerpts below (Figure 7.6), the SURMs acknowledged the value of studying IT, and also recognised the need to learn more about nutrition for themselves and their children.

Figure 7.6: Excerpts of responses from the SURMs

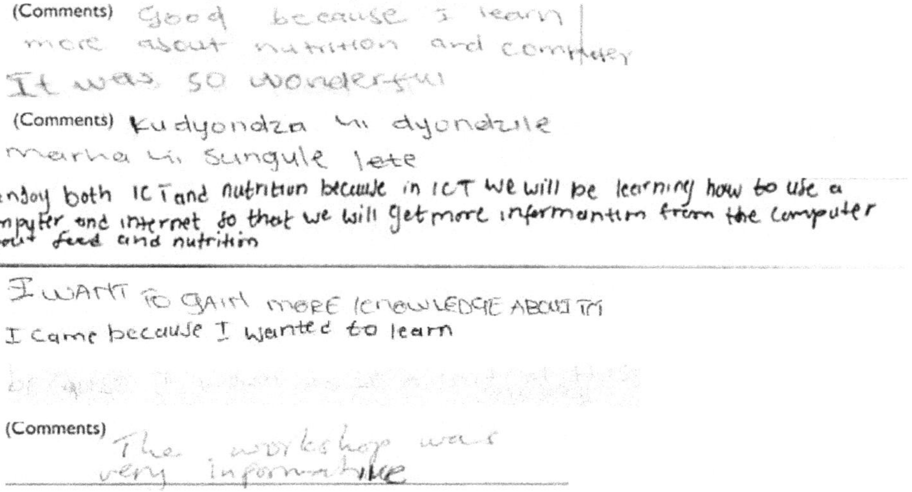

(Comments) Good because i learn
more about nutrition and computer
It was so wonderful

(Comments) Ku dyondza ni dyondzile
marha ni sungule lete

I enjoy both ICT and nutrition because in ICT we will be learning how to use a
computer and internet so that we will get more information from the computer
about feed and nutrition

I WANT TO GAIN MORE KNOWLEDGE ABOUT TH
I came because I wanted to learn

(Comments) The workshop was
very informative

A significant positive statement which summed up the atmosphere in the
workshop was:

> "I really appreciate this project because it encourages us as young
> mothers that we still have a chance to study and it was a great workshop
> I enjoyed myself". (Bombisani)

The SURMs all thought combining IT and nutrition in the same course was a
good idea, with Fanisa looking forward to accessing more information using
the internet:

> "I will use internet to find out more [about] healthy food". (Fanisa)

SL's reflection on the initial workshop foregrounds the importance of 'internal'
motivation versus external motivation. According to him, the workshop managed
to ignite the former:

> "...why are computer courses important ... why is nutrition important.
> I guess your workshop motivated them [SURMs]. You [remote researcher]
> kind of motivated [them], taught them why it is important ... gave them
> ideas before the actual course ... I think that pre-run is really important
> ... That's definitely more successful than was my trial with the high
> school when only an external motivation was from teachers". (SL)

The above feedback is critical, in that it provided a warning of the difficulties
we might have if the course was too technical and loaded with technical IT
vocabulary or medical jargon relating to nutrition. The issue of the translation

of materials into XiTsonga was not explicit in the workshop, but was implied if we wanted to make an impact.

During-intervention stage

The impact of responsive co-teaching on students' learning

Feedback from BM and SL highlighted the importance of having 'real-time' discussions with the remote researcher, to maintain an active involvement as participating researchers. The informal feedback received gave us a good sense of what was happening on the ground. Receiving feedback from two facilitators from diverse cultural backgrounds was also a good way to triangulate the information.

BM and SL were consulted in the early stages of the process to get some feedback on the course's inception, development and delivery. Initial dialogues were maintained via cell phone (WhatsApp and SMS) to set up Skype calls. The two significant interviews about the early classes were recorded on 27 and 31 July, relating to the evaluation of the implementation of the course, presented in Fig. 7.7 below. The themes which emerged from these interviews helped to structure instruments used for the final section of the study.

Figure 7.7: 'Word Cloud' for BM's (L) and SL's (R) interview dialogues

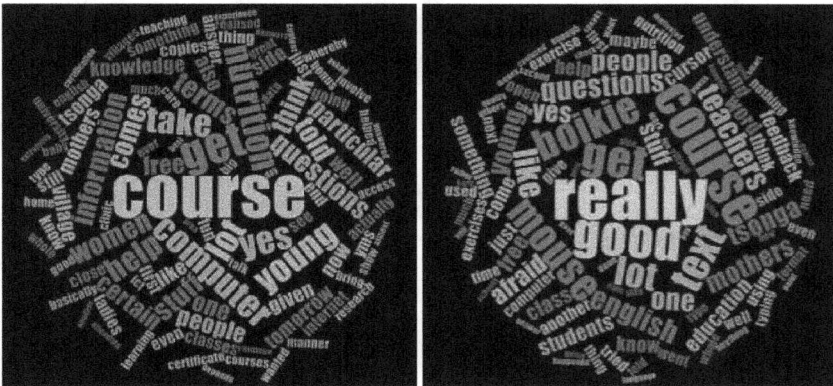

The top five recurring words for BM were: 'course', 'get', 'computer', 'lot' and 'nutrition', while those for SL were: 'really', 'course', 'good', 'get' and 'boikie'. A superficial re-arrangement of these words could reveal: With 'boikie' you 'get' a 'really' 'good' 'course'! However, a deeper reading of the dialogues reveals that both BM and SL:

- share a concern or passion for IT and nutrition training, and are thus committed to the course;

- recognise that they have a shared competence;

- practice relational care;

- have a great deal of respect for each other as professionals and are committed to learn from each other.

It is indeed this ability to recognise that you can learn together and from each other that creates opportunities for learning and development in a CoP. The subsequent interviews with the facilitators indicated that they felt they had been changed by the experience of co-teaching the SURMs. With SL having initially started in a teaching role, delivering the course with BM acting in a support role, he deferred to BM when he realised the cultural/language barrier was inhibiting SURMs' progress, as illustrated in the excerpts below:

> If they don't give me any feedback ... I have no chance to teach them anything. BM is better with the interaction with the young mothers. (SL)

> Like I said, I tried it with English and said they can answer in English and BM can translate it but it didn't work out ... (SL)

> They are more comfortable if I explained in [Xi]Tsonga. Getting them to answer stuff in [Xi]Tsonga. I was explaining questions in English and furthermore in [Xi]Tsonga. Some answered in English and some answered in [Xi]Tsonga. (BM)

One can see that the facilitators developed and built a relationship that enabled them to learn from each other. What is pertinent to note here is their ability to understand the importance of *responsive teaching* – the ability to respond to the contextual needs of the SURMs.

The SURMs responded positively to the teaching of BM and were complimentary about SL's support. A poignant comment was from Faniswa: "He respects us and we respect him".

The results showed that SURMs unanimously experienced this responsive co-teaching with a contextual focus as an enabler: a route to better employment; opportunities for further study; and a means to obtain information and empowerment. Being a life-long learner was one of the attributes that the SURMs seemed to appreciate[3]:

> ... Down here in rural areas it's scarce that people can get such an opportunity to study computers and nutrition. A whole lot of young

---

[3] Note: The SURMs preferred to converse in their mother tongue (XiTshonga), so all excerpts from the interviews were translated into English by BM. Pseudonyms are used instead of real names to maintain anonymity.

mothers down here are pretty much careless with nutrition. It's also advantageous that if ever there is a job post and it requires computer skills, at least I can type. (Bombisani)

The course was fine. It helped me gain more knowledge in terms of the food types I should eat before and after the birth of the baby. So, it pretty much well helped me a lot. I can go on the computer and I look up information on the Internet about nutrition for my baby. (Bombisani)

Post-intervention stage

The value of peer support

In responses to questions relating to course teaching and style, it emerged that SURMs used the course as an opportunity to have their own group discussion to share their experience as young mothers:

We have discussion after the lesson to know exactly about the challenges our young mothers face. (Bonani)

A peer support network appeared to have grown in the group:

They help me when I don't understand. (Enelo)

This was acknowledged by the evaluation feedback given by BM and SL. SL's appreciation of the value of peer support which developed in the classroom is evident:

The most significant thing I found was they started to help each other without asking. They saw one of the women had a problem to log in so others went to that women and helped her to log in. (SL)

The value of context-based teaching

Both facilitators saw that the contextual focus, i.e. the combination of practical IT skills with another subject, offered a valuable way to learn:

With a context, it is much easier to learn the IT skills ... If they have it in context with the topic, it's like linked to each other ... Teaching should always be in the context of some topic. (SL)

BM also highlighted that the course was fulfilling a need for better health education, which is only provided in a limited way by rural clinics:

The only information that they get is from the clinic and at the clinic they are not told what can help them. There is not a lot of health education. (BM)

Echoing BM's sentiments about the critical need for sexual health education is SL, who through his engagement with the SURMs and being in the community observed:

> Education when it comes to sexual diseases is really low–people are not educated … particularly the youngsters–they have no clue … Here it's taboo. (SL)

The above excerpts illustrate that responsive teaching requires the facilitators to be present and available to support others in their growth. It is an example of a pedagogy of 'relational care'. It transcends the content to be learnt and foregrounds the contextual issues at play, and transforms the way in which the SURMs see themselves towards the end of the course. When SURMs were asked to reflect on their learning post-intervention, a new understanding of their roles and identity emerges. A particular awareness of their context is evident in the expressed need for future life skills courses, including advanced nutritional training, childcare, HIV/AIDS, and sexual health:

> As I have attained knowledge on the course, I can go around spreading the gospel about the course itself and what other people can gain from attending the course. (Enelo)

> I want to emphasise on alcohol and drug abuse and HIV. Sexual health education … If people are told more about life skills and how to take care of themselves and also other SURMs coming together, starting projects that can help motivate people to have a healthy lifestyle. (Bombisani)

Discussion and conclusions

In this chapter we inquired into the capabilities of responsive community-based co-research and co-teaching programmes for out-of-school youth. Little has been written about how the needs that SURMs express for extramural learning with IT and for improved nutrition could be used to develop a context-based course through co-researching and co-teaching. The CBPAR framework employed allowed for the intervention to place the community at the heart of co-researching and co-teaching.

The results illustrate that contextualised BAE courses can become a catalyst for SURMs in this rural community to become empowered in controlling and managing their nutrition and that of their young children. However, at a deeper level of analysis, considering Bobsin et al.'s (2017, p. 15) argument that affordances "only exist in practice and in context", one becomes aware of the contradictory nature of affordances. The following four facets of affordances are applied to the results to allow for a deeper level of analysis:

1) Affordances are *relational*. Strong et al. (2014) contend that affordances are neither the product of the object (technology–actant) nor the subject (user–actor). They are relational, meaning that they emerge out of the interaction between the subject and the object.

2) Affordances offer *possibilities of action*. This means that it is not necessary for a particular user to have realised or actualised the affordance for it to exist, but there needs to be a user who could actualise it.

3) Affordances can be *constraining*. Strong et al. (2014) argue that the possibilities of action are not infinite. In other words, certain possibilities are made possible and others are not.

4) Affordances are *goal oriented*. This emphasises the point that human actors have intentionality as opposed to actants (technology) (Strong et al., 2014, p. 55).

These four facets were applied to the SURMs' perceptions of extramural learning with IT and the BAE nutrition course, as outlined below.

Pre-intervention stage

The motivation to attend the first workshop is driven by an internal motivation and the need 'to gain information on IT and nutrition'. The motivation therefore aligns itself with the notion of affordances as being 'relational' and 'goal oriented'. The need arises out of attendance at the workshop, and carries with it an intentionality: the intention 'to learn about IT and nutrition'. This intention is temporal and carries with it 'possibilities of action'. The possibilities of action are actualised by the SURMs through their ultimate acquisition of IT skills (projected future action) in their potential to master the Internet. The Internet will be used 'to find information about feeding and nutrition'. In this regard, the workshop attendance brings to the fore both the 'relational' and the 'possibilities of action' nature of affordances. The future possibilities to learn and act become immeasurable, because the 'why' is internally motivated.

During-intervention stage

In this stage the impact of responsive co-teaching on students' learning is heightened, foregrounding the relational nature of affordances. The course was initially intended to be taught in English. As the classes unfolded, it became apparent that the SURMs were more comfortable when taught in XiTsonga with English terms included where necessary. The ability to respond to the contextual needs of the SURMs, coupled with the respect accorded the SURMs, related to the SURMs' self-actualisation as life-long learners. SURMs project themselves into the roles of gainful employment; they can enrol themselves into positions that require a person with the skill set that they have developed. The nature of affordances as 'possibilities of action' is foregrounded.

Post-intervention stage

In this stage the notions of peer support and context-based teaching are brought to the fore. We see the 'possibilities of action' truly being cast against the constraints of living in a rural environment. This contradiction comes from the complexity of resource provision in rural areas. The lack of childcare facilities in the village becomes the biggest constraint for the SURMs. It constrains the possibility of SURMs attending, volunteering and participating in the future events of the project, due to the precarious nature of this 'hidden' support.

Furthermore, there are the realities of the employment prospects in rural Limpopo and the cost and risk factors which come into play when a single mother has to leave her child/children in care in order to leave the village to work. The higher-order motives to improve the plight of women overall become constrained by the 'context' of practice. This provides an insight into how South Africa's history and context of inequality continue to be 'sculpted and truncated' by socio-economic forces (Donner & Walton, 2013).

The second constraint comes from the struggle of having to negotiate one's identity within a largely patriarchal tribal context. How do SURMs move beyond the taboo around sex and issues of healthy living within this community? The agentic nature of peer support and context-based teaching allows Bombisani, for example, to have hope in the future of the community, where the issues of alcohol and drug abuse and HIV as 'easy escapes' for the youth (Fihlani, 2018) can be confronted head on.

To conclude, the findings of this study highlight the powerful effect of a community education intervention for SURMs in a resource-limited rural area of South Africa. The findings showed affordances as 'possibilities for action' that can be "both enabling and constraining" (Strong et al., 2014, p. 55). We contend that it is not only access to a basic IT and nutrition course, but also economic, social, and cultural dynamics that play a decisive role in our ability to fully grasp the concept of 'affordance' in this context.

References

Balazs, C. L. & Morello-Frosch, R. (2013). The three Rs: How community-based participatory research strengthens the rigor, relevance, and reach of science. *Environmental Justice, 6*(1), pp. 9-16.

Bhana D., Morrell R, Shefer, T. & Ngabaza, S. (2010) South African teachers' responses to teenage pregnancy and teenage mothers in schools. *Culture, Health & Sexuality, 12*(8), pp. 871-883.

Bobsin, D., Petrini, M. & Pozzebon, M. (2017), The value of technology affordances to improve the management of non-profit organizations. *RAUSP Management Journal, 54*(1), pp. 14-37.

Cornwall, A. & Jewkes, R. (1995). What is participatory research? *Social Science & Medicine, 41*(12), pp. 1667-1676.

De Witte, K., Cabus, S., Thyssen, G., Groot, W., & van den Brink, H. M. (2013). A critical review of the literature on school dropout. Educational Research Review, *10*, pp. 13-28. https://doi.org/10.1016/j.edurev.2013.05.002

Donner, T. J. & Walton, M. (2013). 'Your phone has internet–why are you at a library PC? Re-imagining Public Access in the Mobile Internet Era'. *14th IFIP TC13 Conference Proceedings of Human–Computer Interaction*, 2-6 September 2019, Cape Town (pp. 347–364). Cape Town: INTERACT. http://www. interact 2013.org/

Fihlani, P. (2018). *South Africa teen pregnancy: Juggling school exams and baby twins.* https://www.bbc.com/news/world-africa-45889366#

Fraenkel, J. R. & Wallen, N. E. (1993). *How to design and evaluate research in education.* New York: McGraw-Hill.

Glaser, B. G. & Strauss, A. L. (2009). *The discovery of grounded theory: Strategies for qualitative research.* New Brunswick, NJ: Transaction Publishers.

Google. (n.d.). Google Maps directions to Mulamula village in Limpopo Province, South Africa. https://www.google.com/maps/search/mulamula+village+limpopo+province/

Hartnack, A. (2017). Background document and review of key South African and international literature on school dropout. *DG Murray Trust (DGMT).* Retrieved from: https://dgmt.co.za/wp-content/uploads/2017/08/School-Dropout-Background-Paper-Final.pdf

Harwell, S. H. (2003). *Teacher professional development: It's not an event, it's a process.* Center for Occupational Research and Development. http://www.cord.org/uploadedfiles/HarwellPaper.pdf

Human Sciences Research Council (HSRC). (2013). *Audit of technological initiatives for rural development (DRDLR).* http://curation.hsrc.ac.za/Datasets-MJAFAA.phtml

Kevany, K. M. & MacMichael, M. (2014). Communities of knowledge and knowledge of communities: An appreciative inquiry into rural wellbeing. *Gateways: International Journal of Community Research and Engagement, 7*(1), pp. 34-51.

Lave, J. (1991). Situating learning in communities of practice. *Perspectives on Socially Shared Cognition, 2*, pp. 63-82.

Livingstone, H. (2019). *The role of socioeconomic factors in the successful completion of matric education among young mothers in the Soutpansberg East circuit, Limpopo province, South Africa* (Master's dissertation). University of South Africa.

Modisaotsile, B. M. (2012). The failing standard of basic education in South Africa. *Africa Institute of South Africa Policy Brief, 72*, pp. 1-7.

National Department of Health (NDoH), Statistics South Africa (Stats SA), South African Medical Research Council (SAMRC), and ICF. (2019). *South Africa Demographic and Health Survey 2016.* Pretoria, South Africa, and Rockville, Maryland, USA: NDoH, Stats SA, SAMRC, and ICF.

Organisation for Economic Cooperation and Development (OECD). (2006). *ICT and learning: Supporting out-of-school youth and adults.* Organisation for Economic Cooperation and Development.

Strong, D. M., Johnson, S. A., Tulu, B., Trudel, J., Volkoff, O., Pelletier, L. R., Bar-On, I. & Garber, L. (2014). A Theory of Organization-EHR Affordance Actualization. *Journal of the Association for Information Systems, 15*(2), pp. 53-85.

Smith, R. & Turpin, M. (2017). Design science research and activity theory in ICT4D: Developing a Socially relevant ICT platform for Elderly women in Remote Rural South Africa. *14th IFIP WG 9.4 International Conference on Social Implications of Computers in Developing Countries, ICT4D,* 22-24 May 2017, Yogyakarta, Indonesia (pp. 345–356). Cham: Springer. https://hal.inria.fr/hal-01650055

Spaull, N. (2015). Schooling in South Africa: How low quality education becomes a poverty trap. In A. de Lannoy, S. Swartz., L. Lake, & C. Smith (Eds.), *The South African Child Gauge* (pp. 34-41). Cape Town: Children's Institute.

Thompson, R. M. (2016). *Implementation of an integrated ICT and BAE course for young mothers using CBPAR in Limpopo* (Master's dissertation). University of KwaZulu- Natal.

Wenger, E. (1998). Communities of practice: Learning as a social system. *Systems Thinker, 9*(5), pp. 2-3.

Section 2:
Connecting Africa and the world through co-teaching and co-research

Chapter 8

You map our world; we write yours

Kristian D. Stewart

University of Michigan Dearborn, United States of America

Siddique Motala

University of Cape Town, South Africa

Abstract

This chapter reports the findings of a joint assignment between a South African engineering class and a composition course in the United States. Both student cohorts were placed in WhatsApp chat groups to facilitate cooperation as they completed a geographic information systems (GIS) mapping assignment (South African students) and writing assignment (American students). Questions guiding this research stemmed from a desire to connect students outside of localised classroom spaces to the global world. Applying case study methodology to one group, based on data collected such as instructor field notes, the WhatsApp chats that students provided to the instructors, the collaborative mapping assignment which resulted in reflective essays/StoryMaps, researchers noted the tension and possibilities within this collaboration. Discussion includes a commentary on traditional classroom environments, where students are positioned unequally, as limited in providing them with an authentic and worldly perspective adjacent to the power and possibilities of future transcontinental curricular endeavours.

Keywords: transdisciplinary activism, transnational collaboration, higher education, writing, cartography, global citizenship, transcontinental curricular endeavours, glocal education, StoryMap, South Africa, United States

***

Introduction

We are university instructors from opposing disciplinary fields who are passionate about social justice pedagogies. We met at a higher education conference in Cape Town, South Africa, in 2018 and wondered if we could combine the teaching and pedagogical research that we were implementing in our respective classes (composition and GIS) across vastly different contexts. One of us resides and works in South Africa, the other in the United States (USA). In our classroom work and scholarship, we were already interested in social justice education and to what extent we could encourage our students to take an interest in global issues. We believe that there is benefit to students when they are exposed to different people, places, and ideas. We discussed our individualised projects, specifically how our classroom practices addressed issues relevant to the USA and South Africa but were also relevant within our localised communities.

As an example, the writing class Kristi was instructing at the time (which was used as a nucleus for this project) was conceptualised after the election of Donald Trump in 2016. Noticing the polarisation on campus and in the USA, curriculum was meant to 'talk back' to an uptick in racialised and 'America first' rhetoric dominating the national stage. Additionally, Siddique was concerned about the technicist approach to engineering education in South Africa, which focused on maintaining minimum standards and left little room for students to substantially interrogate issues related to ethics.

We each bring to the project different theoretical and methodological points of view. We put into conversation US-based philosopher Kwame Anthony Appiah (cosmopolitanism) with feminist poststructuralist philosophers Rosi Braidotti (nomadic ethics) and Karen Barad (hauntology), as well as affect scholar Michalinos Zembylas (pedagogy of discomfort), and the turn to "glocal education" (Jackson & Han, 2016; Patel & Lynch, 2013) to imagine the possibilities of co-learning with global partners in local classroom settings. Merging our unique backgrounds and theoretical perspectives was done with two aims in mind: to assist with the navigation of the pedagogical process and to aid our understanding of subsequent analysis of the intervention.

Power and possibilities

Since Donald Trump announced his candidacy for the American presidency in 2015, his promise for an 'America first' agenda and his 'Make America Great Again' slogan became mainstream and popularised rhetoric. However, Trump's #MAGA tagline sits adjacent to the many racist remarks (Graham et al., 2021) that have defined both his campaign and his presidency. Additionally, Trump's unashamedly bigoted and prejudiced public rants against people of colour have drawn large support (Newman et al., 2021). The result has been that in some arenas White nationalism has replaced American patriotism, thereby causing some US citizens to challenge any connection to a global world. Trump's call to reject globalism and to embrace an America made only by–and for–largely White America has made socially just and anti-racist teaching practices more challenging in this climate. In fact, Trump signed an executive order banning racial sensitivity programmes and critical race theory, the academic theory that supports diversity training, in the United States Government (Cineas, 2020). Teaching in the time of Trump required a directed effort to remind students that their worlds exist outside of a classroom, neighbourhood, and even country.

South Africa's fractured history also calls for thoughtful ways in which its students can encounter people with diverse cultures and beliefs. Early on in post-apartheid South Africa, the imperatives of nation building took centre stage. This was an attempt at dealing with the legacy of a deeply divided society, mainly along racial lines. The 'rainbow nation', a term coined by Archbishop Desmond Tutu, was intended to symbolise the unity of the diversity of people in the country. 'Rainbowism', however, turned out to be problematic, as it backgrounded issues of structural inequality and silenced people's lived experiences of oppression (Ngoasheng & Gachago, 2017). Furthermore, South African nationalism tends to manifest in an intensification of xenophobic discourse, particularly against other Africans. In South Africa, certain nationalities (for example Nigerians, Somalis, and Congolese) are vilified, and each nationality has developed a pejorative archetype that serves to intensify xenophobic discourse. The public airing of privately held prejudices and fears is currently *en vogue* in right-wing Western discourses.

As we developed this project, both authors saw the need–and the possibilities– that a shared classroom could provide for our students. At the inception, we agreed that Appiah's (2006) *Cosmopolitanism: Ethics in a World of Strangers* would be utilised as a mentor text as we brainstormed the goals for our collaboration. We found Appiah's notion of "cosmopolitanism" to be a useful example as we considered how to combine our classes across time and space. Appiah (2006) explains cosmopolitanism as a metaphor for both the literal act of conversation and as an appeal for people to become citizens of the world who start with the simple idea of developing "habits of coexistence" (p. xix) in order for diverse people to become "used to one another" (p. 78). Central to Appiah is his belief that people should be placed in unique positions where they can learn each other's arguments and beliefs without trying to bend the other to his or her will. Our collaboration was our attempt to place students into partnerships to 'expose' them to varied attitudes, cultures, and languages that exist in other parts of the world. In our complex local environments, we felt a deep commitment to foreground this 'exposure' as vital to our anti-racist and socially just teaching practices.

In addition to Appiah (2006), we were also guided by Braidotti's (2006) nomadic ethics and the new materialist insights of Barad (2007). In a nomadic worldview, the Western, binary construct of difference is eschewed. Western philosophy emphasises universal characteristics of groups, so that categories like 'man', 'woman', 'poor' and 'foreigner' may be created. In today's capitalist world, the human standard continues to be White, able-bodied, male, youthful, belonging to a nation-state and speaking a standard language. Western humanism creates a hierarchy of worth in which women (sexualised others), people of colour (racialised others) and animals, together with non-living matter (naturalised others) are placed lower down than the dominant 'man'. The racialised other is also extended to include non-Western and non-Christian others (Braidotti, 2008). Additionally, Barad advises us on the importance of being attuned to silence. She says that each worldly entanglement matters "not just for what comes to matter but what is constitutively excluded from mattering in order for particular materialisations to occur" (Juelskjær & Schwennesen, 2012, p. 21). Silence, erasure, and avoidance are tactics that have been (and continue to be) used in violent nationalism and colonialism. In bearing witness to the silencing of and pervasive prejudice towards some groups in our classes, we felt that it was our duty to resist such violence.

The student cohorts, location of the study, and collected data

The American cohort consisted of 66 students across three sections of introductory composition on a university campus located in the greater Detroit metropolitan area within the USA. Our largely commuter campus is uniquely located among the largest Arabic-speaking population in North America. In addition, this region is composed of several expat and immigrant enclaves where diverse classroom environments are commonplace. Students enrolled in Composition 106 during the Winter 2019 term were more female (n=40) than male (n=26) and self-identified across multiple racial and ethnic identities (White, 30; Iraqi, 3; Syrian, 2; Indian, 1; Lebanese, 5; Asian, 2; African American, 8; Yemeni, 2; Bangladeshi, 2; Arab, 4; Mexican, 4; Pakistani, 1; mixed-race, 2). Of this cohort, English, Arabic, Spanish, Urdu/Hindi, and Albanian were identified as fluent first languages.

Students in the American course spent the 16-week term examining the theme "What Does It Mean to Be a Global Citizen?" They read Trevor Noah's (2016) *Born a Crime: Stories From a South African Childhood,* excerpts from Appiah's (2006) *Cosmopolitanism: Ethics in a World of Strangers,* and investigated global citizenship and human rights issues through TED Talks, in-class readings, and writing assignments. Eight weeks of the semester were dedicated to working with our South African colleagues.

The South African cohort consisted of 22 second-year engineering students who were studying toward a qualification in geomatics at a university of technology in the Western Cape. The course is an introductory geographic information systems (GIS) course aimed at introducing students to GIS theory and the use of GIS software. All of the students were South African (this was unusual as previous cohorts typically had other African nations represented) and consisted of 11 Black, 8 White, and 3 Coloured students.[1] Typical of an engineering class, it was overwhelmingly male (19 students) with only 3 females. Although English was the language of instruction, only 3 students' first language was English. The rest of the students identified their first languages as Afrikaans (8), isiXhosa (5), isiZulu (4) and Sesotho (2).

Students were placed in purposefully mixed groupings of 6–7 students (Creswell, 2009) via the WhatsApp chat application at the instructors' discretion. Each group generally consisted of two South African students and four US students. Because the collaboration depended on WhatsApp, grouping our students was a critical component of this assignment. Thus, placing our students in groups where they could foster new and affirmative relationships with and among their international colleagues, students 'other' than them, was paramount. Our understanding of otherness has been influenced by Butler (2004) and Staszak (2008). Through the lens of human vulnerability, Butler (2004) urges us to decentre the 'I' in global narratives in order to understand our role as global actors and to view how our lives are "profoundly implicated in the lives of others" (p. 7). In a similar way, Staszak (2008) compliments Butler and reminds us how otherness divides humanity, allows individuals to be placed in hierarchical groups ('us' versus 'them'), and how 'othering' feeds asymmetrical power relationship and discrimination.

Given the aforementioned concerns, making students aware of both unconscious and conscious bias which they may harbour was intentional. Prior to the pairings, in the American classroom dialogue that surrounds White privilege, police brutality toward people of colour, and the immigration debate (i.e., 'America first') led to frank conversations that revealed the positionality students held on all sides of the course themes. Students whose views were in opposition with each other were placed in the same groups. As an example, a student who authored a paper detailing White privilege as a myth was placed in the same group as a student of colour who tried explaining to him how she had been the target of racial profiling by the police. Adjacent to challenging our students' world views, our pairings were intended to encourage global citizenship, cosmopolitanism, and empathy across lines of difference.[2]

---

[1] Race-based terminology was used extensively to entrench the apartheid status quo and is still recognised in democratic South Africa, largely because of government efforts to redress past racially discriminatory laws or practices. We therefore utilise the unfortunate terms 'Black,' 'White,' and 'Coloured' to refer to the racial groups that were officially recognised in the apartheid era and continue to live on in the 'new' South Africa.

[2] The American classroom was set up as a place for open dialogue and communication. Students were often placed in groups as standard classroom practice. The authors understand the sensitive nature of emotional labour and who carries it in terms of

In the South African class, the lived realities of Black, female, and rural students often contrasted with those of White South African students. We purposefully combined students who were different from each other, and these differences were revealed in some of the assignment submissions. The American students also had similar patterns of contrasting lived experiences, largely dependent upon where the students resided–with wealthy western suburbs, Detroit, or largely homogeneous enclaves like the cities of Hamtramck or Grosse Pointe Shores as examples.[3] In the American classes, women and men of colour were purposefully identified to be WhatsApp group leaders. In thinking about these selections, McIntosh's (2007) "privilege walk" comes to mind; therefore, both White female and male students were largely excluded from this leadership role so as to decentre Whiteness within the groups. The groups were additionally mixed across lines of gender, race, ethnicity, and language to the best of our abilities to do so.

The joint curriculum consisted of a mapping and writing assignment that tasked the members of each group to communicate through WhatsApp in order to adequately complete their assignment. In WhatsApp, the students asked each other questions from their assignment briefs. By default, students got to know one another through shared conversation. The South African students were asked to produce maps of the houses of the American students in their group. Thus, they had to produce a set of Cape Town and Michigan maps. Additionally, both cohorts were required to collate information about their colleagues, such as:

-    Describe the population and average income of each suburb.
-    How do you travel to campus?
-    Do you have a job while you are studying?
-    What is the distance from your house to public transport/hospital/ family/friend/your nearest neighbour/grocery store?
-    What is the distance from your house to the ocean/lake/public park?
-    What wildlife visits your property?

These questions were meant to aid the South African students in creating meaningful GIS maps and the American students in 'writing the world' of their colleagues. As a final project, American students were asked to reflect on the

---

representation of the Black experience. Groupings were meant to disrupt privilege and challenge White supremacy culture.

[3] "White Flight" from Detroit in the 1960s and 1970s (Clotfelter, 1976) and "Black Flight" in the early 2000s aided the creation of segregated living spaces resulting in Detroit being one of the most racially discrimitive cities in America (Farley, 2018).

collaboration and to compose the 'world' of their South African colleagues in a multimedia platform combining text and images called a StoryMap (https://storymaps.arcgis.com/), see Figure 8.1.

Figure 8.1: Sample slides from a StoryMap

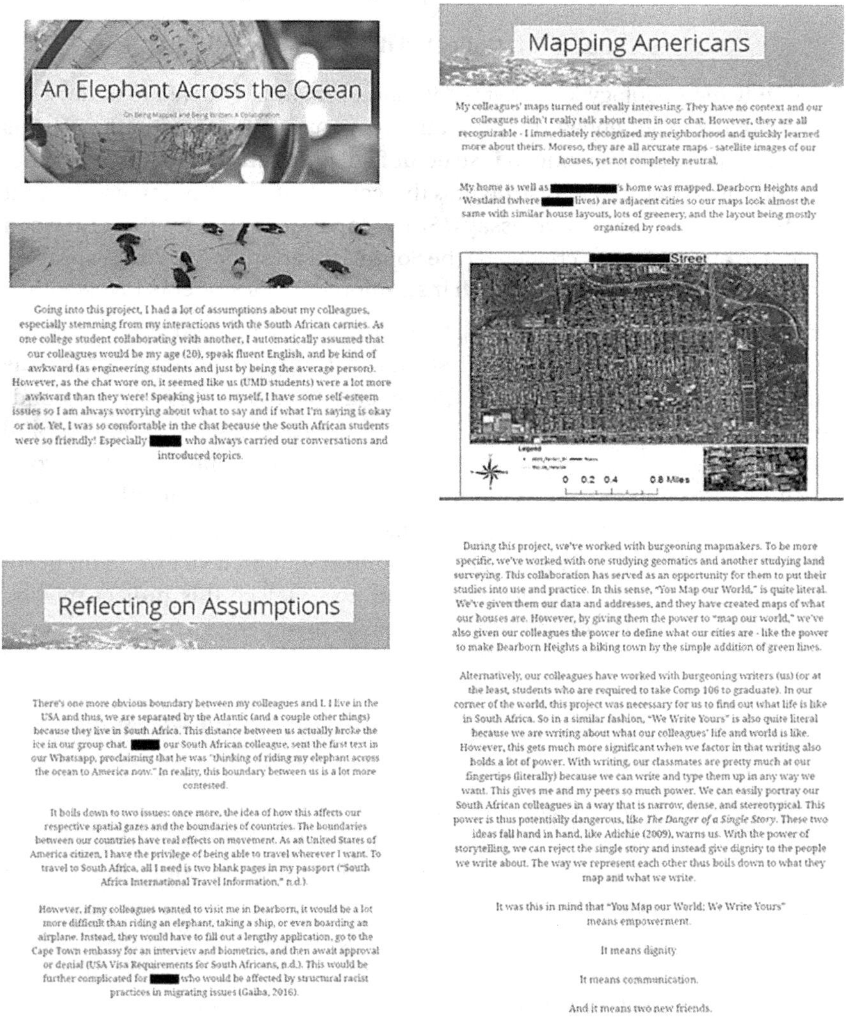

The following questions guided our collaboration:

- Question 1: How might each of our distinct student populations benefit from transnational collaboration?

- Question 2: What might students learn about themselves and each other through global exposure?
- Question 3: What tensions were exposed/highlighted through the collaboration?

Collected data

Case study methodology (Creswell, 2009; Stake, 1995) was selected to understand how students experienced the programme of study over the duration of this course. Collected data included instructor field notes, the WhatsApp chats that students provided to the instructors, the collaborative mapping assignment which resulted in reflective essays/StoryMaps (authored by the American students), and GIS maps created by the South African students. Ethics approval and consent was received from both institutions and all students involved.

Initial data were coded utilising Saldaña's (2012) method for examining qualitative artefacts. During the first round of analysis, holistic coding was implemented to better understand the general direction of the data. Second-round coding included an *in vivo* analysis (Saldaña, 2012) of the chat and instructor field notes and impressions. Findings include one WhatsApp group which, in our opinion, connected more meaningfully than the other groups. Most notably, we discovered the tensions, possibilities, and power relations that revolved around our students' assumptions and preconceived notions of otherness. These themes speak directly to how we see this project moving forward in the future and how other academics might engage in transnational collaboration.

The intersections of discomforting pedagogy, 'glocal' education, and feminist new materialisms

Drawing from the pedagogy of discomfort (Boler & Zembylas, 2003) and nomadic ethics (Braidotti, 2006), we positioned our students in WhatsApp chat groups that would purposefully challenge their long-standing beliefs and encourage them to question the world around them. In agreement with Boler and Zembylas (2003), education is not meant to be neutral or "comforting" nor a vehicle to reproduce the status quo. Rather, students should be placed in scenarios that allow them to question their assumptions about themselves and each other and assist them in working toward examining binaries that form society, like power/freedom and oppressed/oppressor (Bekerman & Zembylas, 2011; Zembylas & Bekerman, 2016). Furthermore, we were guided by the stance of feminist/new materialist theorists such as Braidotti and Barad, who advise on the importance of dealing responsibly with alterity. Barad's (2007) theory of agential realism allowed us to inhabit an in-between space and think diffractively about the relationships between curriculum, theory, and student engagement.

Our quest in this project was for our students to appreciate the juncture where their two worlds met by placing them in direct positions to examine how privilege, power, race, and material access had informed their individual and collective worlds. This is where 'glocal' education steps in. While this project takes place in specific, localised classroom locations, we emphasised the global nature of our learning community. Our 'place' was a departure from a traditional classroom setting and took shape over WhatsApp. In education literature, glocal has been defined as an adaptive education movement that is "outward looking, yet localized" (Jackson & Han, 2016, p. 133) and as a critical merging of global economic, social, and political issues integrated into local classroom contexts (Harth, 2010). Braidotti (2013) advocates that education should help to create communities of learning that look like the societies they reflect, serve, and help to construct. Additionally, these communities should be attuned to social justice, respect diversity, and affirm the positivity of difference.

A glocal approach views education as an interconnected system where stress is placed on recognising the world as a site of study before positioning how personal (and local) stories exist within a larger and global framework of multiple social histories (Barndt, 1997). Soldatova and Greer (2013) have articulated glocal identity as "characterized by acquired multicultural competence" and "based both on local and global experience and knowledge" (p. 474). Dahlberga and Bagga-Gupta (2014) see the world as linked by technology and have created online spaces where students can have cultural transactions without leaving their home environments. These "borderland spaces" (Dahlberga & Bagga-Gupta, 2014, p. 482) become sites for engagement where students can develop cultural awareness. This new environment has been described by Patel and Lynch (2013, p. 224) as a "third culture space" where diverse communities can make connection with each other. As Patel and Lynch (2013) note, glocal ideology is the recognition that cultural wealth and knowledge underpin global communities, and these traits are the building blocks to developing a third culture space.

Lastly, we considered 'hauntology',[4] a term coined by Derrida (1994) and used by Barad (2010, 2017), which refers to traces of the past that haunt the present and future. In this regard, it is important to be attuned to the silences and erasures that may haunt our classrooms. For example, telling past stories of

---

[4] We examine hauntology within this intervention as it relates to anti-racist education in Motala & Stewart, 2021.

racial exclusion and violence are not just recollections of a painful past (for some) but part of difficult existing and future material conditions. Barad (2017, p. 74) points out that "Hauntings are not immaterial, and they are not mere recollections or reverberations of what was. Hauntings are an integral part of existing material conditions".

Findings

What worked, what did not? Tensions, resonances, and dissonances

At the outset, communication between our students was a barrier we had not anticipated. We assumed that students would start talking easily, as they are smartphone savvy and seemingly from a generation that values the use of technology in communication. We found that technology can serve as a platform to minimise the effort it takes to communicate. However, that does not mean students know how to communicate effectively. Students did not know what to say, how to start 'talking', and what to 'talk' about. The US students even requested that the instructor provide them with conversation starters. We also discovered that the US students had preconceived notions of how the conversation should take place. They attempted to control the dialogue and became irritated by what they perceived as non-timely responses from their South African colleagues.

English was the language of communication in the chat, which was both an assumption and a convenience for the American students. The US students had to be constantly reminded that for many of their South African counterparts, English was either a second or a third language. However, some US students took it upon themselves to try and use Afrikaans or isiXhosa in the chats (they did not know either of these languages existed before this collaboration). The US students also had to be reminded about access to material resources, particularly with regard to Cape Town's rotating electricity outages.

As for the South Africans, they occasionally became frustrated that the Americans did not know about the world in the same way as they did. It became clear the South African students had a global awareness (in terms of politics, history, and geography) that the American students lacked. However, both groups agreed that their colleagues were more like them than they first believed. For example, they found it interesting that their counterparts shared similar struggles relating to attending school and holding down jobs. Some American students were shocked that many South African students had the same hobbies that they did. Toward the end, they found commonalities across their lines of difference.

Silences

We were aware of the silences that continue to haunt the daily existence of specific groups of students, particularly those that may be characterised by their intersectionality that spanned gender, race, economic status, and religion: Black, female, Black and female, and Black, female, and Muslim. One of the more troubling findings of the collaboration was that one female South African student of colour was misidentified for the entire collaboration. In short, assumptions were made about her gender, as she was called by her last name– as opposed to her first–in the chat. The American students had no idea that she was female; and by the end of the project, this student felt justifiably enraged.

Another issue of concern was the extent to which history was erased by most of the South African students. There was a clear silencing of South Africa's oppressive and apartheid history by a few of the Black students when questioned by the US students. For example, when a US student asked if there was discrimination in South Africa, the response was "Life in SA is great! We have the greatest quality of food! Our weather is simply marvelous [sic]!" Even though the American students had been studying South Africa and knew of its complicated history, nobody in the group–even the other South African students–troubled these statements.

However, there were some instances of silences being challenged. An example stems from a dialogue between a White South African student and his Black colleague. A US student asked if there was anything they would like people to know about South Africa. The White South African student remarked largely on corruption being combatted and eliminated in the workplace. He also expressed frustration that South Africa was known only for "stuff like racism", which he said is now being addressed openly and "people are becoming less racist". His Black counterpart in the group had a different opinion. He remarked that "history is haunting people" and "people feel oppressed by this situation". He continued, "The history had divided the nation today because each and every person has a scar of what happened".

Unusual to teaching and learning interactions in South African engineering classrooms that typically focus on technical content, this project opened a space that gave the Black student freedom to express a political viewpoint. Perhaps the online presence of the US students gave the student a space to express his feelings of continued oppression, even in the face of the hegemonic view that apartheid is 'over' and people are 'free'. The existence of structural and systemic racism is indeed a spectre that haunts the everyday reality of Black South Africans. Nonetheless, this exchange was small and self-censored. Perhaps this silence was a tactic used in the face of the power relations within the academy–students may have felt that they needed to maintain cordial relations to complete the task and pass the course.

What was created and what was gained

A highlight of the collaboration was a chat group that included Mia (African American, devout Muslim female) and Ben (Afrikaner White male). Mia was the group leader on the American side. This chat, although it included other students, was basically a one-on-one conversation between Mia and Ben that spanned 34 printed pages (the average for the collaboration was 22 pages). Here is an excerpt (spelling and grammar retained as in the original):

> **Mia:** Im African american. My grandfather was half white half native American so i have a bit of that in me
>
> **Ben:** Native american that's pretty cool. Khoisans in africa suffered a similar fate to them.
>
> **Mia:** There was talk of removing andrew jackson from the 20 dollar bill bc he was in office during the trail of tears
>
> **Ben:** Issue with removing every piece of history with bad connotations is you'll just about get rid of everything.
>
> **Mia:** True but i think it was the intent of doing some type of justice for the natives
>
> **Ben:** Theyve done similar here, changed names of places, roads, torn statues down
>
> **Mia:** I know for sure in a lot of public schools they have the curriculum set so that you only know some history but not the full true history
>
> **Ben:** Something happens here for example I remember far more about the french revolution than I do about the khoisan and the bantu.
>
> **Ben:** Coz all we did in history was the damn french revolution
>
> **Mia:** We call that "whitewashing"
>
> **Mia:** Where history is focused on european history and it diminishes other history
>
> **Mia:** American history is centered around the constitution. Leaving out slavery, trail of tears, japanese in concentration camps, the Mexican war and more
>
> **Ben:** Lol, but bare in mind the french revolution is a critically important thing to learn not because its french but because it teaches kids that they must not always accept the status quo
>
> **Ben:** Hell throw in the nuclear tests on the pacific atolls
>
> **Ben:** But the issue will always exist because there is so much history to teach especially in the time frame kids have
>
> **Mia:** Don't get me started on jim crow and KKK
>
> **Ben:** Lol, the list is almost endless

This exchange went beyond surface conversation and dialogue relating to the assignment brief and project, and it is an example of a "third culture space" engagement, as Patel and Lynch (2013, p. 224) have described.

At the end of the project students submitted assignments generated by the WhatsApp chat groups. The American students were tasked with 'writing the world' of their colleagues. They could do this either in essay form or they could submit a StoryMap, which is a multimodal application that allows students to integrate words, videos, and images into a cohesive 'map' of their topic. All submissions from the American students had to include photos, maps, and illustrations gathered from the collaboration as supporting documents to their ideas. The engineering students created layered GIS mapping reflective of their own and their American counterparts' lived experiences.

Interestingly, the StoryMaps and essays provided highly contextualised and nuanced information garnered from the course readings, relationships formed in the chat, and student reflections. As examples, US students commented on how the project increased their spatial gaze, how to be a global citizen, and how their worldly perspective had widened. One student remarked that she learned the importance of making conversation to examine differences. Another said she learned about self-identification, specifically regarding her place in a community and how boundaries (real and imagined) are used to shape such identities. Some South African students entered the collaboration imagining that the standard of living and education of the US students would be significantly superior. Many also expected condescension: "We thought they would undermine us and would be self-centred due to the fact that they have a better education system in their country". The same students were surprised to encounter humble, regular people whose university lives had much in common with theirs. Some were also surprised at the diversity of cultures in the US and that prejudice towards 'others' is not uncommon.

The data collected in the StoryMap essays point to the US students rethinking themselves as they synthesised the course readings and WhatsApp conversations and reflected on the project. The maps and essays became vessels for them to challenge their assumptions and beliefs. We found the final projects to be a beneficial tool of this collaboration and the goals we set forth at the beginning of the project. We were pleased by our students' increased awareness of each other, which we linked to the compassion and empathy we saw displayed in the groups.

Analysis and discussion

We asked ourselves what characteristics moved Mia and Ben's conversation into what Patel and Lynch (2013, p. 224) term a "third cultural space". Mia, as a woman of colour, told the instructor after completion of the course that she had this unusual classroom opportunity to "speak her truth". She also spoke about her extreme curiosity about South Africa and viewed this as an asset for cultural understanding and global knowledge (Patel & Lynch, 2013). Furthermore, Mia stated that she decided to let go of her biases once she met the instructor. She shared that after reading the course description and getting excited about the class, she assumed the instructor would be a strong and powerful Black woman. When she met the instructor (Kristi, a White female) before the start of class, she expressed that she was "stunned". She reported (Stewart, field notes) that at that point she let go of her assumptions. She then applied this open-mindedness to the WhatsApp chat.

All groups engaged in mundane, everyday conversation as encouraged by both instructors at the outset of the intervention. Almost all groups chatted about the weather and their respective universities; all groups shared pictures or memes. As aforementioned, Mia and Ben's group became deeply invested in this project. Mia made herself vulnerable by mentioning her own poverty, which allowed Ben to respond in kind. When we looked further at the data, we recognised the first point in the chat where Mia made herself vulnerable:

> **Mia:** When we (americans) use the term suburb we're talking areas that have a higher income average
> **Mia:** Basically upper middle class and rich people live in them
> **Ben:** Yeah I realised when you didnt understand what I ment by suburb
> **Mia:** I live in an urban area
> **Mia:** Which basically means i live in a place where not everyone is making a lot of money people are poorer

This act on Mia's part negated some silences, as both students used their curiosity to get to know one another. Mia and Ben's interaction ties into the notion of a shared responsibility and burden for the communication act. They displayed mutual vulnerability, what Kwenda (2003) and Keet, Zinn, and Porteus (2009) deem a vital component for cultural justice within asymmetrical power relationships. By taking a risk and being vulnerable, Mia and Ben moved their relationship outside of a classroom transaction for a grade into a cultural connection, before it transitioned into a friendship that lasted past the end of the course (as shared by Mia; Stewart, field notes).

Additionally, and drawing from Zembylas (2005), we question how well students can truly know each other in a limited classroom setting, particularly ones like ours where intersectional features are prominent. In our context we found 'knowability' to be a challenge. For example, on the American side, there was a tension between preparing students via context (i.e., South African history/knowledge) versus allowing students to use their curiosity about their colleagues to drive interactions. Mbembe (2001, p. 1) points out that global discourse on Africa is largely negative–it is a place of lack and "its things and attributes are generally of lesser value, little importance, and poor quality". Perhaps without lessons in South African history, students would have allowed themselves to discover each other without preconceived assumptions and, as Zembylas (2005, p. 139) writes, to allow the "other" to remain dignified.

Barad's (2007) theory of agential realism requires a conception of the relationships between matter, discourse, subjectivity, agency, space, and time. As critical practitioners, we had to be cognisant of our focus and vigilant about what we left out, too. In thinking about silence and Barad's notion of agency, we recognised a relationship between agency and silence that in our case resulted in a 'cost' to students. This 'cost' was clearly marked with the gendered silence the South African student experienced, which effectively erased her. This aligns with Butler's (2015) performativity theory regarding the social, bodily, and behavioural construction of gender. Without commonplace acts of communication in the chat, the South African student was unable to express her gendered identity, thereby minimising her personal and academic agency. Nowhere in the conversation did she express the unique vantage point of being a female of colour in a male-dominated field. The misrecognition of her positionality made her angry and forced us to be more attuned to this specific silence. By bringing attention to areas of silence, we are practising a type of epistemic disobedience (Zembylas et al., 2021) and troubling the normativity of specific categories (such as White and male) that are unquestioned in disciplines such as engineering. To add to this dilemma, no groups asked questions such as 'What is your gender?' or 'How do you identify?' Thus, gendered silences were found across all the conversations.

Interestingly, hauntology revealed itself when the South African student referenced a communal and haunted past (see 'Silences' above). Wolfreys (2002, p. 3), drawing on Derrida and contributing to literary hauntology, writes "the spectral is at the heart of any narrative" and "to tell a story is always to invoke ghosts, to open a space through which something other returns". Haunting foregrounds all narratives as a "powerful form of displacement" (Wolfreys, 2002, p. 1), whether the story is real or imagined as both Wolfreys and Derrida purport. In the earlier chat it was clear that the South African student's response, when asked about discrimination, was shaped by the spectre of a painful past existing in the present moment. However, it was also clear that this space went unexamined and remained a place of reticence, thereby reinforcing both colonial mindsets and violent nationalism within the material conditions of this space (Barad, 2007). The student, alone in his critique of South African history, remained isolated, displaced, and fictionalised.

Narratives articulate the boundaries between the "thought and unthought" as a means to examine relationships between the past and present (Davis, 2005, p. 379). We viewed a direct connection between silence and pain, which could have been the rationale behind the silencing of South African historical facts. Perhaps the expectation of being the sole carrier of the emotional labour of Black pain and experience was too much for the student to bear. Following Braidotti's (2006) reasoning, it would be ethical to provide students with opportunities to intersect with the power relations that shaped such spaces, adjacent to encouraging students to engage affirmatively with their own creative powers. Our expectation was not for students to become vulnerable but to be 'exposed' to other people, places, and ideas. The fact that students went to these vulnerable spaces was a benefit of the collaboration and the way it was structured. The organic nature of the conversations allowed some students to challenge their thinking and preconceived notions of otherness.

Conclusion: Moving toward cosmopolitanism

In writing about critical race theory and counter-storytelling, Delgado (1989) stressed the importance of knowing the *world as is* and the possibilities for what *it could be*. Technology has linked our world and created endless opportunities for people to become connected and exposed to one another's unique ideas and points of view (Appiah, 2006). Through technology, our world is smaller and our access to learning with and from each other attainable. We view classrooms as not ending with brick and mortar; they are sites that are fluid, interdisciplinary, and collaborative across time and space. Providing students this opportunity communicated that they do not walk the world alone; they belong to a global narrative larger than themselves. Designing this assignment so both student groups had to rely on each other for completion emphasised a response and a responsibility (Patel & Lynch, 2013) to their global partners. Hopefully, our students will learn to take this knowledge into other domains of their life when they consider their positionality as part of a neighbourhood and community–and their role as a global citizen more broadly.

At the end of our collaboration, questions remain. How might we utilise silences as a start for instruction (Stewart, 2017), and what could we have done to encourage a disruption of silences (Stewart & Ivala, 2017)? We wonder how we, as instructors, could have structured the course and assignment sequence to better support the intersectionality, diversity, mutual vulnerability, and material conditions of our student cohorts. As for the groupings, we did not wish to control, design, or manage the WhatsApp conversations. We see the value of setting up rules of engagement in co-curricular design between our student populations. However, our collaboration deliberately eschewed or challenged traditional power relations. We wanted to explore what emerged from a classroom that was set up as experimental. Moving forward, we will allow students to set their own rules of engagement at the start of the collaboration to hopefully minimise some of the issues that arose in the cohorts.

Students did not break down the walls between them as we had hoped, but we did see a glimmer of the instruction we wished to impart through the communication of Mia and Ben and the StoryMap/GIS assignments. If this kind of cultural engagement was our goal, how did we fail with the other groups? In short: How do we get students to care about each other, both in local and global contexts? It is clear, after an examination of our data, that our students' knowledge and awareness of each other at a surface level was altered. However, we are still grappling with to what extent students' global awareness and/or assessment of the 'other' was impacted by this project.

Our project with this group of students ended in 2019. Had we continued, we ruminate how events in 2020–the Coronavirus crisis and the Black Lives Matter movement in response to George Floyd's murder–would have impacted our collaboration. This is particularly interesting considering that in response to Covid-19 education across the world has become reliant on technology and cooperation between multiple actors. Would students feel more empathetic to each other in this time of catastrophe? Would they view their worlds as interrelated and intertwined, specifically regarding the global reverberations our students face like racism or poverty?

Our classroom intervention was profoundly relational–embedded in the local, yet intimately connected to the global. Appiah (2006, p. 92) points out that "success in life depends on being enmeshed in a web of relationships". We deliberately sought out new relationships that problematised traditional power relations by focusing on alterity. As we move forward, we hope to better establish classrooms that utilise the world as a site of study and embed the notion of cosmopolitanism as fundamental, necessary, and timely.

References

Appiah, K. A. (2006). *Cosmopolitanism: Ethics in a world of strangers*. New York, NY: W. W. Norton & Company.

Barad, K. (2007). *Meeting the universe halfway: Quantum physics and the entanglement of matter and meaning*. Durham: Duke University Press.

Barad, K. (2010). Quantum entanglements and hauntological relations of inheritance: Dis/continuities, spacetime enfoldings, and justice-to-come. *Derrida Today, 3*(2), pp. 240-268. doi: 10.3366/drt.2010.0206

Barad, K. (2017). Troubling time/s and ecologies of nothingness: Re-turning, re-membering, and facing the incalculable. *New Formations: A Journal of Culture/Theory/Politics, 92*, pp. 56-86. https://www.muse.jhu.edu/article/689858

Barndt, D. (1997). Crafting a "glocal" education: Focusing on food, women, and globalization. *Atlantis,2*(1),pp.43-51. http://journals.msvu.ca/index.php/atlantis/article/viewFile/3473/2764

Bekerman, Z. & Zembylas, M. (2011). *Teaching contested narratives: Identity, memory and reconciliation in peace education and beyond.* Cambridge: Cambridge University Press.

Boler, M. & Zembylas, M. (2003). Discomforting truths: The emotional terrain of understanding differences. In P. Trifonas (Ed.), *Pedagogies of difference: Rethinking education for social justice.* New York, NY: Routledge.

Braidotti, R. (2006). *Transpositions: On nomadic ethics.* Cambridge: Polity Press.

Braidotti, R. (2008). In spite of the times: The postsecular turn in feminism. *Theory, Culture & Society, 25*(6), pp. 1-24. doi: 10.1177/0263276408095542

Braidotti, R. (2013). *The posthuman.* Cambridge: Polity Press.

Butler, J. (2004). *Precarious life: The power of mourning and violence.* London: Verso.

Butler, J. (2015). *Notes toward a performative theory of assembly.* Boston, MA: Harvard University Press.

Clotfelter, C. T. (1976). The Detroit decision and "White flight". *The Journal of Legal Studies, 5*(1), pp. 99-112. https://www.jstor.org/stable/724076

Cineas, F. (2020, September 24). Critical race theory, and Trump's war on it, explained. *Vox.* Retrieved from https://www.vox.com/2020/9/24/21451220/critical-race-theory-diversity-training-trump

Creswell, J. W. (2009). Research design: *Qualitative, quantitative, and mixed methods approaches* (3rd ed.). Thousand Oaks, CA: Sage Publications.

Dahlberga, G. M. & Bagga-Gupta, S. (2014). Understanding glocal learning spaces. An empirical study of languaging and transmigrant positions in the virtual classroom. *Media and Technology, 39*(4), pp. 468-487. doi: 10.1080/17439884.2014.931868

Davis, C. (2005). Hauntology, spectres and phantoms. *French Studies, 59*(3), pp. 373-379. doi: 10.1093/fs/kni143

Delgado, R. (1989). Storytelling for oppositionists and others: A plea for narrative. *Michigan Law Review, 87*(8), pp. 2411-2441.

Derrida, J. (1994). *Spectres of Marx: The state of the debt, the work of mourning and the new international* (P. Kamuf. trans.). New York: Routledge.

Farley, R. (2018). Detroit fifty years after the Kerner Report: What has changed, what has not, and why? *RSF: The Russell Sage Foundation Journal of the Social Sciences* 4(6), 206-241. https://www.muse.jhu.edu/article/704134.

Harth, C. (2010). Going glocal. *National Association of Independent Schools.* https://www.nais.org/magazine/independent-school/fall-2010/going-glocal/

Jackson, L. & Han, A. Y. J. (2016). Internationalising teacher education for a "glocal" curriculum: South Koreans learning to teach Hong Kong liberal studies. *Multicultural Education Review, 8*(2), pp. 99-117.

Juelskjær, M. & Schwennesen, N. (2012). Intra-active entanglements - An interview with Karen Barad. *Kvinder, Koen og Forskning, 12*, pp. 10-23. doi: 10.7146/KKF.V0I1-2.28068

Keet, A. Zinn, D. & Porteous, K. (2009). Mutual vulnerability: A key principle in a humanising pedagogy in post-conflict societies. *Perspectives in Education,*

27(2), pp. 111-119. http://citeseerx.ist.psu.edu/viewdoc/download?doi=10.1. 1.1005.6177&rep=rep1&type=pdf.

Kwenda, C. (2003). Cultural justice: The pathway to reconciliation and social cohesion. In D. Chidester, P. Dexter, & W. James (Eds.), *What holds us together: Social cohesion in South Africa*, pp. 67-80. Cape Town: HSRC Publishers.

McIntosh, P. (2007). White privilege: Unpacking the invisible knapsack. In P. S. Rothenberg (Ed.), *Race, Class, and Gender in the United States: An Integrated Study* (pp. 177-182). London: Macmillian.

Mbembe, A. (2001). *On the postcolony*. Berkeley, CA: University of California Press.

Motala, S. & Stewart, K.D. 2021. Hauntings across the divide: Transdisciplinary activism, dualisms, and the ghosts of racism in engineering and humanities education. *Canadian Journal of Science, Mathematics and Technology Education*, 21, pp. 1-17. doi: 10.1007/s42330-021-00153-7

Newman, B., Merolla, J., Shah, S., Lemi, D., Collingwood, L., & Ramakrishnan, S. (2021). The Trump effect: An experimental investigation of the emboldening effect of racially inflammatory elite communication. *British Journal of Political Science, 51*(3), pp. 1138-1159. doi:10.1017/S0007123419000590

Ngoasheng, A. & Gachago, D. 2017. Dreaming up a new grid: Two lecturers' reflections on challenging traditional notions of identity and privilege in a South African classroom. *Education as Change, 21*(2), pp. 187-207. doi: 10.171 59/1947-9417/2017/2479

Noah, T. (2016). *Born a crime: Stories from a South African childhood*. London: One World.

Patel, F. & Lynch, H. (2013). Glocalization as an alternative to internationalization in higher education: Embedding positive glocal learning perspectives. *International Journal of Teaching and Learning in Higher Education, 25*(2), pp. 223-230. http://www.isetl.org/ijtlhe/ ISSN 1812-9129

Saldaña, J. (2012). *The coding manual for qualitative researchers* (2nd ed.). Thousand Oaks, CA: Sage Publications.

Soldatova, G. & Greer, M. (2013). "Glocal" identity, language fluency and cultural identity. *Procedia - Social and Behavioral Sciences, 86*, pp. 469-474. doi: 10.10 16/j.sbspro.2013.08.599

Stake, R. (1995). *The art of case study research*. Thousand Oaks, CA: Sage Publications.

Staszak, J. F. (2008). Other/otherness. *International Encyclopedia of Human Geography*. https://www.unige.ch/sciences-societe/geo/files/3214/4464/76 34/OtherOtherness.pdf

Stewart, K. (2017). Classrooms as safe houses: The ethical and affective implications of digital storytelling in the university writing classroom. *Critical Studies in Teaching and Learning (CriSTaL), 5*(1), pp. 85-102. doi: 10.14426/cristal. v5i1.102

Stewart, K. & Ivala, E. (2017). Silence, voice, and 'other' languages: Digital storytelling as a site of resistance and restoration. *British Journal of Educational Technology, 48*(5), pp. 1164-1175. doi: 10.1111/bjet.12540

Wolfreys, J. (2002). *Victorian hauntings: Spectrality, gothic, the uncanny and literature*. New York, NY: Palgrave.

Zembylas, M. (2005). A pedagogy of unknowing: Witnessing unknowability in teaching and learning. *Studies in Philosophy of Education, 24,* pp. 139-160. doi: 10.1007/s11217-005-1287-3

Zembylas, M. & Bekerman, Z. (2016). Key issues in critical peace education theory and pedagogical praxis: Implications for social justice and citizenship education. In A. Peterson, R. Hattam, M. Zembylas, & J. Arthur (Eds.), *The Palgrave international handbook of education for citizenship and social justice,* pp. 265-284. London: Palgrave Macmillan.

Zembylas, M., Bozalek, V. & Motala, S. (2021). A pedagogy of hauntology: Decolonising the curriculum with GIS. In V. Bozalek, M. Zembylas, S. Motala, & D. Hölscher (Eds.), *Higher education hauntologies: Living with ghosts for a justice-to-come,* pp. 11–28. London: Routledge.

Chapter 9

Enhancing cultural competence and enriching virtual learning experiences via a collaborative online international learning project

Anisa Vahed

Durban University of Technology, South Africa

Krista M. Rodriguez

Monroe Community College, United States

Fábio de Souza

Federal University of Pernambuco, Brazil

Abstract

Despite living in a global society surrounded by a diversity of cultures, ethnicity, education, social status, and world views, some student populations have limited opportunities to study abroad or engage in cultural exchange learning activities. To enhance cultural awareness, intercultural communication opportunities and team collaborative skills, a collaborative online international learning (COIL) virtual exchange project (VEP) was infused into existing dental academic coursework. A culturally focused VEP enables students from different cultural environments (professional, personal and academic) to collaborate on a team project. The project encourages cultural inquiry and awareness, openness to varied cultural perspectives, and integration of global issues to strengthen global workforce skills such as cross-cultural competence and communication, holistic thinking and technology competency, while learning discipline-specific concepts. Virtual communication technology and social media tools, in co-ordination with a learning management system, were used to strengthen students' virtual engagements and enable acquisition and sharing of discipline-specific knowledge. A need for more rigorous reporting on COIL from the perspective of the students' experiences focused this research on exploration of students' opinions and their experiences of participating in a COIL VEP. Using an exploratory case study research design within a quantitative framework, data were collected via a questionnaire. Students from three different dental professional programmes and geo-located countries (South Africa, Brazil and the United States of America) participated in the study. Positively measured results were found within the categories of project introduction and preparation; cultural and diversity competence; impacts on personal behaviour; quality of learning; course quality and overall experience. Inclusion of COIL in the curriculum is an innovative approach to co-teaching and providing opportunities to cognitively, socially and culturally enrich students' learning experiences while encouraging development of digital and research literacies.

Keywords: digital communication technologies, virtual exchange, intercultural competence, internationalisation, collaborative learning, COIL, South Africa, Brazil, United States

***

Introduction

Globally, internationalisation of the curriculum in terms of teaching and learning is high on the agendas of universities (Leask, 2011, 2015; Leask & Bridge, 2013). One desired outcome from an internationalised curriculum is intercultural competence, which students acquire by negotiating, communicating and working in culturally diverse teams (Leask, 2015). A major challenge for universities in their current curriculum design is to include cultural engagements that are enriching and relevant for both teachers and students, while developing "an appropriate range of knowledge, skills and attitudes in students as current and future contributors to the global knowledge society" (Leask, 2011, p. 7). A collaborative online international learning (COIL) virtual exchange project (VEP) can significantly and creatively contribute to the universities' internationalisation agendas, by infusing cultural, technological and collaborative skills (State University of New York (SUNY), 2019).

The SUNY COIL Centre is one of the leading international organisations focused on the emerging field of globally networked learning. Using VEPs, COIL is a teaching and learning methodology that provides opportunities for intercultural and transnational learning to students from globally diverse geo-locations. Through co-developed and co-taught modules, the COIL VEP brings globally distant faculty and students together for collaborative, experiential engagements through multicultural online and blended learning environments (SUNY, 2019). Faculty establish global partnerships through the SUNY COIL Orientation and Academy instructional modules while learning to design, implement, manage and assess a COIL collaborative project. The COIL VEP design provides opportunities for students to develop an integrated identity as global citizens, encouraging cultural inquiry and awareness, and openness to varied cultural perspectives. By integrating global issues, the project further introduces students to global workforce skills such as cross-cultural competence and communication, holistic thinking and technology competency, which support graduate attributes and discipline-specific learning outcomes.

The COIL VEP reported in this chapter required students to collaboratively investigate infection control practices in both clinical and laboratory environments across three different dental disciplines and geo-located universities. Faculty co-designed the project to meet the specific learning outcomes for their respective courses, team-taught modules and managed assessments both collaboratively and individually, based on their specific course requirements. Most faculty facilitation and oversight was programme-specific and project emphasis varied for each programme. Students explored cultural competency topics and co-constructed discipline knowledge from their respective perspectives of professional practice, particularly researching how differences in culture, economics and technology can intersect to create culturally based health protocols. The design of the COIL VEP included learning modules and activities on team dynamics, roles and responsibilities, cultural impacts and management approaches, in order to address the critical need for strong team interactions, culturally sensitive communication and collaborative co-construction of knowledge.

This chapter first reviews the literature on the dimensions of cultural collaboration and communication, and the various synchronous and asynchronous technologies used to support interactive communication between faculties collaborating virtually. The aim of the study, research design and methodology follow. Finally, the results are elaborated and discussed within the categories of project introduction and preparation; cultural and diversity competence; impacts on personal behaviour; quality of learning; course quality and overall experience.

Literature review

Factors influencing cultural collaboration and communication: Theoretical frameworks

Collaborative learning and intercultural engagement, which are critical for a successful COIL VEP, are impacted by a variety of factors, including global, cultural, social, personal, geographic, institutional and academic considerations. Boschma's (2005) distance/proximity dynamics theory offers a useful conceptual and structural tool to understand the challenges experienced in a COIL VEP, related to geographic, social, cultural, cognitive, institutional and organisational considerations (Table 9.1). Geographical distance "challenges teaching and collaborative learning through the cognition, cultural, and social dimensions of proximities" (Hautala & Schmidt, 2019, p. 184), requiring innovative use of technology, social media and virtual communication tools to meet these challenges. Faculty collaboration, project facilitation and team teaching were critical in addressing the institutional and organisational distance challenges. These included managing and aligning the variances in educational timeframes/constraints, semester sequences, curriculum relevance/goals, resources/commitment and institutional cultures/values/norms, which impact the overall quality of the project (Boschma, 2005). Cognitive proximity/distance factors influence the effectiveness of collaborative interactions, co-construction of knowledge, and achievement of each programme's learning outcomes.

Table 9.1: Dimensions of cultural collaboration and communication

Boschma's distance/proximity dynamics theory (2005)	Impacts on effective cross-cultural communication and collaboration	Hofestede's cultural dimensions theory (2011)
Social proximity		Power distance: Egalitarian vs hierarchical
Cultural proximity		Uncertainty avoidance
Cognitive proximity		Masculinity/femininity
Geographic proximity		Time orientation: Short-/long-term perspective
Institutional proximity		Individualism/collectivism
Organisational proximity		Restraint/indulgence

Managing the variances in students' academic backgrounds and strengths, cognitive levels, language skills, technology competency and communication and writing skills promotes the development of a shared knowledge base and a quality collaborative project outcome. Designing relevant interactive activities to strengthen important social and cultural proximities is critical in fostering: 1. effective team interaction skills, 2. conflict management, 3. supportive collaboration, 4. equal participation, 5. exploration of different perspectives and 6. respect for cultural difference. Building trust and a shared interest takes time and is influenced by varied student pressures that impact social relationships, communication, participation, and motivation, including course loads, clinical responsibilities, financial concerns, cultural dynamics and student-teacher status perspectives. Cultural proximity/distance challenges specifically permeate throughout a COIL VEP, influencing communication, collaboration, motivation, participation, reflection and overall learning (Hautala & Schmidt, 2019).

Dutch social psychologist Geert Hofstede's (2011) cultural dimensions framework further supports the importance of including a strong cultural component and focus within a COIL VEP, and choosing effective technology to engage students in meaningful cultural exchanges. Hofstede (2011) suggests that cultural behaviours exhibited within different societies influence how individuals within that culture build connections, value gender roles, handle uncertainty, distribute power, perceive time, and balance their lives. Within cross-cultural communication, cultural characteristics and values influence communication skills, meaning, interpretation, understanding emotions, and the ability to create a social community. This COIL VEP engaged students and faculty with varied social, personal, ethnic, gender, age, academic, professional, learning styles, institutional and organisational cultural perspectives. As the geo-located student cohorts were themselves culturally diverse populations, the challenges of cultural conflict existed within specific programmes as well as between global partners. Students participating in a COIL VEP require focused opportunities to acquire intercultural and intracultural knowledge, through relevant learning activities that encourage development of cross-cultural skills, cultural awareness and cultural sensitivity/responsiveness, to effectively interact with collaborative partners. This encourages students to understand others, interpret meaning, allow for personal bias (stereotyping), assess values, identify similarities as well as differences, and understand how these influence team dynamics, co-construction of knowledge and achievement of learning outcomes.

Uses of communication technology

Technology is critical in overcoming the cultural challenges endemic within a virtual cross-cultural learning experience, and in providing students with a different perspective of the process of collaboration. From a digital literacy perspective, synchronous and asynchronous interactions/engagements are the two approaches to providing collaborative learning experiences over a virtual platform. Synchronous learning, being instruction and collaboration in real time, involves coincident communication, providing immediate connection and opportunities to develop deeper social relationships (Hautala & Schmidt, 2019). Asynchronous interaction enables students and teachers to engage, process information, and formulate collaborative exchanges at their convenience, but may mask nonverbal cues and culturally specific and emotional contexts which are important for effective cross-cultural communication (Klein & Solem, 2008, p. 263).

Studies have highlighted that online learning should be collaborative and student-centred, with students as active participants in the learning process, to encourage them to adopt a deeper approach to learning and achieve higher learning outcomes (Ambrose et al., 2017; Anderson, 2008a; Picciano, 2017). To achieve these goals, it is critical to utilise applicable technology to teach collaborative skills and support interactive communication for effective globally distanced, synchronous and asynchronous, and culturally focused collaboration.

Social media and digital communication technologies in online learning

Anderson (2008a) argued that emerging best practices for online environments are less 'teacher-centric' and more student–student and student–content focused. Student–student interactions engage peers to investigate multiple perspectives and collaboratively learn through a joint project. Student–content interactions are facilitated by passive and active means in an online environment to change and/or influence learners' understanding, perspective or the cognitive structures of their mind to achieve sufficient levels of deep and meaningful learning (Anderson, 2008a). These interactions are bolstered through the use of various digital communication technologies, such as Skype, Dropbox, Twitter, WhatsApp and Google Hangouts (Abrams, 2019; Khan, Ayaz, & Khan, 2016; Mudawe, 2018; Mustafa, 2018; Veeresh & Kumara, 2017). The aforementioned technologies are known to facilitate greater connectedness, collaboration and more intense relationships, which complement the importance of building social proximity. Concomitantly, the impact of the various interactions mentioned above on collaborative learning embraces Vygotsky's (1978) social constructivism learning theories, which has been supported by various authors (Anderson, 2008b; Cifuentes & Shih, 2001; Picciano, 2017; Smallwood & Brunner, 2017).

Students working together on an authentic case co-construct their knowledge through social interactions. Teachers are active facilitators of the teaching/learning process, rather than authoritative leaders. Several studies have highlighted that learning environments are more effective when they follow student-centred, knowledge-centred, assessment-centred, and community-centred approaches (Ambrose et al., 2017; Anderson, 2008b; Danver, 2016; Picciano, 2017; Truhlar, Williams & Walter, 2019). These interactions can be provided by online learning platforms such as Facebook (FB), which have enhanced capacity to distribute content and support student engagement (Barczyk & Duncan, 2012; Niu, 2019). Contrary to previous arguments on the 'digital divide' (Prensky, 2001, 2005), Barczyk and Duncan (2012, p 118) reported that social media creates a 'digital dividend' as teams of people are enabled "to communicate and collaborate across cultural, geographic and language boundaries", a condition which is necessary in diverse international and multinational workplaces. It is critical that resources and infrastructure are available to promote two-way dialogues to decentralise control over learning and teaching. Social media and digital communication technologies embedded within a learning management system, along with faculty facilitation and guidance, enable teams of people to communicate and collaborate across cultural, geographic and language boundaries.

Within the context of the research reported in this chapter, WhatsApp and FB were used in addition to the Moodle learning modules as formal and supplementary tools for student collaboration and virtual engagements. FB enabled instructors to provide project-related information/content and a discussion forum to facilitate students' participation and interactions. The affordance of the web is to "allow us to envision an e-learning environment that is rich with student-student, student-content, and student-teacher interactions that are affordable, reusable, and facilitated by active agents" (Anderson, 2008b, p. 65).

Facebook and WhatsApp: Strengthening students' virtual exchanges

Padayachee (2017, p. 57) argued that "there appears to be a misconception that merely providing technology can transform education", indicating that challenges exist with how to use technology as well as how to integrate digital technologies into the curriculum effectively. Niu's (2019) review of studies using FB for academic purposes confirmed that FB connects users/learners to build a strong community through more effective information-sharing, creating a sense of belonging within a group, nurturing peer learning through enhanced interactions, and supporting self-monitoring and self-directed learning. Facebook for academic purposes allows greater learner autonomy, enables students to be knowledge producers rather than just knowledge consumers, and encourages taking responsibility for personal learning processes/outcomes.

As FB allows easy access to educational materials and provides a creative means to interact with peers, it can positively enhance communication and collaboration in a VEP, by encouraging student motivation to learn and become self-empowered learners (Souza et al., 2019). A social networking site such as FB also has educational value when used to enhance communication and collaboration between academics, which Niu (2019, p. 1389) terms "academic socialising".

Apart from a teaching and learning tool, FB may be used as a learning management system (LMS) since it allows for student-teacher interactions. However, Niu (2019) cautioned that FB lacked the capacity to upload different file formats, limited online discussion search/review capabilities, lacked an organised structure, and presented concerns about compromised privacy. Facebook does not "always deliver optimal quality of learning outcomes, especially when the teaching content requires learning by doing" (Niu, 2019, p. 1390). The successful adoption of FB can be attained if its capacity is matched with the learning goals and course content. Teachers can achieve this through a well-structured activity plan combining learning tools with predetermined learning objectives, ideally limiting off-topic discussions, student distraction and superficial learning.

The virtual technology WhatsApp is used for expressing ideas; communicating and exchanging information in real time; and supporting student–content, student–student, and student–teacher interactions (Alqahtani et al., 2018; Cetinkaya, 2017; Mustafa, 2018; Rigamonti et al., 2019; Veeresh & Kumara, 2017). A study reviewing social media utilised for teaching infection prevention and control in dentistry (Souza et al., 2019) revealed that WhatsApp was the most cited (64.3%) utility tool used to swiftly access discipline information. Reportedly, a negative aspect of WhatsApp included posting of excessive and/ or irrelevant/off-topic messages, which may lead to 'social addiction' and adversely influence virtual team collaboration.

Scepticism of working in virtual teams

A substantial body of literature documents the challenges associated with team leadership, recognising member talent, equal co-construction of knowledge, building relationship trust, and handling frustration and isolation (Ambrose et al., 2017; Ceo-DiFrancesco & Bender-Slack, 2016; Cetinkaya, 2017; Chydenius & Jadin, 2017; Cifuentes & Shih, 2001; He & Huang, 2017; Hurst & Thomas, 2008; Wihlborg et al., 2018). From their experience with developing soft team skills within an online environment, Hurst and Thomas (2008, p. 466) asserted that even though "trust is a tricky concept", social interaction and building trust are key attributes in team and online learning. They suggest that a vital ingredient to ensure effective teamwork is to create an environment in which participants feel comfortable and trust in the online learning experience.

Boschma (2005) and Hautala and Schmidt (2019) suggest that differing knowledge backgrounds between international partners is a prerequisite for relevant collaborative learning and co-construction of knowledge, although excessive cognitive distance can lead to frustration and lack of interest/ participation. It is therefore critical to assign responsibilities based on academic strengths and skills. In order to develop and nurture a culture that allows for meaningful and trusting relationships between team members, Hurst and Thomas (2008, p. 467) recommended using communication technologies that will help students establish and maintain trust; understand and appreciate diversity; manage their academic and personal lives; monitor the contributions of team members and activity/task progress; and benefit from the team project. A successful COIL VEP requires strong team connections, effective and respectful team interactions, and equal motivation and participation of all members.

Research aim and question

The aim of this study was to elicit students' opinions and learn about their experiences of participating in a COIL VEP. The main question guiding this study was: What did students perceive as the factors that enabled and/or constrained their participation and interactions in the COIL VEP?

Research design and methodology

Following a positivist paradigm, an exploratory case study research design was used to examine the COIL VEP (Yin, 2009). Kumar (2014, p. 155) suggests that a case study design can be used to explore an area "where little is known or where you want to have a holistic understanding of the situation, group or community". Study participants included: the 2018 (n=24) and 2019 (n=10) Dental Technology first-year extended curriculum programme students from Durban University of Technology (DUT); the 2018 Dental Assisting students (n=12) from Monroe Community College (MCC) in New York, United States; and the 2019 Dentistry students (n=10) from the Federal University of Pernambuco (UFPE) in Brazil.

A critical factor was the differences between institutional semester timing and structure, which Boschma (2005) refers to as "institutional proximity/ distance". The Dental Technology programme commenced in February 2018 and 2019. The Dental Assisting and Dentistry programmes commenced in August 2018 and 2019, respectively. These variances limited the length of time for the COIL VEP. A one-month COIL VEP was implemented between DUT and MCC from 27 August to 21 September 2018, and between DUT and UFPE from 23 September to 18 October 2019. In 2018, the DUT/MCC COIL VEP was developed and implemented utilising FB as the main LMS. In 2019 the DUT/UFPE COIL VEP was conducted using UFPE's Moodle LMS and FB as a supplemental tool. All COIL tasks were 'classroom integrated', being closely linked to a specific course syllabus, namely Introduction to Applied Dental Technology (DUT), Dental Specialities Procedures (MCC), and Biosafety and Ergonomics II (UFPE). Students received varied programme-specific course credit for their online project activities, and project emphasis differed for each programme.

As illustrated in Table 9.2, an 'ice-breaker' task introduced the cultural component of the COIL VEP. Students and course facilitators created and uploaded to FB a personal, culturally focused introduction video. Facilitators monitored the team discussion threads on FB and WhatsApp. In 2019 students were required to post all WhatsApp communication interchanges into the Moodle course template for final assessment and grading. Grading rubrics detailing expectations and outcomes were provided for each project task (introduction video, team communication discussions, and infection control protocols final project). After conclusion of the COIL VEP, students completed an anonymised and descriptive questionnaire consisting of four sections: Section A collected students' demographic details; Section B assessed students' use of technology; Section C measured students' use of online tools; and

Section D used a 5-point Likert scale to gather students' opinions about COIL. Three open-ended questions allowed for free responses to solicit perspectives about and suggestions for increased support of learning, improvements of content delivery, implementation of the project, and the effective use of technology within the COIL VEP. Questions included in Section D of the questionnaire were adapted, with permission for use and adaptation, from a post-COIL project survey/questionnaire developed by the Global Learning Experience team at DePaul University in Chicago (Rosita Leon, Assistant Director; email communication to the first and third authors on the 11 April 2018).

Ethical approval was granted via DUT's Institutional Research Ethics Committee (IREC 068/18) and clearance was provided by MCC's Institutional Review Board and UFPE's research office. Written consent was obtained from participating students.

Table 9.2: Overview of activities and tasks of a 4-week COIL VEP

		Task: Individual introductions
WEEK 1	Ice Breaker: Facilitator and student introductions Activity One: Introductory videos ▪ Students/facilitators created and posted an introduction video	❖ Describe your background (cultural/academic/ personal) ❖ Share your interests ❖ Identify your field of study ❖ Share any goals or future perspectives ❖ Tell us something in your 'mother tongue', which may not be English
WEEKS 2, 3 & 4	Collaborative group project Activity Two: case study scenario ▪ Teams used various asynchronous and synchronous communication tools to complete a case study on clinical and laboratory factors impacting infection control	Task: Team members communicated and worked together to discuss and develop content data for assigned project topics: ❖ Infection control practices in the dental surgery ❖ Infection control practices in the dental laboratory ❖ Ethical and cultural aspects of infection prevention and infection control
WEEK 4	Activity Three: Reflection by completing a questionnaire	

Descriptive (univariate and bivariate analysis) and inferential (correlations and Chi-square test) statistics with $p<0.05$ set as statistically significant (SPSS-Version 26®) were used to analyse the data. Factor analysis was performed for data obtained from the Likert scale to identify underlying variables, or factors, and to explain the correlation patterns within a set of observed variables. Content validity was used to ensure that the questionnaire focused on concepts and constructs that emerged from the online learning literature review. The internal consistency of the survey was assessed through Cronbach's alpha.

Results and discussion

In 2018 and 2019 the questionnaire response rate was 69% (n=25) and 90% (n=18), respectively. The social network platforms commonly used by the 2018 students were FB, Instagram, WhatsApp, Snapchat, and Twitter, with 63.3% indicating that they used them daily. Close to 78% of the 2019 students indicated that they commonly used FB, Instagram and WhatsApp. A high percentage of the students (2018 = 80%; 2019 = 88.9%) indicated that this was their first VEP experience. As shown in Table 9.3, the reliability scores for the Likert scale for Question 19 in Section D of the questionnaire exceeded the recommended Cronbach's alpha value of 0.70, which indicates consistency of scoring.

Table 9.3: Reliabilities

Section D – Q19 of the questionnaire		No. of items	Cronbach's alpha	
			2018	2019
I.	Project introduction and preparation	3	0.703	0.779
II.	Cultural and diversity competence	4	0.817	0.881
III.	Impacts on personal behaviour	5	0.836	0.778
IV.	Quality of learning	3	0.845	0.745
V.	Overall experience and course quality	4	0.818	0.942

Table 9.4 presents the Pearson correlations, which were computed across the five sections mentioned in Table 9.3. The relatively high correlations in the summary indicate that impacts on cultural/diversity competence, personal behaviour, quality of learning, overall experience and course/project quality are potential predictors of students' positive experiences of participating in a COIL VEP.

The Mann-Whitney results for all statements in Section D: Question 19 of the questionnaire were significantly different, with p-values less than 0.001. Two statements: "This project experience will affect my future career" and "I would choose another course/subject that includes a COIL module" exhibited p-values of 0.003 and 0.020, respectively. Only one statement showed no significant difference: "I made connections with international students that I will maintain in the future" (p=0.786). The test results from the Kaiser-Meyer-Olkin measure of sampling adequacy (> 0.50) and the Bartlet''s test of sphericity (p<0.05) indicated that the conditions to conduct factor analysis were satisfied (Table 9.5).

Factor analysis was performed for the Likert scale data, to identify underlying themes and explain the pattern of loading within a set of observed variables. In 2018, responses to the statements per section of the questionnaire revealed that students could see the direct link of the statements to the overall theme (Table 9.6). In 2019, the results of the 'Impacts on personal behaviour' section split along two sub-themes, which indicates that students had varying interpretations of the statements within this theme.

Table 9.4: Overview of Pearson correlations

Sections in Q19 of the questionnaire		2018		2019	
		Pearson correlation	p-value	Pearson correlation	p-value
Cultural and diversity competence	Impacts on personal behaviour.	0.661	0.000		
	Quality of learning.	0.509	0.004		
	Overall experience and course quality	0.724	0.000		
Impacts on personal behaviour	Cultural and diversity competence	0.661	0.000	0.815	0.000
	Quality of learning	0.680	0.000		
	Overall experience and course quality	0.724	0.000		
Quality of learning	Cultural and diversity competence	0.509	0.004	0.705	0.001
	Impacts on personal behaviour	0.680	0.000	0.791	0.000
	Overall experience and course quality	0.712	0.000		
Overall experience and course quality	Cultural and diversity competence	0.724	0.000	0.511	0.300
	Impacts on personal behaviour	0.824	0.000	0.567	0.014
	Quality of learning	0.712	0.000		

Table 9.5: Results from the Kaiser-Meyer-Olkin measure of sampling adequacy and Bartlet's test of sphericity

Section of the questionnaire		Year	Kaiser-Meyer-Olkin measure of sampling adequacy	Bartlet's test of sphericity		
				Approx. Chi square	df	Significance
I.	Project introduction and preparation	2018	0.645	40.576	3	0.000
		2019	0.562	17.701	3	0.001
II.	Cultural and diversity competence	2018	0.741	118.260	6	0.000
		2019	0.686	51.990	6	0.000
III.	Impacts on personal behaviour	2018	0.776	157.040	10	0.000
		2019	0.535	38.325	10	0.000
IV.	Quality of learning	2018	0.713	100.255	3	0.000
		2019	0.655	11.340	3	0.010
V.	Overall experience and course quality	2018	0.712	134.718	6	0.000
		2019	0.747	81.824	6	0.000

Table 9.6: Factor analysis

Section D of Questionnaire, Q19 statements	Project introduction and preparation		Cultural and diversity competence		Impacts on personal behaviour		Quality of learning		Overall experience and course quality	
	2018	2019	2018	2019	2018	2019	2018	2019	2018	2019
1. I was prepared for the cultural components and diversity aspects of the project.	0.825	0.762								
2. I was prepared for the technology aspects of the project.	0.712	0.931								
3. I was prepared for the requirements of the project.	0.819	0.818								
4. The COIL project introduced me to a new perspective on culture and diversity.			0.832	0.912						
5. The experience changed my perception of another cultural or diverse group.			0.832	0.970						
6. The experience introduced me to a different worldview.			0.846	0.856						
7. The experience increased my interest in further opportunities for international exchanges.			0.716	0.754						
8. The experience changed the way I behave in interpersonal and cultural encounters.					0.696	0.890				
9. The experience increased opportunities for discussion and debate outside the online class.					0.859	0.853				
10. The experience provided me with skills and knowledge that I will use in the future.					0.797	0.895				

11. I made connections with international students that I will maintain in the future.	0.794	0.942		
12. This project experience will affect my future career.	0.758	0.664		
13. Participating in the COIL project made me feel more engaged with my learning.			0.894	0.732
14. The COIL project directly improved the quality of my learning experience in this course.			0.897	0.848
15. I acquired the pertinent discipline knowledge required by the project case.			0.836	0.857
16. I would recommend a course/subject that includes a COIL module to other students.			0.873	0.958
17. I would choose another course/subject that includes a COIL module.			0.881	0.853
18. Overall, the learning experience in this COIL module was positive.			0.728	0.953
19. Overall, the quality of the COIL module content contributed to a valuable learning experience.			0.727	0.949

Despite a small percentage of students being undecided, Figure 9.1 depicts significant differences in the scoring patterns, with higher levels of agreement observed (above 80%; $p<0.05$) for the culture and diversity, and technology aspects of the COIL VEP. The student perspectives may be attributed to relevant preparatory modules provided prior to the official commencement of the COIL VEP, and the recognised benefits of using FB (Niu, 2019).

Figure 9.1: Scoring on project introduction and preparation

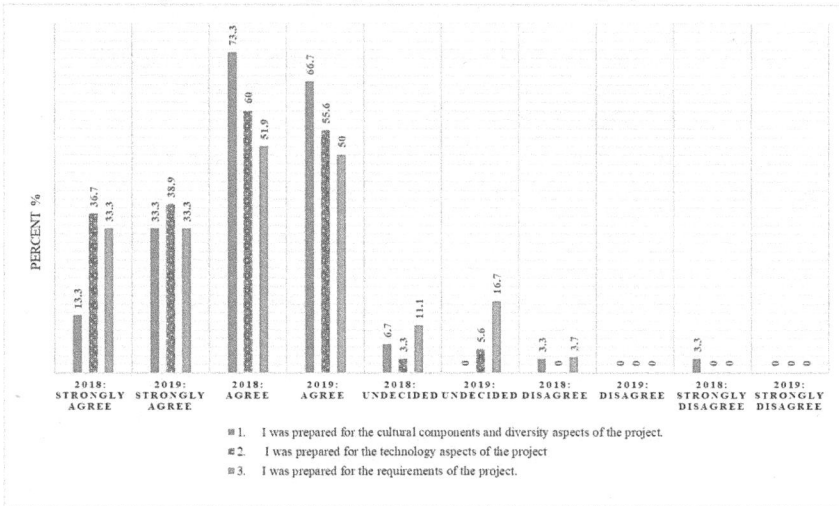

Apart from the 2018 students' responses to Question 5 (56.6%), more than 80% of students predominantly agreed that they acquired cultural and diversity competence (Figure 9.2). Scoring patterns for Questions 4 (2018: p=0.03; 2019: p=0.01), 5 (2019: p=0.05), 6 (2018: p=0.05) and 7 (2019: p=0.02) in Figure 9.2 were significantly different. Consistent with Hautala and Schmidt (2019), social and institutional distances experienced by students due to weak Wi-Fi connectivity at DUT, different university semester structures and time zone differences, could have attributed to a fair percentage of the 2018 students being undecided (32%) or disagreeing (11%).

An interesting finding from written responses, that may influence these statistics, was the concept that students may not view collaboration as being asynchronous as well as synchronous. Excerpts from the open-ended questions support this:

> "The time difference was incredibly frustrating and I do not feel that I gained anything positive from this experience".
> "It was nearly impossible to really collaborate since when one person was available, the others were working, sleeping, at school, etc".
> "Our University has some problems when it comes to Wi-Fi, which prevent us from being able to video call at times".

In supporting organisational/institutional proximity (Boschma, 2005), faculty involved in future COIL VEPs need to provide regular communication, engagement and oversight, while encouraging flexibility in using alternative technologies such as Microsoft Teams and Skype to better manage the variances in semester structure, course differences and time zone constraints. Addressing these challenges supports the development of social proximities for stronger team interactions and effective student collaboration.

Figure 9.2: Scoring on cultural and diversity competence

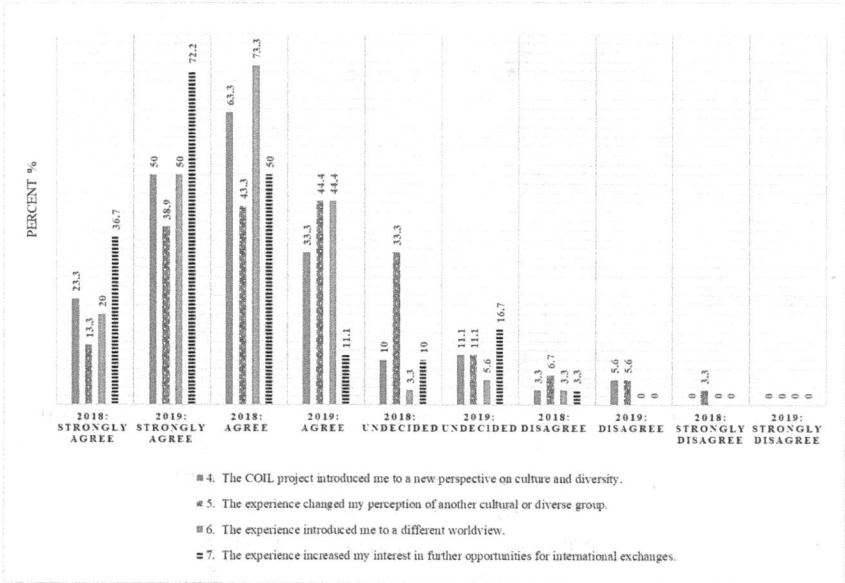

4. The COIL project introduced me to a new perspective on culture and diversity.

5. The experience changed my perception of another cultural or diverse group.

6. The experience introduced me to a different worldview.

7. The experience increased my interest in further opportunities for international exchanges.

With reference to Figure 9.3, contrary to the 2019 results, significant differences in scoring patterns on the 'impacts on personal behaviour' were observed ($p < 0.05$) among the 2018 students for Questions 8 (2018: $p = 0.02$; 2019: $p = 0.06$); 9 (2018: $p = 0.05$; 2019: $p = 0.05$); 10 (2018: $p = 0.02$; 2019: $p = 0.07$); 11 (2018: $p = 0.02$; 2019: $p = 0.07$); and 12 (2018: $p = 0.00$; 2019: $p = 0.02$).

Although present in the qualitative feedback from the 2018 students, there was a higher prevalence of frustration experienced by the 2019 South African students, who conveyed that:

"There was not that much interaction from the overseas students".

"The behaviour of the international student was poor since they were not responding".

"COIL is a good concept but the success of it lies on both ends to communicate. If one end does not co-operate then programme will be unsuccessful".

The above feedback could have contributed to the 2019 'Impacts on personal behaviour' section splitting into two sub-themes (Table 9.6).

Figure 9.3: Scoring on impacts on personal behaviour

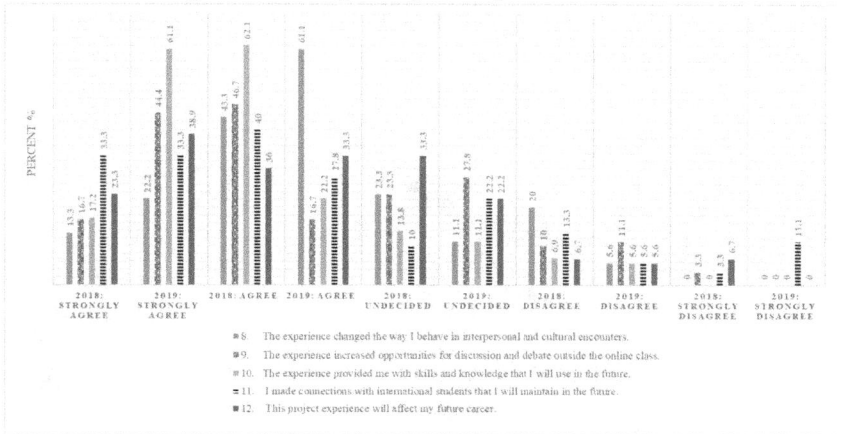

Students recommended that "facilitators need to make sure everyone in the project contribute" and "actively communicate with students during collaboration to ensure that positive collaboration is taking place". Consistent with Hurst and Thomas's (2008) advice, the design of a VEP should include focused activities/ tasks that foster social, cultural, cognitive and institutional proximities throughout the virtual collaboration. One suggestion is to design tasks that prepare students to work effectively in virtual teams by developing attributes associated with assigning accountability, managing flexibility, monitoring progress, using a peer-rating system, and encouraging social interaction. It is important that all students have the same motivation and expectations. Facilitators need to assess cognitive strengths to assign specific roles, use diverse forms of technology to motivate students, and provide consistent and equal expectations during the COIL VEP to create social connection and facilitate sharing of knowledge. It is also critical that facilitators impart the same emphasis for the project in their respective programmes and establish similar course requirements and outcomes.

From Figure 9.4, it can be ascertained that over 75% of the 2018 and 2019 students agreed that the COIL VEP made them feel more engaged with their learning. There were significant differences in the scoring patterns on the quality of learning ($p<0.05$), particularly for Questions 13 (2018: $p=0.003$; 2019: $p=0.005$), 14 (2018: $p=0.001$; 2019: $p=0.007$) and 15 (2018: $p=0.000$; 2019: $p=0.032$). The quality of their learning experience improved as they acquired pertinent discipline knowledge.

Figure 9.4: Scoring on quality of learning

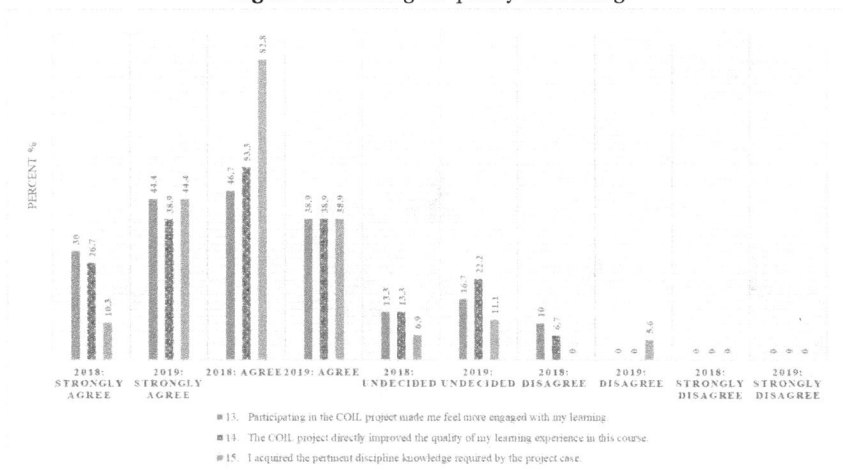

As depicted in Figure 9.5, significant differences in scoring patterns on the overall experiences of the 2018 and 2019 students were observed (p<0.05) for Questions 16 (2018: p=0.034; 2019: p=0.031), 17 (2018: p=0.023), 18 (2019: p=0.003), and 19 (2019: p=0.002). No significant differences were observed for Questions 17 (2019: p=0.114), 18 (2018: p=0.233) and 19 (2018: p=0.883). This could be attributed to students' lack of commitment to completing tasks, which is corroborated by excerpts from 2018 students on the open-ended questions:

> "I think COIL would be exciting and more fun if we all participated in the discussions we had within the groups that were created. I personally feel like students were not participating enough to help us finish the project in time".
> "It should be done with people who want to do it ... some don't want to communicate. They gave us a hard time trying to talk to them".

To enable organisational/institutional, social, cultural, and cognitive proximities (Boschma, 2005), and to engage in meaningful cultural exchanges (Hofstede, 2011), faculty need to establish a focused, inclusive, interactive COIL pre-project training programme. Prime objectives are to establish social connections to foster an understanding of culture/diversity; encourage effective team dynamics; cultivate trust; foster meaningful reflection activities; and communicate/collaborate using diverse forms of technologies, such as co-writing in online documents (Hautala & Schmidt, 2019). Interactive modules and effective technology can bolster student–student and student–content interactions, irrespective of the distance between team partners (Anderson, 2008a), to encourage students to be enthusiastic for and develop responsibility to team members and become stakeholders in the project.

Figure 9.5: Scoring on overall experience and course quality

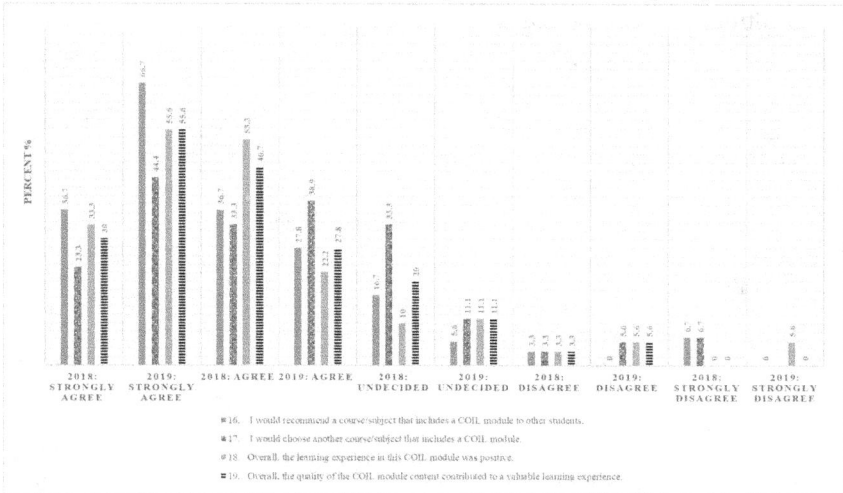

Despite the negative responses, and consistent with Ceo-DiFrancesco and Bender-Slack (2016), and Hautala and Schmidt (2019), students concluded that the COIL VEP is a:

> "Wonderful opportunity, very much appreciate to be part of COIL, it should be done more with other modules. It was great making friends and knowing more about other people from international countries".
> "… good experience, it promotes diversity and give opportunities to connect to the international world".

Limitations and conclusions

The theoretical framework of the study evaluating this COIL VEP may have some limitations; however, there are aspects of the results which can be generally applied. The results add to the body of literature evaluating concerns related to student motivation and commitment, the necessity of pre-training, impacts on team collaboration and facilitator co-ordination, influence of limitations of university resources/infrastructure, and use of digital technologies for successful virtual learning.

Applying Boschma's proximity/distance parameters in the design, development and implementation of a COIL VEP guides facilitators in creating an effective collaborative learning environment. Structured activities encourage students to build social proximity trust, overcome geographical distance, understand collaboration, and manage cognitive proximity to co-construct knowledge. Faculty facilitation and guidance with clearly defined and consistent expectations and outcomes across student cohorts are necessary to reduce students' frustrations caused by student–teacher and student-student interaction constraints, and institutional and organisational variances.

A global partnership includes cultural engagement and requires skills in cultural understanding. Applying Hofstede's research on impacts of cultural behaviour on communication to the development of applicable and focused induction modules on culture and diversity, is imperative in teaching a variety of valuable skills. These skills include cultural communication, sensitivity to cultural difference, and the impacts that cultural behaviours have on intercultural engagements, team dynamics, and fostering of global partnerships and relationships.

A key component for a VEP across geographical locations is the application of digital pedagogy and adequate training for all students. The study results indicate that students' frustration with technology, institutional resources, and time zone differences adversely impacted on communication and collaboration. Facilitators need to evaluate applicable digital communication technologies that will enhance asynchronous and synchronous engagements, assist student communication and collaboration, and promote the exchange of knowledge.

Infusing a COIL VEP into the curriculum enhanced students' sharing and co-construction of knowledge across cultures, disciplines, and societies, while supporting their epistemological development in preparation for their professional field of practice.

The inclusion of a suitably designed COIL VEP is an innovative way to internationalise curriculum and utilise collaborative teaching and learning pedagogy to enrich students' learning experiences cognitively, socially, and culturally, while strengthening digital and research literacies.

Acknowledgements

This work is based on research supported by the National Research Foundation in South Africa. We are grateful to Mr Naeem Seedat's (DUT) commitment to co-constructing the COIL VEPs, Mr Deepak Singh (DUT) for his expert statistical guidance, and Dr Gillian Cruickshank (Queens University in Belfast) for proofreading the article. Deepest thanks to the 2018 and 2019 Dental Technology, 2018 Dental Assisting and 2019 Dentistry students for their participation in the COIL VEP and for making this study possible.

References

Abrams, Z. I. (2019). Collaborative writing and text quality in Google Docs. *Language Learning & Technology, 23*(2), pp. 22-42. doi: 10125/44681

Alqahtani, M., Bhaskar, V., Elumalai, K. & Abumelha, M. (2018). WhatsApp: An online platform for university-level English language education. *Arab World English Journal, 9*, pp. 108-121. doi: 10.24093/awej/vol9no4.7

Ambrose, M., Murray, L., Handoyo, N. E., Tunggal, D. & Cooling, N. (2017). Learning global health: A pilot study of an online collaborative intercultural peer group activity involving medical students in Australia and Indonesia. *BMC Medical Education, 17*(1), Article 10. doi: 10.1186/s12909-016-0851-6

Anderson, T. (2008a). Teaching in an online context. In T. Anderson (Ed.), *The Theory and Practice of Online Learning* (2nd ed.), pp. 343-366. Edmonton: Athabasca University Press.

Anderson, T. (Ed.) (2008b). *The Theory and Practice of Online Learning* (2nd ed.). Edmonton: Athabasca University Press.

Barczyk, C. C. & Duncan, D. G. (2012). Social networking media: An approach for the teaching of international business. *Journal of Teaching in International Business, 23*(2), pp. 98-122. doi: 10.1080/08975930.2012.718703

Boschma, R. (2005). Proximity and innovation: A critical assessment. *Regional Studies, 39*(1), pp. 61-74. doi: 10.1080/0034340052000320887

Ceo-DiFrancesco, D. & Bender-Slack, D. (2016). Collaborative online international learning: Students and professor making global connections. In A. J. Moeller (Ed.), *Fostering Connections, Empowering Communities, Celebrating the World* (pp. 147-174). Richmond: Robert M. Terry.

Cetinkaya, L. (2017). The impact of WhatsApp use on success in education process. *International Review of Research in Open and Distributed Learning, 18*(7), pp. 59-74. doi: 10.19173/irrodl.v18i7.3279

Chydenius, T. & Jadin, T. (2017). *Virtual Teams as part of Internationalization of Higher Education*. Paper presented at the Cross-Cultural Business Conference, Steyr, Austria. https://www.researchgate.net/publication/317014507_Virtual_Teams_as_part_of_Internationalization_of_Higher_Education

Cifuentes, L. & Shih, Y.-C. D. (2001). Teaching and learning online: A collaboration between US and Taiwanese students. *Journal of Research on Computing in Education, 33*(4), pp. 456-474.

Danver, S. L. (2016). *The SAGE Encyclopedia of Online Education*. Tousand Oaks, CA: SAGE Publications.

Hautala, J. & Schmidt, S. (2019). Learning across distances: an international collaborative learning project between Berlin and Turku. *Journal of Geography in Higher Education, 43*(2), pp. 181-200. doi: 10.1080/03098265.2019.1599331

He, J. & Huang, X. (2017). Collaborative online teamwork: Exploring student" satisfaction and attitudes with Google Hangouts as a supplementary communication tool. *Journal of Research on Technology in Education, 49*(3-4), pp. 149-160. doi: 10.1080/15391523.2017.1327334

Hofstede, G. (2011). Dimensionalizing cultures: The Hofstede Model in Context. *Online Readings in Psychology and Culture, 2*(1), pp. 3-26. doi: 10.9707/2307-0919.1014

Hurst, D. & Thomas, J. (2008). Developing team skills and accomplishing team projects online. In T. Anderson (Ed.), *The Theory and Practice of Online Learning* (2nd ed.), pp. 343-366. Edmonton: Athabasca University Press.

Khan, I. U., Ayaz, M. & Khan, S. (2016). Using Skype to develop English learner'' speaking motivation. *Science International, 28*(5), pp. 41-48.

Klein, P. & Solem, M. (2008). Evaluating the impact of international collaboration on Geography learning. *Journal of Geography in Higher Education, 32*(2), pp. 245-267. doi: 10.1080/03098260701728500

Kumar, R. (2014). *Research Methodology: A step-by-step guide for beginners* (4th ed.). London: SAGE Publications.

Leask, B. (2011). Assessment, learning, teaching and internationalisation – engaging for the future. *Assessment, Teaching & Learning Journal, 11.* https://www.leedsbeckett.ac.uk/staff/files/110726_...

Leask, B. (2015). *Internationalizing the Curriculum.* London: Routledge.

Leask, B. & Bridge, C. (2013). Comparing internationalisation of the curriculum in action across disciplines: Theoretical and practical perspectives. *Compare: A Journal of Comparative and International Education, 43*(1), pp. 79-101. doi: 10.1080/03057925.2013.746566

Mudawe, O. M. N. (2018). Google Docs: Potentials and promises for scaffolding supervisory pedagogical practices of EFL/ ESL students' writing dissertation. *Journal of Applied Linguistics and Language Research, 5*(2), pp. 192-206.

Mustafa, E. N. E. (2018). The impact of YouTube, Skype and WhatsApp in improving EFL learner'' speaking skill. *International Journal of Contemporary Applied Researches, 5*(5), pp. 18-31. http://ijcar.net/assets/pdf/vol5-no5-may2018/02.pdf

Niu, L. (2019). Using Facebook for academic purposes: current literature and directions for future research. *Journal of Educational Computing Research, 56*(8), pp. 1384-1406. doi: 10.1177/0735633117745161

Padayachee, K. (2017). A snapshot survey of ICT integration in South African schools. *South African Computer Journal, 29*, pp. 36-65.

Picciano, A. G. (2017). Theories and frameworks for online education: seeking an integrated model. *Online Learning.* doi: 10.24059/olj.v21i3.1225

Prensky, M. (2001). Digital natives, digital immigrants. *On the Horizon: The Strategic Planning Resource for Education Professionals, 9*(5), pp. 1-6.

Prensky, M. (2005). "Engage Me or Enrage M" –- What today's learners demand. *EDUCAUSE Review Magazine, 40*(5), pp. 60-65.

Rigamonti, L., Dolci, A., Galetta, F., Stefanelli, C., Hughes, M., Bartsch, M., . . . Back, D. A. (2019). Social media and e-learning use among European exercise science students. *Health Promotion International, 35*(3), pp. 470-477. doi: 10.1093/heapro/daz046

Smallwood, A. M. K. & Brunner, B. R. (2017). Engaged learning through online collaborative public relations projects across universities. *Journalism & Mass Communication Educator, 72*(4), pp. 442-460. doi: 10.1177/1077695816686440

Souza, F. B., Kim, J. W., Carvalho, E. J. A., Jamelli, S. R. & Melo, M. M. D. (2019). Social media for teaching infection prevention and control in dentistry: Survey of students' perception and comparative study of academic performance. *Journal of Clinical and Diagnostic Research, 13*(4), pp. 1-5.

State University of New York (2019). *COIL Center for Collaborative Online Learning: COIL Course Orientation.* http://coil.suny.edu/index.php/page/partnering-orientation

Truhlar, A. M., Williams, K. M. & Walter, M. T. (2019). Student engagement with course content and peers in synchronous online courses discussions. *Online Learning, 22*(4). doi: 10.24059/olj.v22i4.1389

Veeresh, C. M. & Kumara, T. M. P. (2017). Impact of Whatsapp mediated learning approach on academic achievement of student teachers. *Imperial Journal of Interdisciplinary Research, 3*(9), pp. 210-218.

Vygotsky, L. S. (Ed.) (1978). *Mind in Society: The development of higher psychological processes.* Cambridge, MA: Harvard University Press.

Wihlborg, M., Friberg, E. E., Rose, K. M. & Eastham, L. (2018). Facilitating learning through an international virtual collaborative practice: A case study. *Nurse Education Today, 61*, pp. 3-8. doi: 10.1016/j.nedt.2017.10.007

Yin, R. K. (2009). *Case Study Research: Design and Methods* (4th ed., vol. 5). California: SAGE Publications.

Chapter 10

Learning from coronavirus: Design principles for connected co-learning and co-teaching in online and blended global architecture studios

Jolanda Morkel

STADIO Higher Education, South Africa

Lindy Osborne Burton

Queensland University of Technology, Australia

Mark Olweny

University of Lincoln, United Kingdom

Steven Feast

Curtin University, Australia

Abstract

The coronavirus (COVID-19) pandemic not only amplified current challenges in higher education generally, and in architectural education specifically, it revealed the potential for globally connected practices in learning, teaching and research. We were interested to explore how connected co-learning and co-teaching can be designed for inter-institutional collaboration, in online and blended global studios across cultural boundaries–in this case the global South and North. Employing a collaborative autoethnographic research methodology, and through an in-depth reflection on our respective learning contexts, and educational and professional practices, we formulate four learning design principles for connected co-learning and co-teaching in online and blended global architecture studios. The proposed design principles address current critiques of architectural studio education globally, related to socialisation, asymmetrical power relations, and the mental health of students, and–in online spaces specifically–aspects of social presence, authenticity and embodiment.

Keywords: learning design principles, co-learning, co-teaching, online learning, blended learning, architecture studio, South Africa, United Kingdom, Australia

***

Introduction

"Learning from coronavirus" in the title of this chapter, is a tongue-in-cheek semantic reference to the seminal book *Learning from Las Vegas* (1977), by famous Zambian-born architect Denise Scott Brown and her co-authors Robert Venturi and Steven Izenour. This provocative text, which challenges well-established modernist ways of seeing the city, has for more than five decades served as a reference for architecture students all over the world. In much the same way, we expect the coronavirus, which forced us to reconsider our understanding of space and proximity, to do so in the years to come. Venturi, Scott Brown and Izenour (1977) explored architecture through digital technology rather than building technology (Lehmann, 2019), in terms of new image, media, representation, and the architecture of communication (Vinegar & Golec, 2008).

Even before the sudden global pivot to online learning in response to the coronavirus (COVID-19) pandemic and mandatory social distancing precautions, the four Schools of Architecture that form the focus of this chapter employed technology for blended, flexible, and online learning and teaching strategies that supported authentic and inclusive disciplinary approaches (Burton, 2018; Feast, 2020; Morkel, 2017; Olweny, Ndibwami & Ahimbisibwe, 2020). These technology-mediated approaches not only facilitated interaction and collaboration between students, educators, and external experts but also promoted inter-institutional collaboration.

Through employing alternative technologies for learning and teaching in these contexts, we challenged the status quo of the traditional architecture studio. Although the solutions to the "wicked" problems (Marshall, 2008) that were sought at these Schools of Architecture were not specifically seen to result from formal learning design processes, we propose that, intuitively, learning design was employed to formulate novel solutions that employed digital and online technologies for learning and teaching. This assumption echoes Gross and Do's (1997) observation that, through its focus on design as a disciplinary domain, architecture education offers valuable lessons for the design of learning, regardless of the discipline.

Although the learning designs (Morkel, 2015; Morkel & Pallitt, 2015; Seitzinger, 2016) developed in our Schools of Architecture were driven by context-specific professional, political, socio-economic, and practical demands, they responded to similar challenges associated with the traditionally accepted signature pedagogy of the studio (Shulman, 2005), or what Salama and Crosbie (2020) termed the legacy model. These challenges include asymmetrical power relationships between students and educators, mental health issues caused by stress and workload, and a degree of ritualised teaching practices (Webster, 2008; Burton, 2018; Morkel, 2017; Olweny, 2015, 2017, 2020).

It was our shared appreciation for good learning design and the use of digital technologies for learning and teaching that brought us together and sparked our curiosity. We were interested to explore how connected co-learning and co-teaching can be designed for inter-institutional collaboration, in online and blended global studios across cultural boundaries–in this case the global South and North. Reflecting on our collective experiences prior to and during the first few months of the global pandemic in 2020, we wanted to explore how we might approach complex challenges in a rapidly changing world, and which design principles to employ. There is limited, if any, literature that links learning design with architectural education, or literature on the value of inter-institutional collaboration across cultural boundaries, specific to architectural education.

Guided by the learning design principles formulated in this study, global perspectives and local relevance (Stewart & Gachago, 2016) can be successfully combined across global South and global North contexts to strengthen learning and teaching experiences, better preparing graduates for a fast-changing and globalised world. Two of the Architecture Schools are in Africa and two in Australia. Although Australia is widely recognised as being from the global North, we acknowledge its "awkward global position" (Connell, cited in Fahey & Kenway, 2010) and the assumption that it sits on the "periphery" (Connell, 2014), or to build on Jane Jacobs' analogy, "on the edge of the knowledge empire" (Jacobs, cited in Fahey & Kenway, 2010, p. 106). For the purposes of this chapter, it is worth noting that the two educational contexts situated in Australia are well resourced compared to their African counterparts.

The four Schools of Architecture offer programmes that employ technology for learning and teaching in varying degrees, from fully online to mostly on-ground modes, with blended variations in between. The Professional Master's programme in Architecture at Curtin University is the first accredited fully online Master's in Architecture in Australia (AACA, 2019; Feast, 2020) and it is offered in collaboration with Open Universities Australia (OUA). The Advanced Diploma in Architectural Technology programme at the Cape Peninsula University of Technology (CPUT) is presented in a blended format, comprising online learning supported by office-based mentoring and quarterly one-week block periods on campus. This programme is the result of a university-industry collaboration between CPUT and Open Architecture (OA) (Morkel, 2017; Poulsen & Morkel, 2016)–refer to Chapter 13. The resident programmes in architecture at Queensland University of Technology (QUT) employ digital technologies extensively, in custom-designed, on-campus learning spaces (Burton, 2018; Wilson, 2014). Finally, the Master's and Bachelor's programmes at Uganda Martyrs University (UMU) rely primarily on on-ground teaching, complemented by occasional virtual studio experiments (Olweny, 2015; Olweny, Ndibwami & Ahimbisibwe, 2020).

Methodology

We employed a collaborative autoethnographic (CAE) approach to explore the potential for global collaboration in architectural education, and to describe the approaches and strategies that can be considered (Chang, Ngunjiri & Hernandez, 2012; Laterza et al., 2016). This qualitative research method allowed us to gain a "meaningful understanding of sociocultural phenomena reflected in our autobiographical data" (Chang et al., 2012, p. 23). As described by Chang et al. (2012, p. 17), this is "a qualitative research method that is simultaneously collaborative, autobiographical and ethnographic". The research team involved four researchers–the number recognised by Chang et al. (2012) as an optimal team size for conducting CAE research. The researchers have different kinds of connections with and links to the African continent. Steven Feast, who lives in Perth, graduated from and now works at Curtin University, has not yet visited South Africa. The other authors have close ties with Africa. Mark Olweny is from Uganda and employed by UMU, although at the time of writing he resided in the United Kingdom on an academic contract at the University of Lincoln. Jolanda Morkel was born and raised in South Africa, where she lives and, during the research period, she taught at CPUT. Lindy Burton, who lives in Brisbane and teaches at QUT, was born in South Africa and relocated to Australia shortly after graduating. All of us share a passion for authentic and inclusive architectural education, as well as the innovative use of educational technology to transform learning experiences.

CAE enabled us to recognise and accept the many ways that our personal experiences shaped the research process, acknowledging and accommodating subjectivity, emotionality, and our influence on the research (Ellis, Adams & Bochner, 2010). We therefore see ourselves as part of the research context (Laterza et al., 2016), and as asserted by Chang et al. (2012, p. 22) "simultaneously the instrument(s) and the data source(s)". In line with CAE research methodology, our writing was iterative and alternated between group work and individual work, as suggested by Chang et al. (2012, p. 22), "building on each other's stories, gaining insight from group sharing, and providing various levels of support as we (they) interrogate topics of interest for a common purpose". We started with individual narrative and reflective writing in online documents organised in shared sub-folders in Google Drive. This was followed by 12 weekly 1-hour long online discussions conducted via Blackboard Collaborate, and ongoing asynchronous feedback on each other's writing. These engagements provided the opportunity for reflection, individual meaning-making, and group sharing, probing, collective meaning-making, and writing (Chang et al., 2012).

Our conversations and reflections focused on how we employed, supported, and researched technology in architectural education in African and Australian contexts, towards future inter-institutional collaboration across cultural boundaries, prior to and during the lockdown period. We took the necessary steps to protect colleagues' and students' identity. Where needed, we obtained permissions in writing. During the third live online meeting session, building on previous writings and interactions, we formulated seven themes that guided subsequent conversations, namely connecting:

1) Online and on-ground spaces,

2) The university and the profession,

3) Digital learning and teaching tools,

4) Students and educators,

5) Educators locally and globally,

6) Students and international experts, and

7) Students through peer-to-peer learning.

This inductive approach confirms Laterza et al.'s (2016, p. 5) assertion that "the boundaries of the study are not set in advance". Instead, an "exploratory approach was used, to allow for the open-ended gathering of knowledge on the real linkages and connections in the social reality under examination, rather than the imposition of a theoretical framework driven by the ethnographer's own assumptions about the topic of study" (Laterza et al., 2016, p. 5). Each of the seven thematic discussions were concluded with a set of five observations. Finally, we distilled these 35 observations into four learning design principles for connected co-learning and co-teaching in online and blended global architecture studios.

Thematic discussions

Theme 1: Connecting online and on-ground spaces

Prior to the COVID-19 pandemic, traditional architectural learning spaces existed mainly in on-ground settings, including campus spaces, community sites and architectural practice environments. The use of online technologies in architectural education that we reflected on range from the on-ground studio, supported by occasional virtual cyber studio initiatives at UMU, to the fully online programme at Curtin, and the two blended variations of CPUT and QUT. Although on-ground and online learning spaces are often considered separate and binary, we observed interesting connections–even overlaps–of spaces in the learning and teaching settings that we discussed. An example of such an overlap is the instance of an on-ground (CPUT) studio session when a student stuck his mobile phone to the wall alongside a printed design proposal (Figure 10.1), when he realised that he had forgotten to print out the drawing needed for the feedback studio session.

An occasion when the connection between the online and on-ground studio appeared to be hindered was observed by the CPUT author visiting the QUT Master's studio. Three students and two tutors gathered around a table for a desk critique, commonly known as the 'crit'. The students were clearly absorbed in their respective digital spaces (see Figure 10.2), and it appeared that the crit might have been more productive had it been conducted fully online–with everyone 'present' in the same (digital) space.

Students and educators bring the real world into the studio through referencing digital resources on their laptops, tablets, and mobile phones (Figure 10.3), or mobile communication with external experts, as demonstrated by a part-time student's WhatsApp messaging with his workplace mentor (Figure 10.4). The global switch to online learning demonstrated how easily the move between on-ground and online learning spaces can occur, and how well connected they can be. Considering the unpredictability of the future, a more fluid and flexible approach might be adopted, allowing for migration between the different on-ground and online spaces, learning settings and modes, and allowing choice where possible and as circumstances require.

Many students enjoy remote learning and the proximity to family while studying from home. However, this is not the case for students in poorly resourced environments, who are often dependent on campus facilities for resources, including hardware, software, and internet access. To enable inter-institutional co-learning and teaching in a post-pandemic world that would address unequal access to resources and the internet, a distributed hybrid model can be considered. This would allow students and educators to gather in small groups on-ground, sharing suitable workspaces, hardware, software, and internet access, to connect to other small groups in dispersed locations.

Figure 10.1: Mobile stuck to the wall

Photograph by Caron von Zeil

Figure 10.2: Desk critique and digital devices

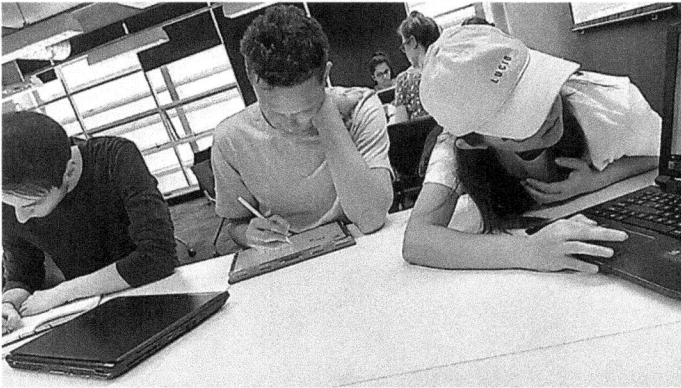

Photograph by authors

Figure 10.3: Mobile phones for references

Photograph by authors

Figure 10.4: Critique via WhatsApp

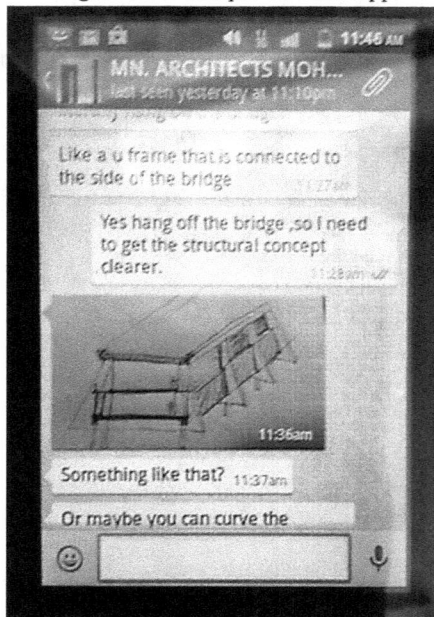

Photograph by authors

We made the following observations related to connecting online and on-ground spaces:

- Adopt a fluid and flexible approach to allow for migration between different on-ground and online spaces and modes.

- Facilitate a range of formal and informal, institutional, and social, synchronous and asynchronous learning settings.

- Ensure good learning design for clear and constructive learning experiences and learning pathways that can be easily navigated.

- Consider the importance of values and community, responding to diverse cultural preferences, and how these could shape learning settings.

- Accommodate unequal needs and circumstances of students, and recognise that these may not be constant but can change over time.

Theme 2: Connecting the university and the profession

All four Schools of Architecture represented in this study value and maintain strong relationships with architectural practices. As part of their Cyber Studio, the UMU invited professionals across the world to join their online studio. Since the students were familiar with the project context, unlike the experts, the students became the 'experts', which built confidence and student agency. At QUT the Professional Practice unit draws on a range of experienced and well-respected professional architects as experts, who meet for regular online learning conversations through which the students and experts are connected, both live and by means of later viewing of the recordings. The CPUT Advanced Diploma students are required to work for professionally registered architects, who provide the mentorship and practice experience required for professional registration.

During the lockdown the authors witnessed a remote site visit which would not have been accessible to students, had it not been streamed online by an architect on his mobile phone. Two of the schools that incorporated substantial online learning components even prior to the outbreak of the pandemic, did so in collaboration with external entities. Curtin University offers a fully online master's programme with OUA (Feast, 2020), and the CPUT part-time blended undergraduate programme is presented in collaboration with OA, a non-profit transformation unit established by the South African Institute of Architects (Morkel, 2017; Poulsen & Morkel, 2016).

Observations based on our reflections on connecting the university and the profession include:

- Create opportunities to position students in expert roles.
- Use technology to connect campus and workplace studios.
- Consider collaboration with external parties who care about education.
- Employ technology to allow students to earn while they learn.
- Encourage students to participate in competitions and professional activities.

Theme 3: Connecting digital learning and teaching tools

Through the rich offering of interconnected formal and informal, institutional, and social, synchronous, and asynchronous digital learning and teaching tools, students are connected to their peers and educators. These online tools are purposely connected to facilitate specific learning pathways. In a study conducted in the part-time blended studio at CPUT, focusing on the use of the webinar as a live online critique platform, it was found that although students do not use the webinar chat function, peer-to-peer interaction was not absent from the synchronous online sessions. What transpired was that these interactions happened on different platforms, for example WhatsApp, that students use as 'backchannels' to support, motivate, and encourage their peers, and to comment on each other's work (Morkel, 2020). In both the Curtin and CPUT cases it was found that students preferred multiple channels of digital communication, and social media, to informally interact with content and different audiences.

Although online learning, and the tools associated with it, were seen to provide an almost instant solution to the sudden closure of campuses and implementation of remote learning, it foregrounded unequal access and equity problems. Students in the global South who did not own laptops, and who could not afford data, were excluded from continuing learning off-campus until they could be provided with laptops and data by the university. In South Africa there was an active Twitter campaign against the reopening of universities while there was a risk that some students might be 'left behind' academically. In the process, six academic weeks were lost. In this context, online learning was not perceived as an equaliser, but rather as a threat to inclusion. A similar scenario played out in Uganda at UMU where the academic year that normally concluded in April continued until August. Rumours on WhatsApp about possible cancellation of the academic year threatened online participation.

Observations linked to connecting digital learning and teaching tools, include:

- Value the human factor and what it means to be human.
- Consider the adoption of multiple tools and channels.
- Accommodate multiple user viewpoints.
- Consider the rapid development of online tools, including virtual reality (VR) and augmented reality (AR).
- Design for inclusivity.

Theme 4: Connecting students and educators

Never had it been so necessary for educators to connect and empathise with students as during the lockdown. Fear about the future dominated, and discussions often switched from learning content and assignment development to survival techniques and coping mechanisms. Educators rapidly needed to diversify their skillsets, to include–in addition to expert facilitation of subject knowledge and delivery–mentoring, counselling, nurturing, and role-modelling. Enabled by technology, private homes which had previously been people's personal sanctuaries quickly converted into lecture theatres, design studios, meeting rooms, offices, and places for 'water cooler discussions'. The co-located activities of family members, housemates, and pets became commonplace in classrooms, and personal artefacts and books were on display for all to observe. Positions of privilege or disadvantage were difficult to conceal, and it soon became evident that online learning favours the privileged.

While attendance seemed to improve when programmes moved online at UMU, students felt exposed and confronted through their inability to hide. Many students disengaged or disappeared when they felt overwhelmed. Some did not want to share their ideas online, out of fear that their creative work would be copied by their peers. Others experienced live online learning fatigue over time, finding it particularly difficult to maintain constant attention to the critique and feedback directed at their peers. Some students–the 'lurk and learners'–simply switched their video cameras off, and others refused to participate. Loss of the nuances and informal cues of communication observed through body language led to reduced on-ground engagement, especially for international students.

Debates were regularly held on whether to record online sessions and what it meant for privacy. One-on-one online 'drop-in' sessions, in lieu of on-ground (office) consultations, helped to support students who felt overwhelmed, exposed, and anxious. Many students demanded rapid responses to their emails and requests for individual and personal feedback, instead of engaging in online group sessions.

Online classroom discussions often started with questions about where people were connecting from, what the weather was like in their respective locations, with apologies for unpredictable background disruptions, and the lack of hair grooming. Tours of personal homes and gardens became commonplace, including pets and children. Displays of humanity and the capacity to laugh when something unexpected or uncontrollable happened provided welcome relief from the mounting stresses of daily life, and the feeling of isolation associated with the new pandemic world. Many students said they wanted to return to on-ground campus settings, because these provide more equitable places and spaces to learn compared to studying from home.

The observations related to connecting educators and students include:

- Provide nurturing care to students as an essential element of effective online teaching.
- Consider that hierarchies of privilege and disadvantage are amplified online.
- Respect students' privacy and relinquish power when teaching online.
- Display humanity and humour to help neutralise anxiety.
- Accommodate both shared collaborative and individual student consultation sessions.

Theme 5: Connecting educators locally and globally

We derived significant benefit from the connections that developed through the methodological approach that underpinned the study. These were framed by our personal and professional experiences, and we appreciated the value of difference and diversity that contributed to the process of co-creation. Through the webinar medium, our home environments emerged as key components of our discussions. In some cases, this provided much needed comic relief, whether from weekly updates of our children and pets, or reports of advertisements displayed on trucks passing by a window. These moments demonstrated the importance of social interaction that enables us–less through programmed steps, than through detours and distractions–to view problems from different positions and perspectives. Our weekly conversations provided much relief and helped us to make sense of our experiences. An example was a demonstration of the contraptions devised by QUT colleagues for teaching drawing online (Figure 10.5), and revealing the conditions under which some UMU students continued their learning activities (Figure 10.6). These anecdotes strengthened the connections between us, while providing useful experiential lessons.

Figure 10.5: Makeshift online teaching aid   **Figure 10.6**: Remote learning conditions

Photograph by Paul Trotter

Photograph by Comfort Tumuhairwe

The coronavirus forced an unprecedented change to the legacy model of the architecture studio (Salama & Crosbie, 2020), disrupting its pedagogical traditions. Our individual experiences as educators, which revealed the importance of global connections, became triggers for delving into the mindset needed for change–not only pertaining to educational approaches, but also to professional trajectories. This was aided by the experiences of colleagues from Curtin and CPUT who had significant previous involvement in online teaching of architecture.

Collaboration across borders, which suddenly became the norm for educators, can be seen as a positive outcome of the move to emergency remote learning and teaching (ERLT). This statement was acknowledged by staff and students in East Africa, who reported on their experiences of online learning and teaching during the coronavirus lockdown (Olweny, Ndibwami & Ahimbisibwe, 2020). We are confident that, drawing on local and global learning and teaching expertise, ERLT practices should transition into authentic and durable learning designs that will reflect transformed curricula, and support relevant and responsible architectural practice.

Discussing the theme of connecting educators locally and globally, we noted the following observations:

- Consider social and personal interaction to share ideas and experiences.

- Remember the role that humour can play to bring people together.

- Accommodate intellectual, practical, and emotional support.

- Find ways to straddle boundaries and overcome time zones.
- Seek diversity when setting up connections.

Theme 6: Connecting students and international experts

The international expert has always played an important role in architectural education, through invited faculty or student presentations, or participation in design reviews. The prestige value of hosting renowned architects is a global phenomenon, increasingly fuelled by the celebrity or 'starchitect' reputation. Over the years UMU hosted prominent international architects–but while educationally invaluable, such events are costly and difficult to sustain. However, hosting international guests via video platforms is technically challenging and dependent on bandwidth.

Despite the challenges, the opportunity to connect students with international experts online was worth exploring. The UMU Cyber Studio (Figure 10.7) was implemented to solve a problem faced by small schools of architecture (Headley, Slee & De la Cruz, 2015), namely to link students in Uganda with architects across the world as tutors for an architectural construction and technology course. This raised several questions about education across borders, including the relationships between global North educators and global South students, and the potentially asymmetrical power relationships. Cyber Studio tutors had limited local knowledge and therefore were reliant on students to provide contextual information, which turned students into the experts. Instead of an unapproachable idol, the expert became an accessible design collaborator. The value of virtual space emerged to break down barriers and build relationships between people across international borders and cultures in an increasingly interconnected and interdependent world.

Figure 10.7: Cyber Studio at UMU

Photograph by authors

Observations that emerged from discussion on the theme of connecting students with international experts are:

- Ensure diversity in the choice of international experts.

- Consider student agency through their localised and indigenous knowledge.

- Employ international experts as accessible and affordable design collaborators, through online technology.

- Use available digital tools and resources, including synchronous, asynchronous, and mobile technologies, and proprietary or open-source software.

- Adopt flexible strategies to meet students, educators, and experts where they are.

Theme 7: Connecting students through peer-to-peer learning

We discovered that social connections helped build student resilience in essential student-led spaces (Stone & O'Shea, 2019), and social media provided safe third spaces (Pet et al., 2017; White, White & Borthwick, 2020) for students to regularly check in with each other in less formal settings. This became especially necessary after group assignments were replaced by individual work, due to mandatory social distancing and self-isolation requirements. Students also missed the opportunity to connect across different year levels or cohorts, as these interactions were not deliberately replicated online.

To assist online students to establish informal social connections, Curtin runs a formative group submission early in the first architecture studio, to introduce students to design thinking, and to each other. In groups of four or five, students produce short videos to introduce the class into their learning spaces, and as a gesture of welcoming. Each student contributes 2–5 seconds of footage to their group to make a short film. Each component follows a similar pattern or theme, and students find creative ways to link their spaces through these videos (see Figures 10.8 and 10.9). This project engages students early in their first studio and introduces them to their peers and to a small group of peers in a low-pressure environment, namely through a formative assessment that is not associated with the burden of performing for grades. Collaboration outside of the formal learning ecosystem is not actively encouraged, but takes place between students once mutual trust is gained. This has led to friendships being formed which continue outside of and beyond the course.

Another example of online technologies connecting students in group work at Curtin is a building science assignment on climate and construction techniques. The on-ground (campus-based) assignment brief on which the online project was based asked students in groups of three to concurrently measure the temperature inside and outside their house (or to find meteorological data to provide the outside air temperature), then analyse the construction methods of each house and compare their thermal performance. When transferred online, this project added another dimension, as students' houses were distributed either across Australia or across the world, resulting in much more varied climatic conditions and construction techniques than the original version of the project offered. Students completed the same analysis of their own house, followed by a joint analysis comparing the performance of each of the houses based on their suitability to their climate. The diversity in location enabled by the online platform deepened the understanding of climate and structure for online students in a way that was not available on campus, where all the students live in the same climate with a much smaller variety of building types.

When asked to give advice to campus students who needed to transition to online education because of the coronavirus, an online Curtin student suggested:

> Don't rely on [public comments] (people generally don't want to be seen as rude for criticising). Form groups with friends to get honest, critical feedback outside of [online classes]. I find this really useful.

In response to a student request, Curtin made a permanently open web conferencing room available for students to meet outside of scheduled classes. This resulted in students forming friendship groups and spontaneously organising Friday night drinks and crit sessions. This informal peer-to-peer support and learning arose from formal collaborations which are designed into the course and enabled by connective technologies. These events were valued more highly than the peer-to-peer learning set up in the formal and structured learning settings, as evidenced by the student's advice above.

Figure 10.8: Creating peer-to-peer connections online

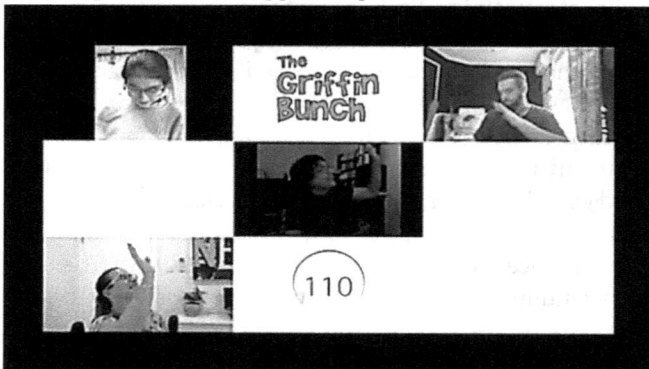

Screenshot by authors

Figure 10.9.a: Linking online and on-ground spaces

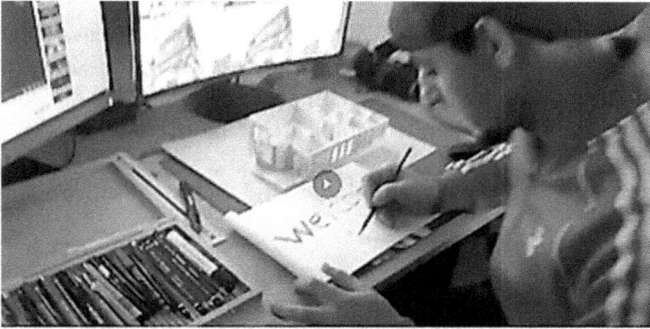

Photograph by Mahmoud Said

Figure 10.9.b: Linking online and on-ground spaces

Photograph by Jack Jaggs Nelson

Observations that emerged from the discussion on connecting students through peer-to-peer learning include:

- Optimise student social networks for peer-to-peer learning and group work.
- Support students to set up social learning spaces that are not necessarily accessible by staff.
- Consider collaborative assignments to facilitate student interaction and build relationships early in the programme.
- Acknowledge a layering of connections and relationships inside and outside of the university, where students find their peers to provide honest feedback.
- Consider students' respective and diverse locations to enrich projects.

Learning design principles

Drawing on the five observations that we formulated for each of the seven discussion themes, totalling 35 observations, we synthesised four design principles for the conceptualisation and implementation of connected co-learning and co-teaching in online and blended global architecture studios.

Principle 1: Employ relevant technologies and techniques through learning design

Central to the seven thematic conversations and reflections on how we employed, supported, and researched technology in architectural education prior to and during the pandemic lockdown period, we identified the need for good learning design to select and optimise relevant technology, and techniques. Through the observation of context and pedagogy, formal and informal, synchronous, and asynchronous on-ground and online modes should be considered, including formal university online platforms and tools, VR, AR and social media.

These technologies and techniques must be explored through deliberate and well-informed learning design. It is the pedagogy–not the technology–that should guide learning design, as well as careful consideration of the student personas and their respective learning contexts (Morkel, 2015; Morkel & Pallitt, 2015; Seitzinger, 2016).

Principle 2: Acknowledge students-as-partners to promote student agency and well-being

To address the asymmetrical power relations associated with the traditional architecture studio (Shulman, 2005; Webster, 2008), or what Salama and Crosbie (2020) refer to as the legacy model, a students-as-partners approach (Cook-Sather et al., 2018) must be adopted. This can address mental health issues and promote student agency (Webster, 2008; Burton, 2018; Morkel, 2017; Olweny, 2015, 2017, 2020, Olweny et al., 2021). Students can be empowered, for example, by co-creating their learning, earning while they are learning, and building confidence through participation in competitions and professional activities. Students' indigenous knowledges and their diverse contexts should be considered in course material and the formulation of assignments and project briefs.

More than showing empathy, educators must employ a nurturing pedagogy (Olweny, 2020, Olweny et al., 2021), by supporting students intellectually, practically and, where possible, emotionally. An awareness of the risk of exposing students, based on cultural or gender difference or, for example, through revealing their home environments and physical appearance through mandatory video sharing, should be cultivated.

Principle 3: Consider flexibility through multiple interlinked learning settings and modes

We found that a range of learning settings, modes and channels should be employed for connected co-learning and teaching, according to their respective affordances. These modes can include formal and informal, institutional, and social, synchronous and asynchronous learning in settings that are connected, to offer optimal and personalised learning opportunities for students according to their unique needs and circumstances.

A fluid and flexible approach that allows for strategic migration between multiple interlinked learning settings and modes will not only be adaptable during times of uncertainty, but also allow student choice and agency.

Principle 4: Recognise humanity, humour, culture and community

We identified the importance that we recognise humanity, humour, culture and community for co-learning and co-teaching design. The need for educators to recognise community, not only in the creation of a studio community, but also considering the students' respective community contexts–not to mention the importance of community for educators–has become more apparent during the recent global lockdown. We observed that students are much more engaged online than they used to be, possibly because of the need for human contact and connection that became apparent during the pandemic. These observations support Wilson's (2014, par 4) argument for the design of the Science and Engineering Centre at QUT by Wilson Architects and Donovan Hill:

> What is the value of a university campus when the majority of courses can now be delivered online? The answer is community. Students want to feel connected to their peers, to their academics and teachers, and to the place where they learn.

Furthermore, the display of humanity and humour, and employing social and personal interaction for learning–also through seeking diversity in the connections, for example through non-local and, where possible, international experts–were emphasised. Also, optimising social networks for peer-to-peer learning was found to enrich these learning experiences, inside and outside of the university. Finally, recognising privilege and disadvantage enabled a more equitable approach to co-learning and co-teaching, and authentic and durable learning designs.

Conclusion

Drawing on the observations generated from the seven themed discussions, we formulated four design principles for connected co-learning and co-teaching across global cultural boundaries in online and blended architecture studios: 1) employ relevant technologies and techniques through learning design; 2) acknowledge students-as-partners to promote student agency and well-being; 3) consider flexibility through multiple interlinked learning settings and modes; and 4) recognise humanity, humour, culture, and community.

The autoethnographic reflections discussed in this chapter draw on and refer to practices and experiences observed in the authors' four contexts, on the campuses and between these learning communities and in their respective networks. We found that many of the assumptions we had made related to global South and global North contexts and cultural boundaries, were not always accurate. For example, although more prominent in the global South, resource constraints were also evident in the global North, and contrary to what we expected, innovation was not necessarily exclusively driven by the global North. The traditional studio methodology has its origins in the global North, and challenging the legacy model (Salama & Crosbie, 2020) is necessary to transform architectural education–perhaps by looking further South.

We suggest that the design principles formulated here can be relevant for connected co-learning and co-teaching for online and blended global architecture studios and other project-based learning contexts more generally. Future research should explore these findings further, by testing the design principles that we formulated in different global South and global North contexts.

Development of the current project with the four authors dispersed across the globe, through webinars, despite all the glitches, provided humorous moments that revealed our vulnerability, and allowed us to share freely. The ease with which these connections could be made demonstrated the potential of future online academic linkages towards co-learning and co-teaching practices across global cultural boundaries. While there will always be the need for a physical presence in the architecture studio, the use of digital media to bridge distance and connect people has proven an invaluable outcome of this unprecedented situation.

Not unlike Scott Brown, Venturi and Izenour's experience of Las Vegas (Venturi et al., 1977), the coronavirus pandemic compelled us to challenge our preconceptions and practices. Central to our learning design response to an unpredictable future lies the deliberate and conscious adoption of relevant technologies, media, and resources, recognising students-as-partners of flexible and multiple learning trajectories, that reject "traditional hierarchies and assumptions about expertise and responsibility" (Cook-Sather et al., 2018, p. 1). As a global community, we should adopt good learning design to address the increasingly complex challenges, by relying on co-learning and co-teaching connections for support.

References

AACA. (2019). *Online Architecture Education and the Australian context.* https://www.aaca.org.au/wp-content/uploads/Online-Architecture-Education-Paper.pdf

Burton, L. O. (2018). *Experimentations in transformational pedagogy and space: The architecture student" experience* (Doctoral dissertation), Queensland University of Technology.

Chang, H., Ngunjiri, F. & Hernandez, K. C. (2012). *Collaborative Autoethnography.* Walnut Creek: Taylor & Francis Group.

Connell, R. (2014). Using southern theory: Decolonizing social thought in theory, research and application. *Planning Theory, 13*(2), pp. 210-223.

Cook-Sather, A., Matthews, K. E., Ntem, A. & Leathwick, S. (2018). What we talk about when we talk about students as partners. *International Journal for Students as Partners, 2*(2), pp. 1-9.

Ellis, C., Adams, T. E. & Bochner, A. P. (2010). Autoethnography: An overview. *Forum: Qualitative Social Research, 12*(1). http://nbn-resolving.de/urn:nbn:de:0114-fqs1101108

Fahey, J. & Kenway, J. (2010). Moving ideas and mobile researchers: Australia in the global context. *The Australian Educational Researcher, 37*(4), pp. 103-114.

Feast, S. (2020). *Lessons from existing online programs.* AASA Webinar Series Webinar #1 What is Good Online Learning in Architecture? [Video]. https://youtu.be/5m-0pUNCJZ0?t=283 [accessed 13 August 2020]

Gross, M. D., & Do, E. L. (1997, September). The design studio approach: Learning design in architecture education. In *Design Education Workshop. Georgia Institute of Technology* (Vol. 8).

Headley, D., Slee, B., & De La Cruz, E. (2015). How do we sketch with someone 1000 miles away?: distance collaboration for designers. *Living and Learning: Research for a Better Built Environment:* 49th International Conference of the Architectural Science Association. Melbourne: Australia.

Laterza, V., Evans, D., Davies, R., Donald, C. & Rice, C. (2016). What's in a "research passport"? A collaborative autoethnography of institutional approvals in public involvement in research. *Research Involvement and Engagement, 2*(1), pp. 1-22.

Lehmann, S. (2019). What is the relevance of the book *"Learning from Las Vegas"?* YouTube, accessed 30 March 2021. Online AIA Conference in Las Vegas, 18 July 2019. https://www.youtube.com/watch?v=F53ese8D21o

Marshall T. (2008). Wicked Problems. In M. Erlhoff & T. Marshall (Eds.), *Design Dictionary Perspectives on Design Terminology.* Basel: Birkhäuser Verlag.

Morkel, J. (2015). *Ideate crea8 iterate: A learning design workshop,* eLearning Update, Caesar's Palace, Johannesburg. https://www.slideshare.net/jolandamorkel/learning-design-workshop-at-elearnigupdate-2015

Morkel, J. (2017). An exploration of Socratic learning in a webinar setting. *Proceedings of the International Conference of the Association of Architectural Educators: Architecture Connects,* 6-9 September 2017, Oxford, UK (pp. 336-344). https://aaeconference2017.wordpress.com/about-2/

Morkel, J. (2020). From Butterpaper to Touch Screen: The Online Desk Crit and the Spaces Between. *AASA Webinar Series Webinar #3 Maintaining Studio Culture in Online Learning* [Video]. https://youtu.be/k2KojqSxs-I?t=2574

Morkel, J. & Pallitt, N. (2015). *Learning Design Workshop Series. E/merge Africa online.* https://www.youtube.com/playlist?list=PLgNzHqwrWe5zbm13bBIM DekDTd3V7wfk3

Olweny, M. R. O. (2015). *Investigating the Processes of Socialisation in Architectural Education Through Experiences in East Africa.* Cardiff: Welsh School of Architecture, Cardiff University

Olweny, M.R. O. (2017). Socialisation in architectural education: A view from East Africa. *Education and Training, 59*(2), pp. 188-200. doi: 10.1108/ET-02-2016-0044

Olweny, M. R. O. (2020). Listen without prejudice: The design studio as a discursive environment (or) Helping students learn in architecture education. *Association of Collegiate Schools of Architecture (ACSA) 108th Annual Meeting, 12– 15 March 2020, San Diego.* http://eprints.lincoln.ac.uk/id/eprint/36309/

Olweny, M., Ndibwami, A. & Ahimbisibwe, A. (2020). *Experiences with online architectural education: Initial results from students and staff in Rwanda and Uganda.* Lincoln: University of Lincoln.

Olweny, M., Morkel, J., Delport, H., Whelan, D., & Ndibwami, A. (2021). Zombies in the Studio: Towards nurturing pedagogical approaches for architectural education in sub-Saharan Africa. *Charrette, 7*(2), 57-83.

Pet, S. R., Silvestri, K., Loomis, S., O'Byrne, W. I. & Kist, W. (2017). 10 Mentored open online communities (MooCs) as a third space for teaching and learning in higher education. In R. Bennett & M. Kent (Eds.), *Massive Open Online Courses and Higher Education: What Went Right, What Went Wrong and Where to Next?*, pp. 137-150. London: Routledge.

Poulsen, L. & Morkel, J. (2016). Open architecture: a blended learning model for architectural education. *Architecture South Africa, 78*, pp. 28-30.

Salama, A. M. & Crosbie. M.J. (2020). Educating architects in a post-pandemic world. *Common Edge, 14*, p. 6.

Seitzinger, J. (2016). 10 *Learner experience powers from experience girl!* iMOOT16 Conference, 26–27 May. https://www.slideshare.net/catspyjamas/10-learner -experience-powers-from-experience-girl-imoot16-agents-of-change

Shulman, L. (2005). Signature pedagogies in the professions. *Daedalus, 134*(3), pp. 52-59. doi: 10.1162/0011526054622015

Stewart, K. & Gachago, D. (2016). Being human today: A digital storytelling pedagogy for transcontinental border crossing. *British Journal of Educational Technology, 47*(3), pp. 528-542.

Stone, C. & "Shea, S. (2019). Older, online and first: Recommendations for retention and success. *Australasian Journal of Educational Technology, 35*(1), pp. 57-69. doi: 10.14742/ajet.3913

Venturi, R., Scott Brown, D. & Izenour, S. (1977). *Learning from Las Vegas.* Cambridge: MIT Press.

Vinegar, A. & Golec, M. J. (Ed.). (2008). *Relearning from Las Vegas.* Minneapolis: University of Minnesota Press.

Webster, H. (2008). Architecture education after Schön: Cracks, blurs, boundaries and beyond. *Journal for Education in the Built Environment*, 3(2), pp. 63-74. doi: 10.11120/jebe.2008.03020063.

White, S., White, S. & Borthwick, K. (2020). Blended professionals, technology and online learning: Identifying a socio technical third space in higher education. *Higher Education Quarterly*, 75, pp. 161-174.

Wilson, H. (2014) *The future of education design.* https://architectureau.com/articles/the-future-of-education-design/

Chapter 11

Emerging principles for online cross-cultural, collaborative research

Nicola Pallitt

Rhodes University, South Africa

Hannah M. Grossman

UCLA/Duke University National Center for Child Traumatic Stress, United States of America

Alice Barlow-Zambodla

e/merge Africa, South Africa

Juhong Christie Liu

James Madison University, United States of America

Neil Kramm

Rhodes University, South Africa

Leah Sikoyo

Makerere University, Uganda

Nompilo Tshuma

Stellenbosch University, South Africa

Abstract

Few studies investigate collaborative processes among researchers (Paulus et al., 2008; Amundsen et al., 2019), yet research collaborations involving multiple researchers have become more widespread. As members of an international collaborative research group, we use a team ethnography approach to examine our research practices. We also investigate the dimensions of our local contexts that both enable and constrain our abilities to connect and collaborate. This chapter discusses our research process and the lenses, ethos and practices that we used to design that process. This is followed by emerging principles based on what we are learning about our own practices, to ensure committed and sustained engagement in collaborative research online, in South Africa, Uganda, and United States.

Keywords: collaborative, cross-cultural, online collaboration, research support

***

Introduction

Collaborative research "can be defined as research involving coordination between the researchers, institutions, organizations and/or communities. This cooperation can bring distinct expertise to a project" (Bansal et al., 2019, p. 137). While other scholars use the terms 'collaborative research' and 'co-research' interchangeably, the authors of this chapter observe that the term co-research is more often associated with participatory research approaches—for example, in the case of Western researchers working with indigenous people to better understand particular practices in a community, or in research done with practitioners who are target participants of a research project. In contrast, collaborative research is not specific to a particular research approach or a specific project—it is about a larger approach to relationships and process-oriented aspects of a project that enables the research to happen in the first place.

Our collaborative research initiative came about through an affiliation between the e/merge Africa[1] network and the Association for Educational Communications and Technology (AECT).[2] Both entities focus on supporting professional communities in the field of educational technology. The organisers of the research initiative created academic mentoring and research groups to support members of these entities. The groups set up within this initiative were collectively titled the International Research Collaborative for Established and Emerging Scholars (IRCEES), and consisted of collectives of researchers and practitioners based in Africa and the United States of America. Within this set-up, established scholars were arranged into groups (with different research interests) as intended mentors, with emerging scholars as mentees. The group to which the authors of this chapter belong–the IRCEES SHM/UL (Supporting

---

[1] An Africa-based online professional development network for educational technology practitioners and researchers See https://emergeafrica.net/

[2] US-based international professional organisation for educational technology professionals. See https://aect.org/

Historically Marginalised and Underserved Learners) Group–indicates our shared interest in supporting marginalised learners.

After our first few online SHM/UL meetings in 2018, we recognised that we were evolving out of the traditional mentorship model envisioned by the organisers of the initiative. Such models can be steeped in hierarchy and status, and often include differential power dynamics that make reciprocity less assured. An ideal mentorship is "a dynamic, reciprocal relationship in a work environment between an advanced career incumbent (mentor) and a beginner (protégé) aimed at promoting the career development of both" (Healy & Welchert, 1990). For the mentorship aspect of our project, we collectively decided on a community of practice approach.

As a group of collaborators, we were individually selected and placed with fellow researchers who shared our interests. Our approach to cross-cultural collaborative research was—and is—a response to challenges that we have experienced with traditional models of academic research. In traditional output-driven and individualistic research cultures, sustainable and mutually beneficial research relationships are hard to achieve. Rarely are the different positionalities of collaborators, their effect on research processes, and the longevity of collaboration acknowledged.

Our reflection has revealed and connected theoretical perspectives and conceptual lenses in the co-creation of our collaborative process. These incorporated experiential learning, social emotional learning (SEL), trauma-informed approaches, cultural influences to cross-cultural research, communities of practice, the Ubuntu philosophy, decolonising academic research and educational technologies, and sociomateriality. Through discussing these perspectives and lenses, we collaboratively reflected and practiced dialogic thinking until we were able to develop a research approach that met our needs both academically and interpersonally.

This chapter provides a rationale for and an examination of our approach. We discuss our team's ethnographic reflections, then share the themes identified as contributing to our strength and success, including emerging principles derived from our practice. These principles can inform other researchers who are trying to co-construct healthy, supportive research collaborations of their own.

Literature review

Collaborative research in academic settings

Collaborative research can optimise choices in relation to defining problems and assembling methodologies, leading to more inclusive interpretation and use of research findings, so as to bring about changes and reframe the power balance (Denis & Lomas, 2003). Challenges associated with collaborative research include ambiguous or uncomfortable roles, conflicting priorities of collaborators, more complex decision making, and concerns about the use of resources and time (Amundsen et al., 2019).

Research into collaborative research appears to be most common in the hard sciences (Bansal et al., 2019) and in the field of technology transfer (Bozeman et al., 2013). Case studies of how researchers use the affordances of various technological tools to do collaborative research with postgraduate students (Lemon & Salmons, 2020) are growing in number and are situated in the broader fields of teaching and learning, and research training. More recently, some scholars have emphasised the importance of decolonising traditionally Western approaches to research and research training (Datta, 2018), and the nature of relationships involved in such approaches. For us, this also involves recentring researchers and putting effort into building relationships, rather than being output-driven. Research collaborations sometimes end once an output has been finalised or when project funding ends. Such outcomes are endemic to output-driven research collaborations.

Research relationships may take a variety of forms, be understood differently across cultural contexts, and involve diverse approaches and perspectives. From the outset, some of these relationships are not equal, and an unequal context makes sustaining them for mutual value even more difficult. Although research collaborations involving multiple researchers have become more widespread, few studies investigate collaborative processes among the researchers themselves (Paulus et al., 2008; Amundsen et al., 2019). We found few articles in which researchers reflected on their practice in a scholarly manner to discuss challenges and share advice, or that focused on supporting relationships among differently positioned collaborators.

Principles for collaborative research

Amundsen et al. (2019) conducted a critical, reflective-in-action study among themselves (three academics working at the same university in New Zealand), collecting and analysing data over a period of 15 months. They acknowledge that there have been efforts within research communities to better understand and measure the effectiveness of collaboration, referring to the work of Marek, Brock and Savla (2015), and Sandoval et al. (2012). They argue that while threads of such models were useful for their study, little is known about processes that contribute to successful outcomes, indicating that further research is needed to better understand elements of a successful collaborative process. They discuss the implications of the dimensions they identified, based on their own experiences, as follows:

1. Acknowledging the affective involves acknowledging fluid, contextual situations that underpin individuals' lives and being, and that any collective has emotional dynamics that when recognised and tended to can assist a group in becoming more effective;

2. Becoming bolder entails not settling for the status quo and harnessing the power of a collective when facing barriers in relation to academic research;

3. Cultivating creativity involves making space for intricate elements that enable collaborative meaning-making; that includes making time for nurturing relationships of respect and working through uncomfortable tensions and frustrations, so that creative ideas and meaningful knowledge can be generated (Amundsen et al., 2019, p. 49).

Our approach has much in common with the ABCs of collaboration shared by Amundsen et al. (2019), as we also emphasise the primacy of the affective, social relationships and an awareness of power dynamics. Our approach (mentioned in the Introduction) emerged in response to upsetting the status quo of a pre-assumed traditional mentoring approach. The cross-cultural and online dimensions of our research collaboration add further complexity.

Theoretical perspectives and conceptual lenses

The range of theoretical perspectives and conceptual lenses that we incorporated for co-creating our collaborative process included: experiential learning, social emotional learning (SEL), trauma-informed approaches, cultural influences to cross-cultural research, communities of practice, the Ubuntu philosophy, and decolonising academic research and educational technologies, as well as sociomateriality. Through these lenses we engaged in dialogic thinking to develop our approach to online cross-cultural, collaborative research.

Experiential learning, SEL and trauma-informed approaches

As collaborators, we consider ourselves a community of learners, becoming better researchers through reflecting on our shared experiences. American educational theorist David Kolb's (2014) experiential learning model involves a situation where learners: 1) experience an activity, 2) share their reactions and observations, 3) process the experience by discussing and reflecting upon it, 4) generalise to connect the experience to the real world, and 5) apply these learnings to future endeavours. This model informed our approach to interviewing skills and survey analysis.

SEL and trauma-informed approaches both consider learners in their physical and sociocultural context, and try to optimise learning based on evidence-based practices. With the SEL framework (common in the mental health and education fields), the broad areas of competence are seen as skills that we hope to foster and develop: self-awareness, social awareness, relationship-building, self-management and responsible decision-making. The Substance Abuse and Mental Health Administration (SAMHSA) conceptualises trauma-informed approaches using six categories: 1) safety, trustworthiness and transparency; 2) peer support, collaboration and mutuality; 3) empowerment; 4) voice; 5) choice; and 6) addressing current inequities (SAMHSA, 2014). Using these categories, we regarded our research collaborative as a learning situation, and considered how we might be more 'trauma-informed' as part of our process. While neither SEL nor trauma-informed approaches are usually associated with cross-cultural research, SEL skills are needed to communicate powerfully in cross-cultural settings (Morris et al., 1999), and these skills are integral to successful cross-cultural collaborative work (Payton et al., 2000). We therefore decided to incorporate the frameworks of SEL and trauma-informed approaches to define and support interpersonal strategies.

Culture and cross-cultural research

Culture involves "a fuzzy set of basic assumptions and values, orientations to life, beliefs, policies, procedures and behavioural conventions that are shared by a group of people, and that influence (but do not determine) each member's behaviour and his/her interpretations of the meaning of other peoples' behaviour" (Spencer-Oatey, 2008, p. 3). Additionally, "culture should be regarded as the set of distinctive spiritual, material, intellectual and emotional features of society or a social group, and that it encompasses, in addition to art and literature, lifestyles, ways of living together, value systems, traditions and beliefs" (UNESCO, 2001, n.p.).

Brislin defines cross-cultural research as "empirical studies carried out among members of various cultural groups who have had different experiences" (1976, p. 215), which enable them to engage in emic analysis to document "valid principles that describe behavior in any one culture, taking into account what the people themselves value as meaningful and important". Cross-cultural research opens the horizon for new perspectives, topics and methods of study, and accommodates the need to unfold multiple layers of complexity in cross-cultural communication, research methods and knowledge-exchange dynamics. Our approach involved positioning our cultural diversity as a strength and taking time to engage in knowledge translation towards shared understandings. It is important for cross-cultural researchers to develop the competency necessary to understand each other (Kim & Bonk, 2002).

Communities of practice

Communities of practice (CoPs) are "formed by people who engage in a process of collective learning in a shared domain of human endeavor" (Wenger & Wenger-Trayner, 2015, n.p.). In the development of a community of practice, learning takes place in pursuing meanings, and the realisation of members' values usually shapes the identity of individuals as well as the group (Handley et al., 2006; Wenger, 1999). Some scholars argue that power relations, ideology and conflict have been poorly explained in relation to CoPs (Contu & Wilmott, 2003; Veenswijk & Chisalita, 2007). This reinforces the importance of combining multiple theoretical perspectives and conceptual lenses.

Ubuntu philosophy

Ubuntu[3] is an African philosophy that positions the individual in terms of their relationships with others (Muwanga-Zake, 2009). It involves recognition of our shared humanity and of the reality that one person's personhood and identity is fulfilled by others. Ubuntu has become accepted as a research paradigm that can inform research agendas and methodologies (Muwanga-Zake, 2009; Seehawer, 2018). As part of our process, we discuss dominant paradigms and approaches to research, again questioning the status quo. Western research cultures are often individualistic and competitive. Muwanga-Zake (argues that "Ubuntu as a research philosophy gives the research process a human face, as opposed to some top-down imposed research processes, and advocates collaboration with the participants and community humanely, with respect to their spirituality, values, needs, norms, and mores" 2009, p. 418). We see Ubuntu as informing the development of our research collaborative, and as rightly positioning an individual in a CoP.

Decolonising approaches to academic research and educational technologies

Decolonisation, "requires action involving resistance to colonization, revaluing traditional Indigenous knowledge, reclaiming equitable ways of interacting to co-create new possibilities, and transforming political and personal histories" (Ritenburg et al., 2014, p. 72). We view decolonisation as part of how we approach cross-cultural collaborative research in "reclaiming equitable ways of interacting to co-create new possibilities" (Ritenburg et al., 2014, p. 72). Decolonising involves questioning dominant paradigms, approaches, theories

---

[3] We acknowledge that the roots of Ubuntu are complex and beyond the scope of this chapter. We encourage readers to engage with the works of Muwanga-Zake (2009) and Seehawer (2018) for further clarification.

and practices as part of our work. Dominant theories and frameworks in educational technologies research come from the global North.[4] This awareness encouraged us to pursue research approaches and literature in similar contexts to our own, characterised by a majority of 'marginalised' students and differential access to technological and other resources.

Sociomateriality

Much research on educational technology usage in African settings focuses on material access to the internet and digital devices. This focus perpetuates a 'digital divide' discourse, viewing people and their practices from a 'deficit' perspective. In contrast, a sociomaterial perspective offers a context-sensitive view of technology usage, in which practices are more complex than material access. Sociomaterial assemblages and entanglements (Gourlay & Oliver, 2018 are then considered part of people's contexts, where "the material world is treated as continuous with and embedded in the immaterial and the human" (Fenwick et al., 2012, p. 6). As Ubuntu and decolonising approaches assist with recognising power relations in a way that is currently lacking in CoPs, sociomateriality enables us to consider online collaborative research and the use of educational technologies as practices, and to contemplate how participation in particular practices is produced and sustained, and related to particular assemblages. Additionally, how "practice becomes reconfigured or transformed is addressed at the nexus of sociomaterial connections" (Fenwick et al., 2012, p. 7).

Digital team ethnography

Digital team ethnography involves collaborative and interdisciplinary ethnographic reflection, enabled by digital tools that create a live source of data which can be recorded and analysed (Beneito-Montagut et al., 2017). This research method, "favours a collaborative, non-hierarchical and dialogue-driven knowledge production process" and involves, "collective sense-making processes in any or all stages of the research process" (Beneito-Montagut et al., 2017, pp. 664-668), which resonates with our approach to collaborative research. As is the case with collaborative research, little is known about how ethnographers work together as part of a team to conduct their research (Beneito-Montagut et al., 2017).

---

[4] 'Global North' (North America, Western Europe, Australia, and Japan) acknowledges the global North-South divide, which is both socio-economic and political. Countries in the global South (Africa, Central and Latin America, and most of Asia) are considered to be 'less developed', given these countries' limited access to resources such as safe drinking water, adequate sanitation, electricity, internet access, and so forth.

Our digital team's ethnography resides in the recordings of online meetings, notes taken during meetings, and other artefacts that we collaborated on, such as recorded online conference presentations and videos reflecting on our shared research process. We have presented several of these recorded conversations as different aspects of our work. The ethnography here illustrates three areas: 1) benefits and drawbacks to our approach, 2) themes of success from shared reflection, and 3) emerging principles of this approach.

Co-creating our approach to cross-cultural, collaborative research

Context

Originally there were 12 members in the group; four left within the first year, and one new member joined. Four collaborators are based in South Africa, one in Uganda and two in the United States (one in Virginia and one in California. There are eight female-identifying and one male-identifying collaborator. Two collaborators were taking a break at the time of writing. Some collaborators did not know each other before the first meeting, while others had met or worked together before. Racial composition is: Asian-American (1), African American (1), African (3), and White (4). Educational backgrounds include: Academic Development, Agriculture, Botany, Cognitive Psychology, Curriculum Studies, Education, Educational Technology, Instructional Design and Technology, Information Systems, Higher Education, Media Studies, Teacher Education, Science Education, and Sociology.

The e/merge Africa network became affiliated to the AECT in 2016, and the IRCEES initiative started in 2017. In 2018, IRCEES organisers invited prospective mentors and mentees (emerging scholars) to apply to join a pilot research support group, through a call shared by the e/merge Africa network and the AECT Culture, Learning and Technology (CLT) division. The intended goals and ways of working across groups evolved over time, although the broad purpose was to:

> ... support each other as a community of practice in developing the abilities to investigate cultural patterns in research capacity, technology adoption, and collaborative possibilities. We will also learn from the process of optimising opportunities to disseminate knowledge and overcome challenges collaborating with people from a wide variety of cultural backgrounds. These will be intentionally leveraged to support access and inclusion through open education resources and research. (IRCEES Charter, 2018)

The authors of this chapter are the members of the IRCEES SHM/UL group (one of the four groups). Identifying all group members as 'collaborators' or 'our group' rather than distinguishing between emerging and experienced scholars, we have been working together consistently for over two years. We have co-designed an interview protocol and survey for educational technology users working in African universities, conducted interviews, co-presented at conferences, and refined our understanding of cross-cultural and culturally situated research as experiential learning.

Our shared goal brought us together and influenced how we designed our approach. To support marginalised learners, one must understand the supports and barriers to learning. Our understanding of identities, intersectionality, inclusion and context compelled us to apply an equity lens in our research. As some of our collaborators were themselves historically marginalised and under-represented learners, this awareness informed our research process and how we can better enable equitable participation among ourselves.

Our approach to facilitating collaboration

As discussed earlier, our approach took a different turn from the mentoring directions initially envisaged. In our work we regularly interrogate the dimensions of our local contexts that enable or constrain our abilities to connect and collaborate. We have a voluntarist approach to skill sharing. Our attitude to division of labour allows members to participate in flexible ways, especially for sustained engagement in collaborative research online.

When launching any initiative, we co-create a shared understanding of the concept. We identify a point for exploration then invite each member to share their perspective, after which someone summarises the contributions and identifies common ground, working towards a shared understanding and agreement. In this process we create opportunities for collaborators to ask questions and triangulate perspectives. Open-ended questions allow collaborators to frame concepts that make the information powerful and meaningful.

Our decision-making processes provide everyone with the opportunity, the right and the responsibility to share their perspectives, insights and opinions. We provide time and space for opinions to be gathered, discussed and evaluated. Even when conversations may seem tangential or off topic, we have found it valuable to continue the discussion.

Our approach to tools and tasks

We meet once a week, for between one and two hours, to plan the research design and determine methods and tools for the research study described in the next section. Starting the meeting with greetings and catching up, we have a weekly call (when it is morning for the American collaborators and evening for our African counterparts). The meeting is held on the Zoom platform, but we regularly have cameras off, to conserve bandwidth and improve connectivity.

It is primarily used to share screens. Meetings are recorded and curated in a shared space (Google Drive). If one of us loses connectivity or is unable to attend, we let the group know via WhatsApp.

During the meetings we work on what we can with those present. There are no strict deadlines. People volunteer to take on either the full task or part of it. If one person needs help finishing a task that is harder than expected, we discuss it and someone volunteers to help. We make time to address issues that are complicating the collaboration or making it less safe, comfortable or enjoyable. We have no true leader. On different projects, collaborators put in varying amounts of time or work. Decision-making is built around self-selecting, instead of being selected for the process.

Collaborative research on educational technology usage in African universities

The general goal of this group is to research access to and use of education technologies in African higher education contexts. We created a semi-structured interview and a survey as part of our research activities. We began with the interview process. Dr Mary Brenner (Professor in the Department of Education at the University of California), as advisor to Dr Grossman (a co-author of this chapter) for her postgraduate studies, graciously led a qualitative interviewing session. After that, we wrote and refined the interview protocol. Next, we collaboratively practised our interview skills. Observed by the group, one group member would conduct the interview on camera with another member. Following each round of practice, we discussed strengths and areas needing improvement. With just-in-time guidance, feedback and collaborative support, we assured ourselves of the quality of our process and our interviewing skills. Then we individually interviewed educational technology experts from universities across Africa. Fourteen interviews have been conducted with educational technology practitioners at universities in South Africa, Kenya, Ghana, Nigeria, Uganda and Botswana.

Similarly, we collaboratively wrote then refined our survey in iterative cycles. We designed the survey in Qualtrics, refining questions using the shared screen functionality via Zoom. This refining process occurred in our weekly online meetings over a period of 1.5 months. It began by interrogating wording and local terminology. For example, the definitions of hybrid and blended learning differ in Ugandan, South African and American contexts. We also compared our survey to others and discussed differences and strengths. For feedback, we shared the interview with e/merge Africa network convener, Tony Carr, given his experience with Africa-wide surveys on educational technology usage. Using Carr's feedback, we refined the survey before deploying it for data collection.

Benefits and drawbacks of a collaborative, experiential research approach

This approach allows us to venture into new contexts feeling supported and protected. In these spaces we know we each have something to offer. The wisdom each of us has helps us all to grow. We co-create the map of our journey as we define the path itself. We have products and outputs; we have also been constantly adjusting the paths to proceed with our research. Because our research is not primarily output driven, we can first attend to ideas, reflections and processes, then adapt the products and outcomes to fit.

This approach is challenging. To co-create and share ideas requires regular meeting times with the whole community. Interpersonal complexities need to be monitored and addressed to keep the process on track. For example, someone may want a task completed faster than our process allows, which can lead to uncomfortable power dynamics and group members feeling their perspectives are under-valued. Recognising how detrimental these dynamics can be, we invest time, energy and social capital into resolving them to everyone's satisfaction.

We use our flexibility to help address time constraints. When there is a concrete product to be made or a new process to be started, a group member will volunteer to take charge of the process (or the aspects of the process they feel they can powerfully contribute towards). If no one volunteers, or if the total labour requirement is not covered, we accept that a project may need to be adjusted. Some of the ways in which we adapt are: inviting outside experts (such as a former academic advisor providing interviewing tips or bringing in resources from our varied networks); using the e/merge Africa network to share survey information to get a survey distributed more broadly; reworking a product (adapting a conference proposal to the reality of where a project was, or creating a new timeline to suit our process); and distributing a survey months later than initially expected.

Our tendency has been to explore as widely as possible, but sometimes there is an outcome for which only a limited time frame is available. We use flexible timelines to get the outputs completed. Whenever forced by external pressures to reassess our progress towards a particular outcome, we modify our process for the product creation. These areas become more complex, as we try not to compromise our approach. Some ways to get things done faster are: meeting in smaller groups, having individuals condense information before group gatherings, and support situations where individuals do the work and the group provides feedback and guidance on the process. These 'speeding up' strategies make things more complex and make us uneasy as it becomes more difficult to keep a shared voice on collaborative outputs (such as this chapter). Nonetheless, we trust each other, and we continue to co-create processes that allow each voice to be included and incorporated. Tables 11.1 and 11.2 indicate collaboratively identified challenges and strengths.

Table 11.1: Challenges in the cross-cultural collaborative process

Challenges	Examples
Geographic location	South Africa, Uganda and Virginia
Time differences	PST 8 am = 7 pm in Uganda
Language/cross-cultural communication	Different definitions of blended/hybrid learning
Cross-disciplinary communication	Media Studies, Agricultural Sciences, etc.
Create meaningful shared spaces	Zoom, WhatsApp, Google Drive, Teams, etc.
Unreliable availability of needed tools and resources	Power and connectivity issues
Keeping motivated	Pandemic initially reduced motivation
Competing commitments	Multiple professional obligations

Table 11.2: Strengths and supports of the cross-cultural collaborative process

Strengths	Examples
Shared resources	Google Drive, Zoom, Qualtrics
Communication and collaborative strategic planning	Brainstorming together
Multiple communication pathways	WhatsApp, Zoom, Teams
Flexible grouping and iterative reporting back	Alice and Hannah write together, then send on
Recording for asynchronous participation	Audio recording of weekly meetings
Creating reminders, supports and deadlines	Checking in on the WhatsApp group

Themes of success from shared reflections

In our dialogic thinking, these are the reflected themes that we collectively think are most influential.

1. Sharing

Sharing has been one of our most successful strategies. Information-wise, we dedicate large amounts of research process time to creating a strong shared understanding of what we are doing, both at the beginning of a process and by monitoring that shared understanding throughout the process. This includes understandings of contexts, processes, terms, roles and responsibilities, but we also share resources, networking connections, processing time, and collaborative reflection, and we often co-write. This focus on sharing is integral to our work, because it creates a network of support and makes us more capable of doing good-quality work.

Sharing results happens alongside strong co-constructed, collaborative understandings of concepts. These conceptual lenses then live in us, individually and collectively. This allows us to introduce relevant approaches and literature to support the under-served populations that we are dedicated to strengthening. Thus, our work spreads beyond our collaborations and supports our communities with broader reach.

2. Adapting based on resources and participation

Another way that makes this work more powerful is focusing on leveraging all available resources. These include expertise, time, physical and technological resources, emotional support and networking. In resource-poor environments, leveraging allows more flexibility than would otherwise be possible. Many of us are experts in one area, but not in others. By combining our expertise, we are able to see what strengths we bring to the project and how it adds value to the whole. We acknowledge and respect that there will be times when individuals will not be able to share much or even participate regularly. This allows people to step away when necessary, but still to recognise that they are welcome and encouraged to return. This might mean the restructuring of a project, a change in the timeline, or even not finishing something we have begun. By catering for changing situations and providing opportunities for adaptation in our process, we support the entirety of our collaboration.

3. Learning by doing

By applying and adapting, we gain skills, strengths and perspectives (lenses). As simple summary knowledge gets fleshed out with real-world practice, we become better at understanding how that information interrelates to make up a conceptual framework, what we currently understand, and where more learning is necessary.

We are learning skills from each other that are necessary for our profession, but were never taught. By using real work and problems to learn from, we become able to identify what we know and where the gaps are; we are able to build in directions we believe in. Many of us do not have as much experience of starting a project or building a process as others do. These tasks come with their own skill sets, which are necessary for success and for systems change, but we are seldom given places in the system to practice them. By creating projects and designing the processes that drive them, we give ourselves a low-risk place to improve ourselves as individuals within this particular group and to improve in the necessary social-emotional, organisational and administrative skills that we need to be powerful in our greater endeavours.

This learning starts as work, but, as we learn, the work gets easier and easier. We move from learning the frameworks to being able to apply the lessons and frameworks we have learnt, to working together more effectively. Additionally, we are able to take our new learning into other spaces. These new conceptual tools add to our overall abilities and expertise, making us stronger researchers and collaborators.

4. Collaborative reflection and feedback in a safe space

We have created a safe space where it is acceptable to make mistakes. We are allowed to be vulnerable with each other. This allows us to share our true perspectives and receive honest feedback from each other, knowing the person is coming from an attitude of collaboration and wanting to build a better whole. We are not trying to prove we are right or show anyone up. We are trying to combine our knowledge and expertise to develop a richer understanding of a shared goal. By reflecting together, we support each other in identifying relevant information, understanding how various influencing factors are related, and deliberating about problem-solving options. The sharing and reflection empowers us all to contribute and to create outputs better than we could alone.

5. Flat hierarchy

We are led by an in-the-moment, co-facilitated decision-making process. We collaboratively decide what we want to learn and what the lessons will be, based on our individually determined needs. People aren't assigned roles or tasks, but instead say what they are willing to do, and we link those pieces together to achieve a whole. This is successful for many reasons. First, we are a diverse group and have differing areas of expertise. Our flat hierarchy allows members to contribute their expertise where they feel it is necessary, without waiting for permission from someone else in the collaboration. Additionally, our consensus decision making affords us the ability to focus our energies on the areas we feel are most important. If we are strong in an area, we rely on our knowledge base and use that to move forward. If we identify that we need support in an area, we determine the best path forward to get that support, and then we incorporate it into our process.

Additionally, our flat hierarchy allows us to guide our project with an equity focus. We all look at our process, identifying places where there is implicit bias, systemic racism, colonial behaviour, oppression and dehumanisation, and then we collaboratively look for another solution to the same issue. We co-identify where there are places that need strengthening and support, and then work together to do the supporting.

Figure 11.1. Emerging principles for online cross-cultural, collaborative research

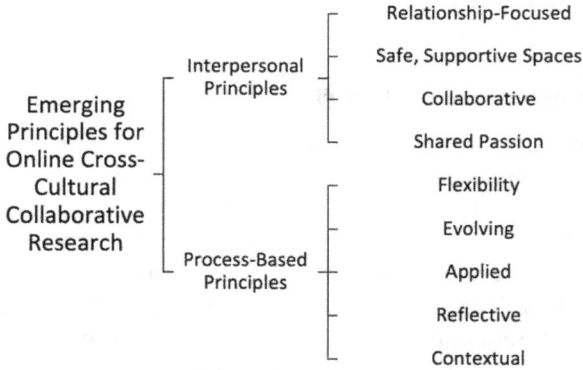

Emerging principles for online cross-cultural, collaborative research

To summarise our work and make our understanding more available to researchers trying to develop similar research groups, we have collaboratively constructed the emerging principles of this approach. These principles are synthesised ideas to frame the process of creating a similar group. The principles are presented in two categories: interpersonal principles and process-based principles (Figure11.1).

Interpersonal principles informed by our reflections

Relationship-focused: Dedicate time and energy to developing and sustaining interpersonal interactions with collaborators.

Example: We always spend the first 10–15 minutes of our meetings talking about our worlds and catching up. These conversations last longer when needed.

Safe, supportive spaces: Work to create a climate where people feel comfortable and capable, contributing to and celebrating each other's achievements. These spaces have built trust among us. Academic research is often highly competitive and can be very individualistic, with people 'climbing on the backs' of others. We have built enough trust to allow us to be vulnerable with each other, to have uncomfortable conversations, to give and receive negative feedback, and to address problems when they need to be addressed.

Example: When a suggestion is made for a research process that inadvertently goes against our shared values, we reflect and discuss how it conflicts with the values. Then we look for another solution.

Shared passion: We are all individually motivated to do the work and appreciate others' passions, which we incorporate into the work where relevant. Even if those passions are not our own, we recognise the importance of integrating them and adapting based on individuals' strengths.

Example: One member of our team brought a trauma-informed approach to our work. After discussing and engaging with the framework, other researchers felt comfortable and competent to apply the framework elsewhere.

Process-based principles informed by our reflections

Flexibility: A flexible structure allows for growth. Account for people's lives and other responsibilities when planning and doing the work. Give room for plans to change and make it easy for collaborators to support each other.

Example: Initially our meeting time was on a Friday. This made it difficult for collaborators who had to commute to their work site, so we changed the meeting day to Thursday to accommodate this need.

Evolving: Accept and embrace the fact that you need to be involved in a dynamic process which will lead to growth and change. Trust that the process will take you to good places. Dedicate time to reflect on progress and understand the directions in which you are evolving, then leverage the synergies that emerge.

Example: We began with a much more top-down, hierarchical structure, which dissolved as we reflected. Our now-flat hierarchy was a result of this evolutionary process.

Applied: Use experiential learning to practice and improve individual and collaborative skills through contributing to the group.

Example: Through hands-on collaborative practice, group members are now much more confident with research ethics reviews, interviewing and survey development.

Reflective: Use reflection as an intuitive guide to support your process. Take time to share diverse perspectives.

Example: We used reflection to come up with project design elements, group presentations, and even this chapter. Everything we do involves iterative processing and reflection.

Contextual: Be sensitive to context. Integrate contextual factors in all steps of the process.

Example: When we created our surveys, we had each person analyse how that survey would be interpreted in each collaborator's local context. We edited for local understandings of terms and phrasing, to make the survey questions more relevant and clearer.

Conclusion

Often the interpersonal and process-based principles go hand in hand, and we need to pay attention to all of these. Acknowledging that traditional research approaches to collaboration might not be productive for your group will create a flexible and equitable space for collaborators. Recentring researchers in ways that are new or initially uncomfortable may be necessary. This was especially important for us, given that we continued to work together through the pandemic and became more attuned to each other's needs, not just as individuals but as human beings.

We drew on a range of theoretical perspectives and conceptual lenses to engage in dialogic thinking and reflection to co-create our approach to online cross-cultural, collaborative research. Depending on the perspectives and lenses collaborators are drawing on, the approach and principles that are co-created may be different to ours–this is fine. Collaboration need not end once an output is complete or a project has ended. Shared reflection can result in further development and strengthen collaborations in unforeseeable ways. Let these emerge, work with them, and share your approaches with others.

References

Amundsen, D., Ballam, N. & Cosgriff, M. (2019). The ABCs of collaboration in academia. *Waikato Journal of Education, 24*(2), pp. 39-53.

Bansal, S., Mahendiratta, S., Kumar, S., Sarma, P., Prakash, A. & Medhi, B. (2019). Collaborative research in the modern era: Need and challenges. *Indian Journal of Pharmacology, 51*(3), pp. 137-139.

Beneito-Montagut, R., Begueria, A. & Cassián, N. (2017). Doing digital team ethnography: being there together and digital social data. *Qualitative Research, 17*(6), pp. 664-682.

Benson, A. & Barlow-Zambodla, A. 2018. *International Research Collaborative for Established and Emerging Scholars (IRCEES) Charter.* Internal project documentation.

Bozeman, B., Fay, D. & Slade, C. (2013). Research collaboration in universities and academic entrepreneurship: the-state-of-the-art. *Journal of Technology Transfer, 38*, pp. 1-67.

Brislin, R. W. (1976). Comparative research methodology: Cross-cultural studies. *International Journal of Psychology, 11*(3), pp. 215-229.

Contu, A. & Wilmott, H. (2003). Re-embeddings situatedness: The importance of power relations in learning theory, *Organization Science,* 14(3), pp. 283-296.

Datta, R. (2018). Decolonizing both researcher and research and its effectiveness in indigenous research. *Research Ethics, 14*(2). pp. 1-24.

Denis, J. L. & Lomas, J. (2003). Convergent evolution: The academic and policy roots of collaborative research. *Journal of Health Services Research & Policy, 8*, pp. 1-6.

Fenwick, T., Nerland, M. & Jensen, K. (2012). Sociomaterial approaches to conceptualising professional learning and practice, *Journal of Education and Work, 25*(1), pp. 1-13.

Gourlay, L. & Oliver, M. (2018). *Student Engagement in the Digital University: Sociomaterial Assemblages*. London: Routledge.

Handley, K., Sturdy, A., Fincham, R. & Clark, T. (2006). Within and beyond communities of practice: Making sense of learning through participation, identity and practice. *Journal of Management Studies, 43*(3), 641-653.

Healy, C. & Welchert, A. (1990). Mentoring relations: A definition to advance research and practice. *Educational Researcher, 19*(9):17-21.

Kim, K. J. & Bonk, C. J. (2002). Cross-cultural comparisons of online collaboration. *Journal of Computer-mediated Communication, 8*(1), JCMC814.

Kolb, D. A. (2014). *Experiential Learning: Experience as the Source of Learning and Development*. Upper Saddle River, NJ: FT Press.

Lemon, N. & Salmons, J. (2020). Collaboration and co-research. In *Reframing and Rethinking Collaboration in Higher Education and Beyond: A Practical Guide for Doctoral Students and Early Career Researchers*. London: Routledge.

Marek, L., Brock, D. & Savla, J. (2015). Evaluating collaboration for effectiveness: Conceptualization and measurement. *American Journal of Evaluation, 36*(1), 67-85.

Morris, M. W., Leung, K., Ames, D. & Lickel, B. (1999). Views from inside and outside: Integrating emic and etic insights about culture and justice judgment. *Academy of Management Review*, 24(4), pp. 781-796.

Muwanga-Zake, J.W.F. (2009). Building bridges across knowledge systems: Ubuntu and participative research paradigms in Bantu communities, *Discourse: Studies in the Cultural Politics of Education, 30*(4), pp. 413-426.

Paulus, T., Woodside, M. & Ziegler, M. (2008). Extending the conversation: Qualitative research as dialogic collaborative process. *The Qualitative Report, 13*(2), 226-243.

Payton, J. W., Wardlaw, D. M., Graczyk, P. A., Bloodworth, M. R., Tompsett, C. J. & Weissberg, R. P. (2000). Social and emotional learning: A framework for promoting mental health and reducing risk behavior in children and youth. *Journal of School Health, 70*(5), pp. 179-185.

Ritenburg, H., Leon, A. E. Y., Linds, W., Nadea, D. M., Goulet, L. M., Kovach, M. & Marshall, M. (2014). Embodying decolonization: Methodologies and indigenization. *AlterNative: An International Journal of Indigenous Peoples, 10*(1), pp. 67-80.

Seehawer, M.K. (2018). Decolonising research in a Sub-Saharan African context: Exploring Ubuntu as a foundation for research methodology, ethics and agenda, *International Journal of Social Research Methodology, 21*(4), pp. 453-466.

Spencer-Oatey, H. (2008). *Culturally speaking: Culture, Communication and Politeness Theory* (2nd ed.). London; New York: Continuum.

Substance Abuse and Mental Health Services Administration (SAMHSA). (2014). *SAMHSA's Concept of Trauma and Guidance for a Trauma-Informed Approach.* HHS Publication No. (SMA) 14-4884. Rockville, MD: SAMHSA.

Sandoval, J., Lucero, J., Oetzel, J., Avila, M., Belone, L., Mau, M., ...Wallerstein, N. (2012). Process and outcome constructs for evaluating community-based participatory research projects: A matrix of existing measures. *Health Education Research, 27*(2), pp. 680-690.

UNESCO. (2001). *UNESCO Universal Declaration on Cultural Diversity.* Paris: UNESCO.

Veenswijk, M. & Chisalita, C. M. (2007). The importance of power and ideology in communities of practice: The case of a de marginalized user interface design team in a failing multi-national design company, *Information Technology & People, 20*(1), pp. 32-52.

Wenger, E. & Wenger-Trayner, B. (2015). *Introduction to communities of practice: A brief overview of the concept and its uses.* https://wenger-trayner.com/introduction -to-communities-of-practice/

Wenger, E. (1999). *Communities of Practice: Learning, Meaning, and Identity.* Cambridge: Cambridge University Press.

Chapter 12

Participatory action research in digital storytelling: Using mobile technology to co-create social change in Kenya

Antonia Liguori

Loughborough University, United Kingdom

Daniel Onyango

Hope Raisers, Kenya

Melaneia Warwick

Loughborough University, United Kingdom

Michael Wilson

Loughborough University, United Kingdom

Abstract

This chapter reflects on the outcomes of an ongoing transnational partnership between Hope Raisers, a youth-led NGO based in Korogocho slum in Nairobi, Kenya, and the Storytelling Academy at Loughborough University in the United Kingdom (UK). A group of researchers and artists explore the value of digital storytelling as a tool for participatory action research (PAR) through an exploration of the challenges and opportunities of applying this tool to facilitate online and face-to-face conversations. The focus is around issues of global interest from a local and personal perspective. A number of case studies are discussed to demonstrate the impact of a digital storytelling mobile lab, via PAR, on a group of stakeholders including community members, Nairobi-based artists and UK-based researchers.

The case studies recount the processes of exploring hybrid forms of storytelling (digital and performative) to co-design a public event focused on waste management and to develop community-led solutions to the design of urban spaces. The methodological, social and cultural challenges faced while applying PAR approaches to facilitate the digital storytelling process are addressed. There is critical reflection on the ways in which workshop participants and other storytellers were supported in shared, collaborative and asynchronous projects from different, non-traditional learning locations. Through this, it is demonstrated that, while PAR approaches promote social justice, there are a number of ethical dilemmas to tackle and protocols to develop. In this way the authors share different ways of applying a culturally appropriate and practical PAR approach to address societal issues and create social change.

Keywords: digital storytelling, co-creation, video editing, community building, social justice, PAR, mobile technology, Kenya, United Kingdom

***

Introduction

The idea of utilising participatory action research (PAR)-based digital storytelling as a set of creative tools for the co-creation of knowledge within Kenyan communities was the original motivator for creation of a digital storytelling lab based in the Korogocho slum in Nairobi, Kenya. Over the past years, that area in particular, and Kenya as a country, have been experiencing a polarisation of opinions that has often degenerated into violence. Since its origin, Nairobi has had a long history of marginalisation and inequality: 70% of the population lives in slums that occupy only 5% of the total land area (World Bank, 2006). The growth of the slums is alarming, as witnessed in Korogocho, the fourth most populous slum in Nairobi. High densities, congestion and high unemployment characterise the area. Local issues include a scarcity of accessible and potable water, use of the area to house one of the largest dumping sites in Africa, and inadequate or absent infrastructure, education, electricity and living and community space for people (Höök et al., 2012).

As an NGO committed to community development, Hope Raisers felt that different methods were needed to try and help the community to articulate their lived experiences related to some of these challenges. They identified digital storytelling as a useful tool to expand the dialogue around sensitive issues in the area. In particular, they wanted to maximise the potential of the digital component of the digital storytelling methodology, by spreading stories via mobile phones to reach out to a larger number of people. Kenya is leading the continent in terms of smartphone penetration and internet usage, and has a 91% penetration of mobile subscriptions compared to Africa's 80%. Globally, Kenya has the highest share of internet usage from mobile phones as compared to desktops (Namunwa, 2019).

The participatory action research (PAR) approach is built around the commitment to include its participants as collaborative partners in its research processes, so that they become fully conversant with them. Co-researching is a relatively new term that sits under the PAR umbrella (Martin et al., 2019). It defines collaborations between academics and community members that involve co-production and co-creation of research processes and outputs. In this chapter we will look at such ongoing collaborations between Hope Raisers (a grassroots organisation based in the Korogocho slum in Nairobi) and the Storytelling Academy at Loughborough University in the United Kingdom (UK). By critically reflecting on our experiences and illuminating the learning that has been co-created, we aim to highlight and prioritise the value of the different knowledges and ways of thinking involved in the co-developed research processes. We will reflect on this through the lens of technology and its role in supporting researchers from the UK and communities from Kenya in processes of interrogation of local and global issues, knowledge production and critical imagination.

New funding programmes, such as the UK Arts and Humanities Research Council Connected Communities Programme (started in 2011), and the more recent Global Challenges Research Fund (GCRF, started in 2015), have enabled a fundamental shift in power dynamics within collaborative research processes. These new funding opportunities have paved a new way for academic researchers to begin working collaboratively with communities within the UK and across the globe. This involves recognising selected or self-selecting communities as repositories of local knowledge, and recasting them as co-researchers, co-creators and co-producers of research (Facer & Enright, 2016). The GCRF was launched to "support cutting-edge research that addresses the challenges faced by developing countries [and] promote challenge-led disciplinary and interdisciplinary research".[1] It enabled Loughborough University's storytelling research team to meet and start working with artists, activists and project managers from Hope Raisers.

The term 'community' is used in four different ways within the context of the case studies in this chapter. Firstly, communities are situated within a shared geographical area that may vary in scale, depending on whether they are a subsection of a slum, such as Bega kwa Bega in Korogocho, or a particular area of a city such as downtown Nairobi. Secondly, the community speaks to its members–those participants who fit the relevant inclusion criteria within the ethical protocols developed. They have either self-selected into the project

---

[1] GCRF forms part of the UK's Official Development Assistance (ODA) commitment, which is monitored by the Organisation for Economic Cooperation and Development (OECD). See https://www.ukri.org/research/global-challenges-research-fund/

community, through a process of expressing interest after a recruitment drive, or have been initially identified by community leaders, teachers and organisers and agreed to participate. Additionally, we draw on the notion of communities of practice (CoPs), which we understand to mean a group of people who share a common concern, a set of problems, or an interest in a topic, and who come together to fulfill both individual and group goals (Wenger-Trayner et al., 2014). Critical to this category is an allegiance to three characteristics: a shared domain or point of interest; the community itself, where people interact and learn together; and shared experiences, stories or tools. In each of the case studies described, the CoP consisted of a selected group of academics, community leaders and change makers, community members and research partners. The CoP mapped knowledge, identified gaps and set out ways forward by investigating "who knows what and what are we missing?" (Wenger, 2015, p. 3). Finally, community development is perceived as that which adds value to the community and the CoP. It may create breakthrough ideas, new knowledge, and new practices, and develop and disseminate best practices, guidelines, and strategies for their members' use (Banks et al., 2019).

Ethical considerations had a large part to play in developing and conducting the case studies outlined in this chapter. In order to adhere to ethical protocols and approvals, involved conversations took place with community partners. These included considerations of the most appropriate methodologies and tools to apply to the projects, and community partners guided the UK team on what would work best in the field. In coming to viable approaches, we drew on local expertise and knowledge around cultural appropriateness, technical and other literacies, safety, risks, and the likelihood that community members would engage.

While it is true that new technologies can "visualize, validate, and transform social inequalities" (Akom et al., 2016, p. 1287), digital tools were carefully considered as they presented a possible barrier to participants developing digital storytelling literacy. The cloud-based software we chose to train our participants needed only the level of technological literacy used to operate a mobile phone–something that we first ensured all potential participants were able to do, via our recruitment processes. In addition, we ensured that there were enough Kiswahili-speaking facilitators available to offer training and support if needed.

Ethical protocols were co-developed for each of the case studies discussed, as part of the Loughborough University ethical approval process. Project partners advised on the best ways to recruit participants, including whether translations were required or whether other models of ensuring understanding were needed. Ethical consent did not stop at the important form- filling stage, however–it was treated as a sustained and situated concern, where the local environment enabled the team to develop contextualised decisions as needed, in order to build and maintain trust (Warwick, 2015).

We do not want to suggest that there have been no challenges in the co-researching process, or that the positive outcomes here necessarily represent the norm. In fact, from the analysis of previous experiences of research collaborations and partnerships relevant to the field of global development, it has been acknowledged that GCRF criteria do address many of the familiar historic concerns of African partners, while also potentially reproducing structural inequities within the South (Grieve & Mitchell, 2020). When it comes to participation in international research collaborations (Mitchell et al., 2018; Rose et al., 2019), evidence from recent studies in the African education space clearly presents the challenges faced by 'emerging' African institutions which lack an international profile, in terms of gaining access to valued international partnerships. Nevertheless, our experience is an insightful demonstration of how a shared interest in a specific methodology, delivered through community-led and context- tailored approaches such as digital storytelling, can overcome, if not annul, some of the difficulties of the current UK–Africa co-researching context.

Methodology–PAR in digital storytelling as a tool for community development

"Our lives and our cultures are composed of a series of overlapping stories, if we hear only a single story about another person, culture, or country, we risk a critical misunderstanding". – Chimamanda Ngozi Adichie, 'The danger of a single story', TED talk, 7 October 2009

The PAR approach emerged in the late 1990s, where it had an ideological link to research related to marginalised people (Kemmis & McTaggart, 2005, p. 273): "participatory research has long held within its implicit notions of the relationships between power and knowledge" (Gaventa & Cornwall, 2001, p. 70). It was informed by the traditions of participatory research and the destabilisation of traditional hierarchies of knowledge by action research, but differed from action research by its desire to focus on better understanding of particular contexts and populations (Kemmis & McTaggart, 2005, pp. 272-284). PAR was aligned to arts-based and inclusive research practices in its change-making concerns–contrary to action research, that is not always focused on the flattening of power structures in research relationships (Schostak & Schostak, 2008; Kemmis & McTaggart, 2005, pp. 292-293).

Imperatives related to access are also found in the intent of PAR; it is built around the commitment to include its participants as collaborative partners in its research processes, so that they become fully conversant with them. By placing the site of expertise with these populations, it acknowledges and seeks to give voice to the tacit knowledge they hold. In short, PAR has an emancipatory goal, that is realised by engaging a community and putting social change in the hands of the research participants. This adjustment of traditional research roles can place knowledge creation and the sharing of research findings on participants, and this can present interesting challenges in the tensions between group problem solving and leadership, shared power, and facilitation.

When approaching digital storytelling within PAR as a core methodology for community-led projects, we think about 'technology affordance' as a way to refer to change-making strategies that might not have been possible without digital technologies (Chan & Sage, 2019). e-PAR approaches have evolved to enable young people to critically research their worlds and develop active strategies for change via a wide range of digital tools and technologies, such as the internet, photography, video and music production software (Flicker et al., 2008). e-PAR approaches have been used effectively as a co-researching strategy that makes the most of the familiar through the technological fluency which young people have attained, by providing them "with the freedom to see and express their worlds using new and familiar creative technologies" (Flicker et al., p. 289).

In our case studies, we drew on technological approaches and made use of a range of communication tools for PAR in order to engage young people in community action. We also used these approaches with older participants, but in more supported ways that would enable them to access the technology at their own pace. One example here was the inclusion of extra facilitators to provide one-to-one assistance where needed.

The self-reflective and creative process defined as digital storytelling was first developed and applied in the San Francisco Bay area at the Center for Digital Storytelling, today StoryCenter (see www.storycenter.org). The original process (Lambert, 2013; Lambert & Hessler, 2018) includes five activities for a standard digital storytelling workshop: story-circle, script writing, audio recording, video editing, screening. These activities require, where possible, connection to the internet and the use of various software and hardware in different phases, such as programs for audio and video editing installed on computers, phones or tablets; audio recorders; and video cameras. The team involved in the case studies were open to adjusting the process and the use of technology as needed. This happened to suit different environments and local needs (Liguori & Bakewell, 2019).

In previous experiences, digital storytelling has revealed its potential to bring new voices into public debate (Constant & Roberts, 2017; Goldstein et al., 2013; Liguori et al., 2021; Valentine & Sadgrove, 2014), as stories facilitate the sharing of memories and knowledge in order to directly impact a particular life

(Polkinghorne, 1988). Stories can generate empathy and trust in the audience, and at the same time demonstrate their usefulness, because they "have the power to give meaning to human behaviors and to trigger emotions" (Bourbonnais & Michaud, 2018, p. 1). This happens because stories may be perceived as vectors of truth, and therefore have the potential to bridge the micro-macro divide by creating the opportunity to produce counter-narratives, both at the individual and broader community levels (Mattaini & Huffman-Gottschling, 2012; Roscoe et al., 2011; Vodde & Gallant, 2002). As discussed above, this bridging is often facilitated and expanded through the use of digital technology. Critically, the use of digital storytelling can enhance participants' capacities for self-representation and agency (micro-level outcomes), and can produce counter-narratives at a broader community level (macro-level outcomes), especially when shared in the digital realm (Chan & Sage; 2019).

By proposing digital storytelling as a social process for community development, during which each storyteller and each story-listener has an active role, we argue that digital stories convey various understandings of facts with social interest, and stimulate a shared and communal 'holistic thinking' (Meadows & Kidd, 2009) of the world around us. PAR, and within it co-researching, has offered us the tools to understand the existence of multiple truths, and to recognise the importance of what Nigerian novelist Chimamanda Ngozi Adichie described as "the danger of a single story" (Adichie, 2009). Only by consistently reminding ourselves to apply those tools alongside a process of honest reflexivity, is it possible to avoid 'critical misunderstandings' of the environment in which we work. Additionally, as we are utilising digital technologies to enhance the narrative process at individual level, and the production of alternative stories at community level, we are keen to explore how grassroots knowledge is unlocked in the co-creative process (Liguori, 2020). We also seek to analyse the potential impact and implications of 'sharing' the digital output online from a variety of perspectives.

Case studies

CMiiST

The GCRF project 'Creative Methodologies to Investigate Sustainable Transport' (CMiiST)[2] was the beginning of the ongoing collaboration between the team at Loughborough University and Hope Raisers. Over three years we co-developed a number of community-led initiatives, and delivered impact in terms of global visibility of the outputs produced locally. CMiiST was a cross-disciplinary and

---

[2] See https://cmiist.wordpress.com/

cross-institutional network, funded by the Arts and Humanities Research Council and led by the Stockholm Environment Institute, University of York, UK. The main ambition was to create an equitable partnership that could work through creative methodologies to co-design responses to questions of sustainable transport in Nairobi (Kenya) and Kampala (Uganda).

Loughborough University ran an agenda-setting workshop in Nairobi in April 2017, that led to a follow-on opportunity of collaboration. The project was funded through the British Academy GCRF Cities and Infrastructures Programme. It aimed to inform transport professionals on how inclusive transport could be achieved. Creative methods used included urban dialogues, where the city planners and dwellers came together to discuss their mobility options, participatory mapping (PGIS) and Minecraft design, among others. Hope Raisers and Loughborough University worked with local stakeholders in Nairobi to create a series of arts-led workshops and digital storytelling activities designed to raise awareness of transport issues, and to engage the community in a public conversation around possible ways forward to address the situation. In addition, the project team ran creative photography events, such as researcher training in the utility of wearable cameras as a data collection tool (Warwick, 2020), and photography hangouts to reimagine urban locations.

My Mark: My City

The first project run through the new Hope Raisers' mobile digital storytelling lab was 'My Mark: My City', a UN Live-led initiative. This project addressed local community members' views on the future of the Dandora dumping site which straddles the Korogocho slum. This 30-acre site holds 850 tonnes of solid waste, and despite being declared full in 2001, is still in operation. The My Mark: My City initiative was launched worldwide in 2019 by UN Live, the Museum for the United Nations. UN Live's ambition is to dramatically increase the number of people who are actively working on global challenges. The museum, which is currently focusing on digital engagement activities, was established as an independent non-governmental organisation based in Denmark, with a cooperation agreement with the UN. Instead of just inhabiting a building, UN Live will be a global, bottom-up platform which meets people at eye-level. The pilot initiative was conceived to explore how cities will look in 1 year, 10 years', and 100 years' time.

The collaboration with UN Live in September 2019 gave Hope Raisers and Loughborough University the opportunity to co-design a digital storytelling workshop and a public event to tackle issues related to climate change. Hope Raisers organised discussions with 10 local community leaders, through which it emerged that local concerns were particularly linked to the impact of the Dandora dumpsite on the slum dwellers' daily life. We anticipated that community members would want to share their views on the visible environmental and health impacts of the dumpsite, such as air pollution, fire, violence and occupational disease. We were also interested in establishing what potential impacts community members might perceive. The main idea behind this collaboration was to use the new mobile digital storytelling lab to co-design a public forum for storytelling as part of a 3-day workshop, and from this to publish community members' stories online.

Digital stories were created as a tool to assist the community to find possible solutions for the future management and potential transformation of the dumpsite in the next 10 years. These stories gave voice to various perspectives and highlighted emerging conflicting views between those who recognised the financial benefits of working illegally at the dumpsite, and those who strongly complained about the negative impact on their health and security. To unfold the motivations behind those opposite perceptions and identify possible ways forward, the research team from Loughborough proposed to adapt and reframe a traditional form for conflict resolution from Sardinia, Italy, called 'The Reasons', and used for community reconciliation (Bakewell et al., 2018).

In Korogocho the public event was designed as a mock court, where nine workshop participants acted as storytellers and were asked to voice their very different stories on the effect of the dumpsite. The youngest of the storytellers acted as a judge, embracing the role of a visionary, moderator and community inspirator. Over 100 community members were in the audience; 10 of them were chosen by the judge to be part of a jury that helped the judge in framing a 'verdict' that could offer a conciliatory view on the possible future use(s) of the dumpsite. A songwriter and two musicians were also involved in the creative process, and in the public event to compose a community song that could embed all the individual stories.

My Mark: My City developed a hybrid approach to storytelling that drew on both digital storytelling and face-to-face performance. It also gave the opportunity to explore how and at which stage the two different methods supported the community, to expose and address their sometimes conflicting perspectives, interests and priorities. In the post-event evaluation, the feedback from the community illuminated their ambition to create lasting environmental change. They proposed to upscale this type of creative debate, enhanced via Hope Raisers through digital storytelling, to take a step forward in terms of community action for change. In particular, they suggested engaging with the relevant change-making authorities to follow up on some of the recommendations elaborated through their digital stories and during the public storytelling event. Those recommendations included a deeper understanding of the Korogocho community's vulnerability to climate change, and greater consideration of indigenous knowledge to build community resilience and inform climate mitigation strategies. Community members also expressed their desire to see more young local practitioners trained to deliver the creative methods applied, to make participation more effective and sustainable in the long term.

Future Yetu

The Future Yetu (Our Future) project showcased Hope Raisers' technical and methodological development in their partnership with Loughborough University, as well as an opportunity for them to influence policy making. Future Yetu was funded by Cities Alliance in the Spring of 2020 under the 'Local Innovations for New Climate Realities in Cities' programme; it is coordinated by Hope Raisers and includes a member of the Loughborough University team on the steering committee. The project activity started at the end of July 2020, with the aim of positioning digital storytelling as a creative methodology for dialogue between community and local government. This was with the aim of informing a climate adaptation plan at city and county level. The digital storytelling methodology has been applied as a tool to enhance the capacity of Korogocho and its neighbourhood community to anticipate and plan for adequate livelihoods, and to become more resilient to shocks and stresses triggered by climate-related hazards.

Future Yetu has adopted a two-fold approach to ensure the sustainability of the project initiatives. At first edutainment programmes (such as digital storytelling, screening climate change adaptation films, community outreach and a moving exhibition on privately owned minibuses called *matatu*) were developed to reach a large number of communities within a given year, so that the cost per community would decrease as opposed to serving few communities in a given year. Afterwards, relationships with local communities and the Nairobi metropolitan service environment department were built, to maximise the impact and sustainability of the initiative.

Twelve local young volunteers were trained in the digital storytelling practice, and have been delivering workshops within the community and with Nairobi county government officials, to develop stories and dialogue around climate adaptation strategies. The main challenge was the perception of the person-centred digital storytelling approach that some participants had, during a workshop[3] in which two classes (community members from informal settlements and county officials) were asked to socialise, dialogue and co-create stories, despite existing power dynamics within the group: a few felt uncomfortable, and somebody even expressed disdain.

---

[3] Video documentation of the workshop is available here: https://youtu.be/jy6eFnkXAKM

Yet the fact that Hope Raisers was successful in leading a bid that will expand on work originally co-designed with the Loughborough University team offers interesting insights into the dynamics within this partnership. Only three years after their first engagement in a digital storytelling workshop with Loughborough University, Hope Raisers are envisioning the ways forward for their community. This shift in leadership is a highly desirable legacy from this collaboration, but also a clear demonstration of the validity of the digital storytelling methodology, when co-designed with its 'beneficiaries' and tailored to the context, both in terms of culture and infrastructure.

Discussion

Setting up a mobile digital storytelling lab that gives community members access to tablets and easy-to-use mobile applications for audio recording and video editing made the creative and participatory approaches described in these case studies even more accessible. The challenge is that there is more demand for use of this portable technology than Hope Raisers can offer with the technological support currently available. Furthermore, in the informal settlements the risk of possible burglary or the security of the equipment is perceived by some community members as a barrier to their desire to be involved in the process and work with that technology, if they are asked to keep those tools with them for a relatively long time. This raises issues in terms of how workshop facilitation is set up and managed during the creation of digital stories. We have concluded that removing equipment to a safe overnight location is a daily practice worth undertaking.

There were a number of shared, key learnings that emerged from the running of the projects discussed. While the majority of participants had access to mobile technology, there was often a low level of digital literacy among the elderly and some of the women. We were working with mixed groups, where participants were progressing at a different pace, depending on their IT skills. Some felt intimidated during their first encounter with a tablet, but their interest in sharing their stories and the feeling of being empowered by that process diminished initial barriers. Indeed, mutual learning among members of the same community proved to be the most effective way of transferring information on how to use technology from younger to older generations. It represented a natural solution for technical knowledge transfer, over having English-speaking 'experts' in digital storytelling trying to overcome the language barriers, while demonstrating the steps to create digital stories. In this way, the local digital storytelling expertise of Hope Raisers enabled both Swahili and tribal languages like Luo to be the lingua franca of the workshops, making participants feel at ease more quickly and feel that they were owners of the research process.

These different levels of digital literacy could suggest working with more homogenous groups, where participants would work at the same pace, without feeling frustrated by their need for step-by-step guidance. The effectiveness of peer learning in the cases discussed has proved that digital storytelling can also facilitate the intergenerational passing of knowledge and skills, while storytellers are expressing themselves and the creative process is enabling dialogue. Both factors need to be considered while designing a workshop, and facilitators should choose how to balance these, depending on the most achievable and desired goal in each specific context.

Another challenge was the fact that the culture of sharing personal stories on a digital platform was new to the slum community, where often community members are afraid to be overexposed online and of possibly being victimised or bullied. Even if the use of technology is appealing to them, careful consideration is required to make storytellers aware of the implications of sharing their videos online. We have found that additional training opportunities for local workshop facilitators were necessary, to address those issues that go beyond the technical delivery of the workshop.

In our work, the fact that community members in the slum started to experience the power of using simple technology to share their story, made them realise that they did not have to wait for a journalist or a media expert to make their stories more visible. In fact, their main take-away message was that through storytelling they have the tools to organise themselves, debate, reconcile conflicting views, and potentially mobilise the whole community.

Conclusion

Applying digital storytelling as a tool to co-design PAR projects to address global challenges revealed the potential for researchers and NGOs to use simple technology to share education content with the community, and for the people involved in the process to have the opportunity to enhance their self-confidence. This approach also manifested multiple transitions in terms of power dynamics: the first one was discussed during some of the workshops, when community members realised that digital storytelling was offering them a tool for more effective and meaningful public participation, in particular by sharing their stories digitally. Although participation is extensively provided in the Kenyan Constitution, through a process of devolution, communities are not yet empowered to exchange views and influence decision-making. Digital storytelling could potentially offer the platform for a concrete shift in that direction.

The second transition has become tangible in the change of leadership within the co-researching team, when the Future Yetu project was awarded to Hope

Raisers. Reflecting on both those transitions, the biggest lesson learned by the researchers and the artists and activists involved in the process is that, if we are looking for solutions regarding some societal challenges, these solutions are within the communities. It is important to understand that they are the ones providing knowledge: they are not the beneficiaries–as a funding organisation would think–but are key in feeding up ideas with their knowledge. Digital storytelling offered a platform to reinforce even more the fact that the community remains the inspiration for and the owners of local knowledge.

The creative process experienced with those local communities undoubtedly put the story in their hands, generating self-advocacy and community advocacy as the most powerful result. While setting up the digital storytelling lab in one of the biggest slums in Nairobi, we have witnessed competing and often hidden interests to either eliminate or keep slums in their current state. The growing diffusion of mobile devices offers an unprecedented opportunity to empower local communities through new, creative ways of using technology. This can occur despite the challenges in terms of infrastructure, such as the cost of equipment, an often inefficient and expensive internet connection, and digital literacy.

Looking forward, an additional opportunity for grassroots organisations arises also from the current transformation of the education system in Kenya. Hope Raisers' ambition for the near future is to connect their community-led projects with formal education, and use their digital storytelling mobile lab as an opportunity to embed experiential knowledge into formal learning processes. Yet to achieve that, there is a challenge not yet addressed: to expand their current range of actions and projects (both in terms of technology, and to extend their interventions to other areas of Kenya), local Nairobi-based NGOs would need more equipment and more training opportunities. In particular, what is required is to increase the professional capacity of their staff and volunteers to work in a context that requires skills that go beyond technical abilities.

One of the defining characteristics of our research process was the nature of the collaboration between the research partners: a group of researchers from a leading UK research-intensive university and an NGO founded by young artists and activists from an informal settlement in Nairobi. One of the key learning points that emerged from this collaboration was the value of a partnership involving very different kinds of organisations, which acted as a catalyst for mutual learning. While the Loughborough team contributed academic and practical expertise in applied storytelling, Hope Raisers brought expertise in the lived experiences of the Korogocho community, as well as considerable experience of working within that context and achieving impactful outcomes.

It was exactly the differences in the skills that each partner brought to the project that enabled us to learn from each other, and to challenge our own learned orthodoxies. The necessary starting point was a mutual respect for each other's expertise and knowledge, whether acquired through a background in university research or gained through a life lived in the Nairobi slums. In this way, the collaboration required us to think differently–and for that, we certainly owe each other a debt of gratitude.

References

Akom, A., Shah, A., Nakai, A. & Cruz, T. (2016). Youth Participatory Action Research (YPAR) 2.0: how technological innovation and digital organizing sparked a food revolution in East Oakland. *International Journal of Qualitative Studies in Education,* 29(10), pp. 1287–1307).

Banks, S., Hart, A., Pahl, K. & Ward, P. (2019). *Co-producing research: A community development approach.* Bristol: Policy Press.

Bakewell, L., Liguori, A. & Wilson, M. (2018). From Gallura to the Fens: Communities performing stories of water. In L. Roberts & K. Phillips (Ed.), *Water, Creativity and Meaning: Multidisciplinary Approaches to Human Water Relationships.* London: Earthscan, Routledge.

Bourbonnais, A. & Michaud, C. (2018). Once upon a time: Storytelling as a knowledge translation strategy for qualitative researchers. *Nursing Inquiry,* 25(4), pp. 1-7. https://doi.org/10.1111/nin.12249

Chan, C. & Sage, M. (2019). A narrative review of digital storytelling for social work practice. *Journal of Social Work Practice,* 35(1), pp. 63-77. doi: 10.1080/02650533.2019.1692804

Constant, N. & Roberts, E. (2017). Narratives as a mode of research evaluation in citizen science: Understanding broader science communication impacts. *Journal of Science Communication,* 16(4), pp. 1-18.

Facer, K., & Enright, B. (2016). Creating Living Knowledge: The Connected Communities Programme. *Community-University Partnerships and the Participatory Turn in the Production of Knowledge, Arts and Humanities.* Bristol: Research Council.

Flicker, S., Oonagh Maley, C., Ridgley, A., Biscope, S., Lombardo, C. & Harvey, C. (2008). e-PAR Using technology and participatory action research to engage youth in health promotion. *Action Research,* 6(3), pp. 285-303.

Gaventa, J. & Cornwall, A. (2001). Power and Knowledge. In P. Reason & H. Bradbury (Ed.), *Handbook of Action Research: Participative Inquiry and Practice.* London: Sage.

Goldstein, B., Wessells, A., Lejano, R. & Butler, W. (2013). Narrating resilience: Transforming urban systems through collaborative storytelling. *Urban Studies,* 52(7), pp. 1285-1303.

Grieve, T. & Mitchell, R. (2020). Promoting meaningful and equitable relationships? Exploring the UK's Global Challenges Research Fund (GCRF) funding criteria from the perspectives of African partners. *European Journal of Development Research,* 32, pp. 514-528. doi: 10.1057/s41287-020-00274-z

Höök, M., Jonsson, P., Skottke, E., & Thelandersson, M. (2012). *Korogocho streetscapes: Documenting the role and potentials of streets in citywide slum upgrading.* Nairobi: UN Habitat.

Kemmis, S. & McTaggart, R. (2005). Participatory action research: Communicative action and the public sphere. In N. K. Denzin & Y. S. Lincoln (Eds.), *The Sage handbook of qualitative research,* pp. 559-603). Thousand Oaks, CA: Sage Publications Ltd.

Lambert J. (2013.) *Digital Storytelling.* New York: Routledge.

Lambert, J. & Hessler, H. B. (2018). *Digital storytelling: Capturing lives, creating community* (5th ed.). London: Taylor and Francis.

Liguori, A. & Bakewell, L. (2019). *Digital storytelling in cultural and heritage education: A pilot study as part of the 'DICHE' project.* Loughborough University. https://hdl.handle.net/2134/38037

Liguori, A. (2020). Unlocking contested stories and grassroots knowledge. In P. P. Trifonas (Ed.), *Handbook of Theory and Research in Cultural Studies and Education,* pp. 465-479. Cham: Springer. doi: 10.1007/978-3-319-56988-8_35.

Liguori, A., McEwen, L., Blake, J. & Wilson, M. (2021). Towards 'Creative participatory science': Exploring future scenarios through specialist drought science and community storytelling. front. Environmental Science, 8, 589856. doi: 10.3389/fenvs.2020.589856

Martin, S. B., Burbach, J. H., Benitez, L. L. & Ramiz, I. (2019). Participatory action research and co-researching as a tool for situating youth knowledge at the centre of research. *London Review of Education,* 17(3), pp. 297-313.

Mattaini, M. A. & Huffman-Gottschling, K. (2012). Ecosystems theory. In B. A. Thyer, K. M. Sowers & C. N. Dulmus (Eds.), *Human behavior in the social environment theories for social work practice,* pp. 297-325. Hoboken, NJ: Wiley.

Mitchell, R., Asare, S. & Rose, P. (2018). *Equity in international research collaborations: Evidence from the African Education Research Database.* Cambridge Global Challenges Annual Conference. https://www.educ.cam.ac.uk/centres/real/downloads/GCRF%20annual%20conference%20(Mitchell%20Asare%20Rose%202018).pdf. Accessed 27 July 2020.

Namunwa, K. (2019). Kenya leads Africa in smartphone useage. *Business Today.* https://businesstoday.co.ke/kenya-leads-africa-smartphone-usage/

Polkinghorne, D. E. (1988). Narrative Knowing and the Human Sciences. Albany: State University of New York Press.

Roscoe, K. D., Carson, A. M. & Madoc-Jones, L. (2011). Narrative social work: Conversations between theory and practice. *Journal of Social Work Practice,* 25, pp. 47-61.

Rose, P., Downing, P., Asare, S. & Mitchell, R. (2019). *Mapping the landscape of education research by scholars based in sub-Saharan Africa: Insights from the African Education Research Database.* Cambridge: REAL Centre, University of Cambridge. doi: 10.5281/zenodo.3242314.

Schostak, J. & Schostak, J. (2008). *Radical Research. Designing, Developing and Writing Research to Make a Difference.* Oxon: Routledge.

Valentine, G. & Sadgrove, J. (2014). Biographical Narratives of Encounter: The significance of mobility and emplacement in shaping attitudes towards difference. *Urban Studies,* 51(9), pp. 1979-1994.

Vodde, R. & Gallant, J. P. (2002). 'Bridging the gap between micro and macro practice: Large scale change and a unified model of narrative-deconstructive practice'. *Journal of Social Work Education*, 38, pp. 439-458.

Warwick, M. (2015). Shaping an NHS ethics application for research with people with profound and multiple learning disabilities: Creative strategies from a participatory arts practice. Journal of Arts and Communities, 7(3), pp. 167-176.

Warwick, M. (2020) 'Shifting the gaze: The use of wearable cameras in research', in M. Nind & I. Strnadová (Eds.). *Belonging for Individuals with Profound and Multiple Learning Difficulties: Pushing the Boundaries of Inclusion*. London: Routledge.

Wenger-Trayner, E., Fenton-O'Creevy, M., Kubiak, C., Hutchinson, S. & Wenger-Trayner, B. (Eds). (2014). *Learning in Landscapes of Practice: Boundaries, identity, and knowledgeability in practice-based learning*. Abingdon: Routledge. http://www.routledge.com/books/details/97811380221...

World Bank. (2006). *Kenya Inside Informality: Poverty, Jobs, Housing and Services in Nairobi's Slums*. Water and Urban Unit 1, Africa Region. Report No. 36347-KE. Nairobi: Word Bank.

Chapter 13

Understanding our complicity: Reflections on an international collaboration

Daniela Gachago

University of Cape Town, South Africa

Mark Dunford

Digitales, Goldsmiths College, University of London, United Kingdom

Abstract

In this chapter we reflect on an international project funded by the South African National Research Foundation and the British Council that brought together 36 early-career researchers and practitioners from South Africa and the UK for a three-day research workshop held near Cape Town. As part of the steering committee of the project, our ambition was to explore commonalities and differences in access to higher education, achievement within it, and success after graduation for students from marginalised or disempowered communities. The project, part of the Newton Researcher Links Grants, entitled Widening Access and Success in Higher Education (WISH), focused on the arts and the creative industries. We adopted an active design process, where ideas could be identified, explored and contested. Using the established Open Space methodology, we set up spaces for participants to identify and interrogate research questions, so as to establish a sustainable opportunity for future research collaborations. Our group had to navigate differences in terms of power dynamics that come with race and gender, academic or institutional hierarchies, geographical differences, disciplines, and those between academics and practitioners. Using the Theory of Change as a means to structure our chapter, we reflect on the process and various strategies employed in this workshop. This included setting up online pre-workshop spaces for participants to meet, the importance of external facilitation, the complexity of working with a large group, and difficulties in establishing spaces where power could be held to account. We conclude by exploring our own learning and considering how the diverse cohort helped us challenge our preconceptions, habits and beliefs.

Keywords: Open Space methodology, online collaboration, online dialogue, international academic collaboration, transformative learning, theory of change, arts and creative industries, South Africa, United Kingdom

***

Introduction

Looking back on her experiences in an intercontinental research project, Leona Vaughn (2020, n.p.) considered that:

> *This journey has been one of mutual learning – no single one of us had all the answers to how we guarded against power imbalances.*

> *Instead we acknowledged them as they appeared, big and small, discussed them with empathy and worked through how to change the dynamic.*

> *Constantly.*

> *That was the biggest lesson about properly ethical and anti-colonial work. We have to keep actively doing it.*

> *Even when it's uncomfortable or outside of our professional cultural norms and traditions.*

Widening Access and Success in Higher Education (WISH) was funded by the British Council's Newton Researcher Links Grants and the South African National Research Foundation (NRF), bringing together 36 academics and practitioners from the United Kingdom (UK) and South Africa (SA) to address issues of student access to higher education and success within their studies and employability. The programme culminated in a three-day workshop held near Cape Town in October 2017. A mix of participants from different countries and disciplines engaging with difficult concepts created opportunities for growth–but also revealed fault-lines and triggered conflict. As part of the steering committee of this project, we shared many of Vaughn's (2020) sentiments. We also experienced a distance between aspiration and the reality of what could be achieved across a complex, dynamic and time-limited project, similar to other authors' experiences in North-South collaborations (see for example Boughey & McKenna, 2021). In this chapter, we reflect on and interrogate these complexities, and use our experiences to offer lessons that others undertaking comparable work may find valuable.

Theory of Change

Our chapter makes critical use of the Theory of Change (ToC) (O'Flynn & Moberly, 2017) approach to project planning and evaluation, as a means to structure an interrogation of WISH. ToC is an iterative and open methodology and is frequently used as a framework for project evaluation (Davies, 2018). ToC helps in the analysis of project goals, and allows diagnostic exploration of how its participants are served by the processes used and actions taken. ToC as a methodological tool is process-driven, which, in principle, enables assumptions and theories to be made explicit and built into a cycle of understanding (Nkawe, 2013). Ashton (2007, p. 42) defines ToC as "the implicit assumptions held by practitioners and participants about why the activities they choose for addressing a particular problem will work".

Working backwards from goals defined at the outset, ToC provides the means to understand assumptions and explore the efficacy of particular interventions, and to see how–or indeed if–they contributed to the achievement of the overall aim. This allows "a diagnostic lens through which to view implementation in order to illuminate the connections of successive step-by-step results to final results, thus filling in the black box" (Ashton, 2007, p. 43), as shown in Figure 13.1 below.

Figure 13.1: Theory of Change steps (O'Flynn & Moberly, 2017, p. 1)

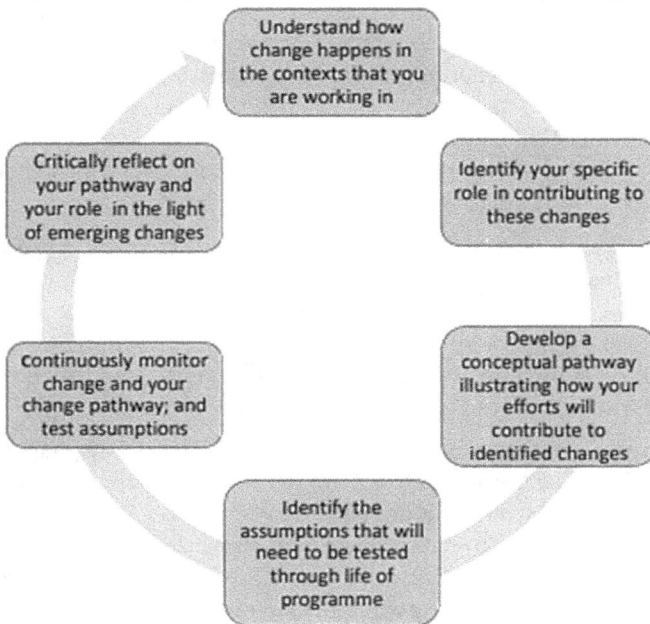

The ToC is pliable; it allows different entry-points into the process, hence, it offers scope for us to draw on a range of evidence gathered during WISH, and our own personal reflections. Nkwake (2013, p. 167) notes that the ToC allows programme designers to understand assumptions, by creating scope to articulate clear questions, that can be translated into observable measures and outcomes that can be reviewed and interpreted. This approach allows us to ask: what, if anything changed as part of WISH, and to explore the significance of any changes. It allows us to understand whether the goals of WISH were achievable or just too aspirational; if we worked with the right people; and what, if anything, we would do differently if we implemented the project time again. It also permits reflection on the limitations of our own influence, and positioning of our work in the wider dynamics of change happening across higher education (HE) in the UK and SA.

Temporary distance creates scope for reflection, but it also means that perceptions may change and memories fade. We mitigated this by drawing on our past and contemporary reflections and collaborating on this chapter over a long period. While we have spoken to others who were at the workshop, and been guided by their feedback and recollections, we recognise that this is a partial and subjective reflection. We acknowledge that other project members might have different opinions and recollections of the project; another combination of authors from the project could have produced different opinions in their reflections and in fact some have already done so, as in the case of a documentary completed by a filmmaker who attended the workshop as an evaluator, and to capture the workshop experiences as required by the NRF/British Council (Nava, 2020). Freeman (2010) stresses the importance of hindsight as not being only "about memory, but also about narrative", and has a process of both generating and interrogating a narrative, which enables one to gain perspective on decisions taken.

The ToC operates as a critical, structural device which highlights our biases. Thus, it creates opportunities for fuller evaluation which recognises both the human dimensions (such as our biases) of the project and the unique elements within it, enabling us to address complex questions. The boundaries of the ToC are limited by authorship: it is the author who frames, shapes and asks the questions; who decides the order and limits of the discussion.

This chapter presents our personal reflections, manifestly shaped by our identities. Based in the UK and SA, we are white, European academics of different genders drawing on our privilege. We shared a draft of our chapter with other participants, to receive feedback and reveal some of our blind spots. We recognise that our account comes from a position of the organising team. And as a result it is limited, partial and subjective, and is a view that invites others to respond, challenge and tell another story.

Theory of Change steps

Our approach follows a modified version of the six steps of the ToC model in which we explore:

1. Our role in addressing change within the specific and radically different contexts in which we were working in the project

2. How change happens within HE contexts

3. The conceptual pathways we took to achieve change in the project

4. The assumptions, expectations and design principles which framed the project

5. How we tested assumptions through monitoring and evaluation of the range of activities within and after WISH

6. Reflections on project process and implementation

Step 1: Identifying our role and understanding the contexts within which the project was implemented

Like many academic collaborations, WISH grew from long-standing professional connections, in this case between academics based at the University of East London (UEL) in the UK and Cape Peninsula University of Technology (CPUT) in SA. We shared a research interest around digital storytelling for social justice, complemented by the commitment of each institution to widen access to and success in HE. A call from the NRF/British Council under the Newton Researcher Links Grants for proposals for workshops to bring early-career researchers (ECRs) from the UK and SA together, provided an opportunity to further develop our research, establish new networks and build collaborative ideas for new projects. Our proposal sought to bring together researchers, educators, students, practitioners, employers and policymakers from the UK and SA to explore practical and implementable ways of supporting access, participation, success and employability (APSE) of diverse students, within and beyond the creative industries in Higher Education.

Both institutions were working to address APSE among underrepresented and/or disadvantaged groups in HE and the labour market. Our particular concerns centred on recruitment, academic progression and post-graduation employment opportunities: low participation in HE, underachievement during studies and low success rates due to poor employment opportunities, and adverse social and economic development. WISH sought to break the cycle by focusing on these three strands of developmental activity (access, success and employability), which were of particular concern to both researchers and each institution.

Unlike many other workshops funded in the Newton Researcher Links Programme, we decided not to follow a traditional conference or symposium model, but to create an open, conversational and experimental space. A space which could be used to co-create longer-term project proposals addressing the above mentioned areas of the project focus. Our hope was that the projects co-created could be taken forward after the workshop, and we could avoid the trap of creating an 'academic talk-shop' where the world outside academia had little influence on the shape or direction of the conversation. This approach of facilitating the workshop was conceived as an open and democratic programme where all voices carried equal weight, and in this respect, it was forward-looking and developmental rather than reflective.

A small lead team with three academics from UEL and CPUT respectively, took responsibility for the development and delivery of the overall project. We, the two authors of this chapter, had organisational responsibility with accountability to the British Council as well as a leadership role, while the other four members were selected based on their seniority and ability to support ECRs in UEL and CPUT, a key specification of the funding guidelines. Their seniority also guaranteed local institutional support. The team comprised three men and three women, but only one person of colour, and four were of European descent.

The organising team issued a call for participation, requesting submission of three relevant challenges or 'wicked' questions which prospective workshop attendees would like to work on. By wicked questions, we refer to problems of sufficient complexity and interdependence to defy simple resolution, in both academia and civil society (Buchanan, 1992; Goodyear, 2015). Participation was split into three ways, with a third of attendees coming from the two host universities, a third from other HE institutions (HEIs), and a third from industry. Industry participants were primarily drawn from policy-making institutions, funding bodies, Non-Governmental Organisations (NGOs), creative industries and HE learning and development. Participants were selected on the basis of their ability to address questions driving WISH, and especially around support for students after completing their degrees, and potential for future collaboration.

The programme was structured to ensure that an equal number of participants came from the UK and SA. We worked to balance seniority and aspiration, so participants were drawn from across academic and professional hierarchies. We also worked at creating a balanced mix across gender and race. Participants included discipline-specific academics, academic developers, learning technologists and managers, and practitioners from a range of different sectors outside academia. The latter work-based group was of particular importance in terms of the overall balance, providing a counterweight that could ground the conversation around experience in the world of work after students graduated and thereby informed discussions around the relationship between subsequent employment and academic life. Questions around employability were a major concern for all involved, and the industry practitioners were able to ensure that this remained at the forefront of discussions.

The final piece in the recruitment phase of participants saw the appointment of a specialist external facilitation team. This was supposed to provide an authoritative, neutral voice to guide the process and ensure equity between participants. Sourcing external facilitation provided an interesting example of how the lack of diversity in structures can be problematic. As is common with these kinds of projects, there was no funding for external moderation, as most of the funding went into travel and accommodation. We therefore needed to reach out to our various networks in Cape Town to identify and recruit possible support at no or very low cost. It is vital to note that the facilitation market in Cape Town is still predominantly white, so the first contacts we received were from white facilitators, who offered pro bono work. After informing the larger group that most of the people who expressed interest for facilitation were white, we received resistance and heavy critique. It was felt that such a process, especially when dealing with sensitive or charged issues such as decolonisation and transformation, could not be solely facilitated by a white individual. The organising committee responded and recruited a diverse facilitation team.

Step 2: How does change happen in different HE contexts?

The workshop's main focus was to understand in more detail how change happens in HE across two contexts: SA and the UK. At the time of writing this chapter, much about the future shape of HE is very uncertain globally. Recent years have seen the arrival of third-party education providers, funders, education technology companies, and start-up colleges and universities, which have now become part of the sector. There has been a rapid growth in transnational education (now seeing a downturn), which generally involves universities from the Global North setting up campuses or agreements with partner institutions, to see 'their' degrees awarded in the Global South, or engaging overseas learners via distance learning. Such transnational activity by UK universities increased by 72% between 2007/8 and 2012/13, and by a further 10% between 2013/14 and 2016/17 (Bennell, 2018, p. 31). Similar developments can be seen in SA, where the number of private institutions of higher learning are rapidly expanding (Ivancheva et al., 2020; Swinnerton et al., 2018) due to the demand for more flexible online learning.

COVID-19 presented an unprecedented challenge for the sector, which may well lead to programme closures and university mergers (Khumalo, 2020) as the medium-term financial impact becomes clearer and income from a large pool of international students is not so certain (Team WonkHE, 2020).

Universities are traditionally very slow to change. School and faculty management roles often rotate among senior academics every three to five years. This, and the principle of academic freedom in relation to teaching and research, means line management hierarchies are not as clearly defined as in many other sectors. A degree of academic autonomy often means that proposed change is likely to require cross-institutional consultation and a certain amount of flexibility, even when the impetus is from the very top. It requires gaining buy-in from academics and managers across the university. Where the drive for change comes from others other than senior management, the likelihood of success often depends on alignment with the strategic goals or values of senior leaders (Bruckman & Cavalho, 2018).

A further challenge for a project like WISH is that universities are elitist institutions, which work to support and uphold existing structures of white supremacy and patriarchy (Mosoma et al., 2019). In the UK, widening access to students of colour and from non-traditional backgrounds has often been the focus of institutions granted university status from 1992 onwards and ordinarily characterised by poorer resourcing and lower prestige[1]. In the UK, Black academics represent only 2.5% of academic staff, and even less if level of seniority is taken into account (HESA, 2018-19). In this context, individual staff wishing to institute change by challenging existing power structures and lack of transformation at these institutions may be taking a significant professional risk by speaking out (Noxolo, 2020). In SA, a recent report confirmed that while some progress has been made towards demographic transformation of academic staff generally, and specifically in relation to the recruitment, progression and retention of Black South African academics, progress is slow, particularly in the more research-focused/historically white institutions. In SA, significant barriers still exist in the university system, and black and female academics remain underrepresented (Mosoma et al., 2019).

Elitism goes hand in hand with established sets of beliefs and assumptions about teaching and learning, which present a fundamental challenge to radical and transformative changes like decolonisation. Institutional anxiety around changes to curriculum or teaching methods may be framed as a concern over a threat to academic standards, and definitions of standards and quality may be confused (Sharp, 2017). Internal perceptions of academia as a space of intellectual 'neutrality' reinforce existing power relations and maintain historical inequalities

---

[1] https://eacea.ec.europa.eu/national-policies/eurydice/content/types-higher-education-institutions-91_en

(Andrews, 2018, p. 140). Changes to learning, teaching, and the curriculum may come into conflict with academic freedom, or perceptions of it, as seen in recent debates arising around highly problematic research stemming from a South African university (Makoni, 2020). However, in the case of decolonisation, some internal imperatives, such as internationalisation strategies in the UK, may arguably prove to be 'unexpected allies' (Last, 2018). Challenges from larger-scale protests, such as Rhodes Must Fall (#RMF), Fees Must Fall (#FMF) or Black Lives Matter (#BLM) can begin to overturn assumptions and may provide an impetus to reshaping university priorities. Staff development, including mentoring and experiential learning, can be a key factor here (Vandeyar, 2019). This does not always sit easily with academic identities, and requires care and sensitivity to ensure that it meets academics' needs as well as institutional agendas.

Linked to this, Vandeyar (2019) argues that in SA decolonising curriculum content alone, without academics engaging in and enacting a shift in values and deep reflection on positionality and systemic inequalities, will not be enough to create systemic lasting change. For a country such as SA, student protests have meant widespread disruptions, ongoing trauma and the need to rethink the identity and role of HEIs (Hlatshwayo, 2021). These protests have highlighted the inequality that persists in the country's tertiary education system and pointed to the need for fresh approaches to addressing systemic problems in HE. In particular, the protests have drawn attention to the need to not only create epistemic access for diverse communities of students (Quinn & Vorster, 2019); but also the call for inclusion of student voices into the curriculum design process, and co-creating spaces where all students can flourish (Cook-Sather, Matthews & Bell, 2019; Ngoasheng et al., 2019).

Step 3: Conceptual pathway taken to achieve change within WISH

The centrepiece of WISH was a three-day workshop, preceded by an online development period where participants worked through the three different themed groups via a shared programme of readings and exercises. These groups used a combination of webinars conducted through Skype and sharing of information, resources and discussion via an asynchronous online communication platform, Slack.

The preparatory work enabled participants to get to know each other, and to refine and refocus the wicked questions. The intention was to lay solid foundations for the face-to-face workshop by establishing common knowledge and a shared sense of identity. Participants were grouped using the three project themes; each group was led by two academic mentors from the organising team, one from UEL and the other from CPUT. The five-week online phase included at least three synchronous online meetings using Skype. We set up a mailing list on Google Groups for communication and used Slack for continued engagement and sharing key readings. A series of Slack channels were established: one for each group, one for announcements about the project, and another for general chats and discussions. We set up a Google Drive folder for the 30 participants to share resources and other working documents.

Participants gathered for the three-day workshop in Cape Town in October 2017. With looming student protests and risk of campus closures, we used a conference venue outside Cape Town, on the Noordhoek beachfront. The three-day workshop was preceded by a meeting with students–a stakeholder group initially overlooked in the planning. While the funders criteria were clear on the importance of including practitioners in this project, students were not part of the desired stakeholder group and not included in the approved proposal. Some participants alerted us to the lack of student voices during one of the pre-workshop meetings. CPUT students were approached through lecturers involved in WISH and the Dean of Student Affairs' Office, and included, for example, members of the Student Representative Council (SRC) and student associations, such as HIV/AIDS counsellors. The engagement with participants in the project and the SCR may have provided the UK participants a more tangible sense of the policy drivers and related discontents within South African HE. However, there was no UK student participation, and CPUT SCR participation was limited as they were not included in the original budgeting; hence both SA and UK students were inadvertently marginalised and SA participants were not exposed to a glimpse of UK student issues.

As a follow-up to the workshop, we scheduled a series of meetings to take some of the project ideas further. We planned both face-to-face (local) meetings and online meetings for ongoing cross-continental collaboration. In the absence of ongoing support from either the lead institutions or the funders, it proved difficult to get everyone together with the same commitment, however individual participants took project ideas further.

Step 4: The assumptions, expectations and design principles within our approach

Early in the project journey, the organising committee identified five values that underpinned the design of the WISH project: embracing diversity, co-creation, openness, unconferencing, disruption and passion-led practices. These drew on design thinking, which has been widely adopted in universities around the world (beyond the design disciplines) as a learning paradigm that nurtures creative problem solving and multi-perspective collaboration (Von Thienen, Royalty & Meinel, 2017). Berger (2010, p. 3) defines design as a "way of looking at the world with an eye towards changing it". It allows for diverging and converging thinking, provides tools and activities to promote creativity and challenge assumptions and habits in academia, and is a mindset characterised by problem orientation, collaboration, generosity, learner empathy, resilience, etc. (Gachago et al., 2017; Goodyear, 2015). The five values under which the WISH project was designed are discussed below in some details:

Embracing diversity

Our call for proposals focused on bringing together people from SA and the UK, with different professional and academic backgrounds to address subjects of shared interest. We wanted to draw insights from these different voices and catalyse a fresh view around the subjects.

Co-creation

From the start we were clear that we wanted participants to own the workshop process and have as much say as possible in how the workshop would be facilitated and run. This was embedded in the pre-workshop phase, and also in how we sought to react constructively to participants' feedback to ensure that the workshop was designed in an iterative way.

Openness

We decided to follow the Open Space methodology2 for the workshop, focusing on co-creation and open structures. Open Space convenes groups around a specific question or task and gives them responsibility for creating their own agenda and experience. The facilitator's role is pivotal- the key task is to enable all participants to raise a question, before standing back and letting others explore this in greater depth. Open Space allows for the emergence of collective knowledge drawn from the expertise of participants. It starts from an assumption that this expertise is readily available, as the right people are together and can be drawn upon when needed. Rather than working from a set programme, Open Space allows for responses to needs and interests that emerge organically from conversations and situations, assuming equity among participants and placing parity on everyone's opinion.

Unconferencing

We sought a loosely structured conference or workshop; emphasising the informal exchange of information and ideas rather than a conventionally

---

2 https://www.involve.org.uk/resources/methods/open-space-technology

structured programme. Unconferencing[3] starts with questions and organises a programme as the conversation evolves. It is participant- and interest-driven so everyone can share knowledge and present ideas as needed.

Inviting disruption

Given the complex issues we were dealing with and it being a time of campus shutdowns and student protests in SA around study fees (#FMF), and the diversity of participants, we expected–indeed encouraged–the workshop participants to ask tough questions and allow for difficult conversations. We saw these challenges as a means to conceptualise our shared understanding of the structural problems underpinning WISH, and catalyse the development of new projects or activities that could facilitate change around the identified challenges.

Passion-led practices

Participants were invited because of their passion for certain ideas, rather than their academic credentials or professional standing. Opportunities were deliberately given to young academics to share new ideas. The workshop strove for debate and sharing rather than production of traditional academic outputs.

Step 5: How we tested assumptions through monitoring and evaluation of the range of activities within and after WISH

Embracing diversity

Reflection 1: *When we met with the facilitators to discuss the programme we intentionally built in spaces for participants to share their work. We knew that we had selected quite a large and very diverse group. We wanted to make sure that we gave everyone an opportunity to share their backgrounds and practices. I remember one exercise well, the marketplace, where participants shared some of their work … it was great, but I kept thinking, too much to take in in too little time.*

WISH participants came from different backgrounds and we knew from the outset that a three-day workshop would not necessarily allow for robust engagement, unpacking and understanding of each individual's motivation to participate in the project. Time was needed to understand how everyone might contribute their personal experience, professional or academic values, and academic knowledge. To pre-empt this, we had created space and time in the

---

[3] https://unconference.net/welcome/

online phase for people to establish connections and explore areas of common interest. Pressures of time meant connections and exchange of ideas didn't happen equitably across the three online groups established. Some people had started meeting and sharing, while others came in with little pre-workshop contact. One consequence of this uneven preparation and limited time spent face to face was a lack of appreciation of each other's strengths and values, which in turn led to difficulties, impacted on working relationships and contributed to misunderstanding and even conflict during and after the workshop.

We had anticipated conflict around the shared history of colonialism between the UK and SA. As a result, UK attendees were warned not to come across as 'giving or helping' South African participants. However, we were unprepared for other conflicts which arose. The absence of student voices and retrospective invitation of SA (CPUT) students to a hastily organised pre-workshop session caused unhappiness (as UK students voices were not sought), set up troubled hierarchies at the outset, and meant that their input was missing in both the preparation and delivery of the programme. We had also expected some tensions between academics or policymakers and practitioners, especially those whose work focused on more practical concerns rather than deeper historical forces. The language used to frame the programme seemed too academic for some of the participants, with terms such as 'wicked questions' considered off-putting, whereas for others the focus on tangible outcomes and personal relationships was too far removed from academic work. Academic hierarchies also made it difficult for junior academics to engage on an equal basis with more senior colleagues.

Taken together, this meant it was harder to gather people together in working teams with similar goals or motivations. A fuller and more rounded exploration and acknowledgement of difference and complexity at an earlier stage might have allowed more fruitful and intellectually productive dialogue, including where there were serious and potentially unresolvable conflicts.

Passion-led practices

Reflection 2: *For me, one of the most painful moments of the workshop happened somewhere in the middle of the process. Issues of transformation, and in particular around the intersections of race, gender, culture, belonging continued to pop up but with very different responses. While for some these conversations seemed essential and incredibly urgent, others seemed to respond with impatience as if they were mere distractions to the process. I remember this one moment so clearly, where one of the UK participants, a woman of colour stood up and shared a very personal story about her son, a young black teenager, being bullied and victimised at his school, based on his skin colour. It was a* *heartbreaking story, and there was absolute silence when she was done. Until another participant stood up and asked, but how is this relevant to our workshop? I felt gutted, paralysed, not knowing what to say or do.*

Questions of social justice lay at the heart of the workshop and were a core value for both UEL and CPUT. Our workshop happened when, in particular in SA, historical inequalities, the legacy of Apartheid and absence of meaningful change in HE had gained significant prominence through student protests. Not all the South African participants were equally affected by these debates and conflicts, and for many of the UK cohort it was a new and relatively complex agenda. Individual perspectives and responses were shaped by race and gender, personal values, background, experiences or geographical location. Different reactions were triggered by many of the conversations. For some participants, these moments of conflict were unnecessary barriers within the workshop that restricted the scope to achieve whatever goal they had set up for themselves. However, for others, these were key moments to address fundamental, life-changing questions that were an essential component of their academic and non-academic identities. From this perspective, the workshop process, in particular its role in making visible and interrogating structural inequalities, had become the priority.

It became clear that in particular the term 'decolonisation' divided the group: for some, it was just another term currently in vogue, which could be used synonymously for internationalisation, contextualisation or student-centred learning, while for others it was an all-encompassing, radical change of how to be, think and act in and beyond academia. These two perspectives clashed early on, and we realised that we had not prepared adequately for how to handle conflict when it occurred. Facilitating conversations like this requires a firm grounding in critical and transformative theory (Ngoasheng et al., 2019), as well as considerable ability to articulate and hold such difficult emotions with empathy and compassion.

Addressing social justice work on an individual level can be difficult and necessitates an openness and a willingness to allow oneself to be challenged and therefore made vulnerable. While some participants openly embraced this, others were more reticent. We had promoted WISH as an opportunity for honest and open conversations, yet the space was not necessarily completely ready for that. In some ways, we created an opportunity for participants to be hurt by encouraging them to be vulnerable while not providing the necessary protective culture of witnessing or support (Ngoasheng et al., 2019).

Facilitating disruption

Reflection 3: *On the final day, participants were asked to post ideas or themes for projects proposals, to share them and sign up to work together to develop their preferred projects. …. We–as the accountable organisers–felt we were a long way from meeting the goal set in our application to the British Council and approved by them. … The sense of unity or purpose that had been apparent at the start of the workshop, and in the formative events, was simply no longer there and there was a mutinous grow. Attempts to set up a group that could draw more disaffected or distanced participants back by addressing "overarching" themes of WISH gathered some interest but when the larger group split into smaller sub-groups, it was immediately apparent that the "overarching" group was exclusively male and this was justifiably challenged by a female participant. The group then dispersed quickly. With the advantage of hindsight, we needed stronger, more assertive facilitation at this point, and, quite probably, at others throughout the workshop. We could–and perhaps should–have allowed people to drift away, to reflect, to leave. … yet group dynamics and an overall sense of duty kept pulling people together.*

Open facilitation is not yet a well-established practice in either SA or the UK, and for many participants it was unfamiliar and potentially discomforting. While we spent time before and during the workshop explaining the purpose and process underpinning these approaches, some participants felt 'lost' and might have been more at home with a conventionally structured process. It is often hard to change established practice, and in a context where academic or work deadlines drive much of our lives, finding resources for more open dialogue without immediately obvious short-term benefits is often difficult. This resulted in varying levels of commitment and engagement.

Our experience was that however fairly the space is set up to be, hierarchies and power dynamics will reveal themselves and play out. Borrowing from social justice work, one needs to create space where marginalised voices are consciously expressed and listened to (Boughey & McKenna, 2021; Ngoasheng et al., 2019). The often dominant voices–be it because of gender, race, hierarchy, or geographical belonging–need to be made to pause, reflect and take a step back, so they can listen attentively rather than respond with defensiveness or disengagement. This, in some ways, goes against open facilitation techniques, which establish parity in spaces for equal engagement. Starting from an assumption that open spaces can be created which are inherently more democratic can mask or shield pre-existing hierarchies, rather than working to expose and confront them. Facilitating an open space embeds difference in the process and makes it harder to interrogate power dynamics as they emerge; it can also lead to new hierarchies or disenfranchisement, either between facilitators and participants or within participant groups. The rhetoric and reality of open space can be different and success requires both a clear commitment to the process and a willingness to cede power, influence and voice as part of this.

Open spaces necessitates careful listening from all involved. Facilitating open space is a skilled and complex task. A successful workshop requires a fully engaged and energised group and there is no doubt that the facilitation team had to work hard to get everyone up to speed, especially with such a fluid programme. This exciting, dynamic and exploratory approach requires participants to respond honestly and constructively to what is taking place in the immediate space. However, if the facilitation team doesn't pick up nuances quickly and sensitively on participants' honest and sometimes challenging responses, a workshop like this can quickly fracture or even descend into conflict.

For instance, the conflict described in the reflection above could have been a watershed moment, an opportunity to shine a flashlight on intersectionality and power that haunted WISH. However, after a brief consultation with the organising committee, the facilitation team decided not to unpack this conflict but to move on, in order to reach their objectives for the hard pressed schedule. The simple pressure of time and the need to reach predetermined goals restricted the capacity to reflect adequately on issues thrown up in a complex process.

Co-creation

Reflection 4: *When we finally met up again for our first follow-up meeting, I looked around and saw mainly participants from the decolonisation group. None of the many project ideas brought us together. We were there because we were passionate about social justice and we liked each other. Something bonded us, our experiences in WISH felt special. We wanted to work together.*

Reflection 5: *There was no substantial UK follow up. Internal restructuring at UEL meant that staff left–two of the three organisers departed within months–so the glue was lost and there was no scope to take activity forward with institutional backing. ... This was a real loss and led many of the UK participants–me included–to question the value of the programme. The reading group went on and some of us regrouped again at the decolonial transformations event at the University of Sussex. But in terms of what WISH had sought to achieve, it all felt like a lost opportunity.*

The initial WISH proposal emphasised the co-creation of a collaborative programme. We shared– and continue to do so–a commitment to the idea of co-creation where shared ownership means shared responsibility. Setting up a culture of co-creation takes time and, most importantly, a common negotiated and mutually understood intention based on shared values and shared commitment to tackle the hard work of transformation.

Building relationships takes time and care. Only one of the groups managed to meet regularly during the pre-workshop phase, which built the necessary bonds and created a shared understanding. In contrast, the two other groups struggled with negotiating meaning and terminologies, and there was not the same sense of direction. This contributed to difficulties in establishing a shared purpose and common outcomes across the three groups.

One consequence was that there were many ideas at the end of the workshop, but no clear direction or means to take them forward. Commitment rested purely on personal engagement and motivation, and one's sense of urgency to engage in processes of change. In the end, only one group managed to continue their collaboration through online meetings and local activity (although individual participants continued working together outside their groups). As one tangible outcome, some participants at CPUT submitted a research proposal and embarked on a co-creation process that led to conference presentations, a co-created book chapter, and the design of a short course on co-creation, offered at four institutions in the Western Cape with the online support and encouragement of international partners. Another initiative that came out of the workshop was the invitation of some South African participants to a UK-based conference hosted at the University of Sussex, which provided a further opportunity to share work and experiences. Connections established during the workshop have seen participants work together on local and international projects. These outcomes depended on the establishment of trusting relationships and a shared passion for this (often difficult) work.

Step 6: Reflections on the process and project implementation

WISH took place during 2017, and this reflection has been written some three years later. The passage of time has allowed us to consider what happened during the workshop, to understand the good and the bad. Working with ToC has provided a means to structure our reflection and has worked as an invaluable guide, by forcing us to externalise, commit to and write down the sometimes implicit principles on which our work was based.

In *Rules for Radicals*, Saul Alinsky (1971, p. 12) states that "the basic requirement for the understanding of the politics of change is to understand the world as it is. We must work with it on its terms if we are to change it to the world we would like it to be". We found a mutual understanding of terms, such as widening participation and defining student success, but others– such as decolonisation–proved much more complex and divisive. While social justice and transformation was the overarching theme of the workshop, we didn't work hard enough to engage with the specifics of change in HE in either the UK or SA. Beyond lack of contextual knowledge between the participants from the different countries, there were other, much more critical differences in commitment to addressing systemic inequalities within HE and within the group.

WISH was based on five principles/values, and reflecting on these we came to the conclusions outlined below.

Embracing diversity

All shared a commitment to diversity, yet there were also multiple conceptions of diversity across WISH. From the outset, and despite the goodwill of all involved, structural limitations within the funding programme and the common white European background of the two primary organisers limited WISH in different ways. No matter how well meaning, the project was set up as a response to a particular opportunity–and was shaped and constrained by it. This led to shortcomings within the programme which restricted the scope to respond creatively and productively to the challenges posed by embracing diversity.

Starting with its basis in a mostly UK-derived funding opportunity, which placed the European partner in a position of power, this project was set up in problematic ways. Challenges and requirements attached to that funding, including expected outputs; limited support in terms of student involvement; and lack of provision for workshop facilitation, pre-workshop preparation and post-workshop follow-up; left little space for the important and complex work of building trust, finding a shared sense of purpose, and engaging deeply with questions of participants' privilege, power and positionality.

Electing a predominantly white and European core team, and omission of students from the eligible group of participants, further entrenched these problems. Reflection showed us how, as a predominantly white organisational committee, we set up spaces that were potentially violent to people of colour. In some instances, we were challenged early enough, but at other moments we were complicit in not insisting on continuation or exploration of difficult conversations, but rather supporting the facilitators to move on towards a predetermined outcome.

Passion-led

Participating in WISH required a significant personal investment in terms of time and an openness to personal and professional transformation. Time is a precious commodity and goodwill was needed to secure the involvement of hard-pressed professionals, especially during the preparatory online phase. One consequence is that some people were better prepared and also more engaged than others; this unevenness affected contributions and engagement during the workshop. It is also clear that for processes that are not remunerated, shared passion is an essential driver for sustained commitment, especially for freelancers.

Open space facilitation

The open space facilitation method applied in this workshop relied on participants' willingness to engage in the workshop and subsequent activities. It also valued process-based work, as much as, or possibly more than the intended outcomes. In this respect, it was experiential; of the moment rather than long term. Stressing a requirement for projects or outcomes required people to come together in a constructive way beyond the three-day workshop, something which the open facilitation process could not adequately engineer and in the absence of confirmed post-workshop resourcing, this was quite possibly an unrealistic aspiration from such a short period of engagement.

Disruption

Our commitment to co-creation and the use of Open Space established some opportunities for constructive and candid dialogue. This meant we needed to create spaces that intentionally foregrounded marginalised voices and challenged dominant ones, whenever conflict arose. Open Space and its emphasis on parity is insufficient in this regard. It also requires potentially difficult identity work that not all participants had signed up for.

Co-creation

Integral to the Newton Fund Programme is an assumption that participants have the wherewithal and commitment to collaborate beyond a short, funded period. However, this is not necessarily the case, especially for those lacking ongoing institutional support. Furthermore, co-creation implies and necessitates a shared investment of time and energy. We saw these factors present difficulties for WISH participants after the workshop. Project-based outcomes such as those originally planned would be easier to achieve with structured provision built into funding models.

Conclusion and recommendations

In conclusion, where WISH fell short most visibly, was that its founding principles, our assumptions, our ToCs, were negotiated between project organisers addressing stipulations of the funding programme, but not confirmed in agreement with the recruited project participants. More work ahead of the workshop, to negotiate principles and accommodate a diversity of perspectives, might have contained conflicts when they arose and allowed for the kind of vulnerability needed to work with sensitive issues such as intersecting identities and power hierarchies (Boughey & McKenna, 2021).

If we had to run this workshop again, we would:

- Be more intentional on establishing diversity across all levels (from management/steering committee to participants' selection to students' involvement to facilitation etc)

- Work to be more explicit about values and principles underlying the project and what participant engagement in it meant, including openness to discomfort, and to uncovering structural inequalities around race, class and gender.

- Be much more careful in how we set up and ensured commitment during the initial online phase

- Engage a facilitation team more adept or experienced in handling difficult conversations

- Create spaces and opportunities for a process of constructive, active listening

- Be more explicit in terms of mid- and long-term ambitions and undertake the strategic planning needed to reach them over time

- Be more open to what can happen–whatever that is–and be able to respond to it.

Richard Sennett (2012, p. 19) draws a distinction between dialectical conversations, where common ground is found through synthesis, and the dialogical, where a conversation does not resolve itself in a shared agreement yet people become more aware of their own position and that of others. WISH project leaders needed to work harder to find ways to accommodate and hold dialogical conversations and sustain the attentive, compassionate or empathetic listening required to achieve success across groups working with them.

Reflecting on this process was not easy or straightforward. Forcing ourselves to return to these spaces of conflict and discomfort, exploring our own shortcomings and complicities as organisers, took effort but also showed us how essential it is to go back and interrogate such experiences as a means to fully understand. The individual and collective gains, pains and learning we discovered as we looked back on our collaboration, on the moments of joy but also the moments of discomfort, show how deeply impacted we were. While not leading to the amount of individual projects that we might have wished for, WISH started something much larger, that uncovered much deeper-lying conflicts and systemic structures that shape all our lives.

Coming back to Vaughn's quote at the beginning, transformation is not a singular, one-off event; it's an ongoing continuous and active effort, *even when it's uncomfortable or outside of our professional cultural norms and traditions.* This kind of work can clash with institutional practices and how to move from such an experimental space back into shared, institutional contexts needs both mindful preparation and follow-up in order to protect all concerned. This needs sustained buy-in and support by the funding partners, institutions and individuals involved. Creating short-term spaces for transformation, as WISH was intended to be, carries risks that we all need to account for.

Acknowledgements

This was a difficult and sometimes awkward chapter to write, especially as it was so focused on our personal experience. Particular thanks go to Dr Marita Grimwood for her invaluable advice and input at key points throughout the lengthy writing process. We are also very grateful to Dr Xena Cupido and Asanda Ngoasheng, who gave constructive commentary, pointed to blind spots and shared their own perspectives and recollections. We would also like to extend our gratitude to our reviewers.

References

Alinsky, S. (1971). *Rules for Radicals.* Vintage: New York.

Andrews, K. (2018). The Challenge for Black Studies in the Neoliberal University. In G. K. Bhambra, D. Gebrial & K. Nişancıoğlu (Eds.), *Decolonising the University,* pp. 129-144. London: Pluto.

Andrews, K. (2020). 'Black Studies as the science of liberation.' Conference paper (online), *Student-led Decolonising the Curriculum Conference,* Birmingham City University, 4 June 2020. https://www.youtube.com/watch?v=E_5EJ4hiX-I&t=555s

Ashton, C. V. (2007). Using Theory of Change to enhance peace education evaluation. *Conflict Resolution Quarterly,* 25(1), 39-53. doi: 10.1002/crq

Bennell, P. (2018). Transnational higher education in the United Kingdom: An up-date. *International Journal of Educational Development,* 67, pp. 29-40

Berger, W. (2010) CAD *Monkeys, Dinosaur Babies, and T-Shaped People: Inside the World of Design Thinking and How It Can Spark Creativity and Innovation.* New York: Penguin.

Boughey C. & McKenna, S. (2021). Interrogating the power dynamics in international projects. *Critical Studies in Learning and Teaching (CriSTaL),* 9(2), 64-82. https://www.cristal.ac.za/index.php/cristal/article/view/448/317

Bruckmann, S., &Carvalho, T. (2018). Understanding change in higher education: an archetypal approach. *Higher Education,* 76(4), 629–647. https://doi.org/10.1007/s10734-018-0229-2

Buchanan, R. (1992) Wicked Problems in Design Thinking. *Design Issues,* 8, 5-21.

Cook-Sather, A., Matthews, K. E. & Bell, A. (2019). Transforming curriculum development through co-creation with students. In L. E. Quinn (Ed.), *Reimaging Curricula: Spaces for Disruption*, pp. 107-126. Stellenbosch: African Sun Media.

Davies, R. (2018). Representing theories of change: Technical challenges with evaluation consequences. *Journal of Development Effectiveness*, 10(4), pp. 438-461. doi: 10.1080/19439342.2018.1526202

Freeman, M. (2010). *Hindsight – The Promise and Peril of Looking Backward*. Oxford: Oxford University Press.

Gachago, D., Morkel, J., Hitge, L., Van Zyl, I. & Ivala, E. (2017). Developing eLearning champions: A design thinking approach. *International Journal of Educational Technology in Higher Education*, 14(1). doi: 10.1186/s41239-017-0068-8

Goodyear, P. (2015). Teaching as design. *HERDSA Review of Higher Education*, 2(2), pp. 27-50. http://www.herdsa.org.au/wp-content/uploads/HERDSARHE 2015v02p27.pdf

HESA. (2018-19). *2018-19 statistics on academic staff in UK Higher Education by ethnicity.* https://www.hesa.ac.uk/data-and-analysis/staff/working-in-he/ characteristics

Hlatshwayo, M. (2021). The rupturesinour rainbow: Reflectionson teaching and learningduring#RhodesMustFall. Critical Studies in Learning and Teaching (CriSTaL), 9(2), pp. 1-18. https://www.cristal.ac.za/index.php/cristal/article/ view/492/314

Ivancheva, M. P., Swartz, R., Morris, N. P., Walji, S., Swinnerton, B. J., Coop, T. & Czerniewicz, L. (2020). Conflicting logics of unbundled higher education in an unequal society. *British Journal of Sociology of Education*, 0(0), pp. 1-18. doi: 10.1080/01425692.2020.1784707

Khumalo, K. (2020). Government has identified 6 universities as high risk. *Sunday World.* https://sundayworld.co.za/education/government-has-identified -6-universities-as-high-risk/

Last, A. (2018). Internationalisation and interdisciplinarity: Sharing across boundaries? In G. K. Bhambra, D. Gebrial & K. Nişancıoğlu (Eds.), *Decolonising the University*, pp. 208-230. London: Pluto.

Makoni, M. (2020). Sparks fly over study on black students and biological sciences. *University World News.* https://www.universityworldnews.com/post. php?story=20200609201341525

Mosoma, D., Msengana, B., Mgwebi, T., Mosoetsa, S. & Bawa, A. (2019). *Report of the Ministerial Task Team on the recruitment, retention and progression of black South African academics.* Pretoria: Department of Higher Education and Training.

Nava, O. (2020). Decolonising the Curatorial Process [video] https://vimeo.com/ 464558806?fbclid=IwAR1_IcXwJ_siBPoRk5KP0ZFS01wf7TBuuONSWezz2elR 7GkqpWNQoT7M3wA

Ngoasheng, A., Cupido, X., Oyekola, S., Gachago, D., Mpofu, A. & Mbekela, Y. (2019). Advancing democratic values in higher education through open curriculum co-creation: Towards an epistemology of uncertainty. In L. E. Quinn (Ed.), *Reimaging Curricula: Spaces for Disruption*, pp. 324–344. Stellenbosch: African Sun Media. doi: 10.1093/0198294719.001.0001

Nkwake, A. M. (2013). *Working with Assumptions in International Development Program Evaluation*. Cham: Springer.

Noxolo, P. (2020). (Post)COVID-19 online learning: opportunities and dangers for black students and staff. Conference paper (online), *Student-led Decolonising the Curriculum Conference*, Birmingham City University, 11 June 2020. https://www.youtube.com/watch?v=0pXVs60HETE&t=2816s

O'Flynn, M. & Moberly, C. (2017). *Theory of Change*. Intrac. https://www.intrac.org/wpcms/wp-content/uploads/2017/01/Theory-of-Change.pdf

Quinn, L. & Vorster, J. (2019). Why the focus on curriculum? Why now? The role of academic development. In L. E. Quinn (Ed.), *Reimaging Curricula: Spaces for Disruption*, pp. 1-22. Stellenbosch: African Sun Media.

Sennett, R. (2012). *Together: The Rituals, Pleasures & Politics of Cooperation*. London: Penguin.

Sharp, K. (2017). The distinction between academic standards and quality: Implications for transnational higher education, *Quality in Higher Education*, 23(2), pp. 138-152.

Swinnerton, B., Coop, T., Ivancheva, M., Czerniewicz, L., Morris, N. P., Swartz, R., ... Cliff, A. (2018). Researching emerging models in an unequal landscape. In N. Bonderup Dohn, P. Jandrić. T. Ryberg & M. de Laat (Eds.), *Mobility, Data and Learner Agency in Networked Learning*, pp. 19-34. Cham: Springer.

Team WonkHE. (2020). *The restructuring regime – money, but at a cost*. https://wonkhe.com/blogs/money-but-at-a-cost/

Vandeyar, S. (2019). Why decolonising the South African university curriculum will fail. *Teaching in Higher Education*, 25(7), pp. 783-796. doi: 10.1080/13562517.2019.1592149

Vaughn, L. (2020). Can research be anti-colonial? *COVID 19 Race & Risk Project Blog*. https://covid19raceandrisk.wordpress.com/2020/07/08/can-research-be-anti-colonial/

Von Thienen, J., Royalty, A. & Meinel, C. (2017). Design thinking in higher education: How students become dedicated creative problem solvers. In Zhou, C. (Ed.), *Handbook of research on creative problem-solving skill development in higher education*, pp. 306-328. Hershey, PA: IGI Global.

Afterword:
Progress, power, pride and pleasure in co-teaching and co-researching

Maha Bali

American University in Cairo, Egypt

I give a workshop, offered around three or four times a year to Egyptian academics, broadly called 'Scholarly Collaboration', in which I emphasise the different actions we need to take before a successful partnership is to occur. These steps, which I brainstormed after a 'Spotlight' presentation that I gave at the eLearning Africa conference, that inspired further thinking via a blogpost titled *Modes of Seeking Collaboration* (Bali, 2016), are: listening, broadcasting, targeting (actively seeking specific collaborators), and ongoing interaction. Briefly, what I meant by each is:

Listening mode refers to reading what others write, present, or mention on social media posts. Two important elements here help expand the circle of people we can potentially collaborate with. One is finding ways to listen serendipitously to people whose research interests may not fully align with ours, whose demographic background (culture, discipline, research approach) may be different from ours, thus opening doors for potentially rich collaborations. We listen to learn, of course, not only for an instrumental goal of seeking collaborators. But one of the key things we need to do when listening is to notice and remember names, connecting names to research interests. How many times have I seen people miss an opportunity to meet the author of a book they're reading, because they didn't pay enough attention to their name? How often do you cite an article with multiple authors as 'et al.' and not notice that the fourth author, whose name you never say aloud, is someone you now know?

Broadcasting mode is when you announce your own interests and intentions, which of course we do when we publish or present at conferences, but we can also do in micro ways (especially early on in an area of our interest), such as when we just blog or tweet or such. This is not in the sense of explicitly advertising that we are seeking collaborators, but in the sense of putting ourselves out there, announcing who we are as academics and what we do, so that others may know us, or know of us. There is a kind of making ourselves vulnerable, sometimes an embarrassing process of shameless self-promotion.

It can also happen in a more directed way of seeking collaborations in more specific ways (see Targeting, below)

Targeting/actively inviting mode refers to when we target particular individuals for particular collaborations. It can be broadcast or done privately. Doing lots of listening helps you choose someone whose interests align; doing good broadcasting increases your chances of either being invited by others (e.g. to contribute book chapters or to special issues, or to co-author or co-teach), although chances of these collaborations working well are more dependent on the fourth, 'interactive mode'.

Interactive mode refers to ongoing relationship-building with others, like responding to blogs or social media posts, establishing personal relationships with other academics. In person, this may mean speaking privately after a presentation, chatting over coffee or lunch in the hallway; online this may mean responding to tweets, amplifying another's work, and establishing private DM conversations beyond the public ones. The ways in which this mode builds cultural capital, and how dependent it is upon meeting in person at conferences, fosters academic gatekeeping that makes it difficult for African scholars (who have little funding to travel, even within Africa, to meet others) to build. This is why I co-founded Virtually Connecting[1], a grassroots organisation that challenges academic gatekeeping by creating hybrid hallway conversations at conferences, connecting speakers and participants at in-person conferences with virtual participants who could not attend in person. Access to presentations and broadcasts is not what people like me are missing out on–those are accessible in various ways–it's those rich connections that people build when they meet and network at events.

In the Scholarly Collaboration workshop that I offer, many of the participants work at poorly funded institutions, and what they want is ways to find research partners at European institutions in order to do more ambitious STEM-based research. They come in less interested in local collaboration, whether within their own institutions or across institutions in Egypt, the Arab world, or Africa. Their attitude comes from three complicated, interconnected factors: the complex tacit hierarchies of power and corruption within local institutions, that makes them wary of collaborating locally; the problematic academic promotion criteria, that valourise single authorship and publication in international journals; and the colonialist assumptions underlying academic publishing, that value well-funded research coming from Northern/Western countries using global North methodologies, equipment and criteria, rather than research that would come from the global South.

---

[1] http://virtuallyconnecting.org/

It makes me realise how privileged I am, as a social scientist, in how much research I've been able to produce, largely with no funding at all. I'm also not in what is called in American institutions 'tenure-track', so no one counts my publications or requires me to publish in certain spaces for certain reasons. I tend to do research on topics of my choice, with whomever I choose, in whatever venue we agree upon (usually Open Access journals, which may not always be those with the highest impact factor). Because I am extremely active on social media in all the modes of listening, broadcasting, continuously interacting and occasionally targeting collaborators, I can often seek collaboration with particular people appropriate for a purpose, and build this collaboration on a foundation of an existing ongoing relationship. I am also often invited to contribute to specific spaces, whether by journal/book editors, or by potential collaborators.

Once we find or choose our collaborators, the process begins. We often hear people talk about collaborative teaching and research with diverse others as something to be celebrated. It should be, because it's often a major feat of affective labour and conflict resolution and teamwork, which no one prepares us for when we're doing a PhD consisting of solitary research for years and years. It's such poor preparation for how to do good, solid research with others, and navigating the power dynamics, challenges, potential self-development and eventual joy in the journey itself. All of this is invisible labour that's completely separate from our pride in the product of our labour. Co-teaching is similarly full of challenges and negotiations, as well as sparks of brilliance and moments of pleasure–the pleasure of sharing what is happening in our classrooms in ways (again) that we usually only ever do alone.

I have had so many collaborations over the years, from research to co-teaching, to open public scholarship, that I felt would be difficult to capture concisely. So instead, I set out to offer ten separate 10-word stories that express some of my thoughts and feelings concisely. I ended up with these 12:

Positive moments:
The journey and relationships are more significant than any product.
The moment my brainwave collides with yours and sparks fly.
I teach better now because we talk things over together.
Collaboration is joy we create by suffering together in solidarity.
You wrote for us when my life was in shambles.

Challenging moments:
We had a fight and she deleted the Google Drive.
When men edit me without suggesting, my voice feels erased.
My co-author is passionate about a theory I don't understand.
When they invited me into the grant, I felt tokenised.

Pleasure in our collaboration is dampened by your colonial gaze.
You smile despite jealousy that my name is remembered more.
We pulled our submission because the peer reviews were colonising.

I want to say that in all of these, I grow as a person and a professional through each of my collaborations, and I am inspired by this quote from Bakhtin (1984, p. 287):

I am conscious of myself and become myself only while revealing myself for another, through another, and with the help of another … I cannot manage without another, I cannot become myself without another.

Perhaps this comes from being an extreme extrovert, and I don't know for sure how my introverted collaborators feel about our interactions–I have never thought to ask them!

I am always conscious that the majority of my research and teaching take place in English, which is not my native language, but my first language. I am very conscious of the colonial implications of this, of being a hybrid Westernised elite, living in my fully Egyptian identity, working at an American-style institution, and how my identity as an academic is influenced by colonialist assumptions. In the process, I too like to seek collaborators from around the world, though I collaborate in co-teaching and research with colleagues in my department, in Egypt, the Arab world, and Africa, as well as Arab/African diaspora colleagues, and also collaborate with many in the global North. This reminds me of how many steps those of us from the global South may need to take in order to be understood by our collaborators:

We [the minorities] and you [the dominant] do not talk the same language. When we talk to you we use your language: the language of your experience and of your theories. We try to use it to communicate our world of experience. But since your language and your theories are inadequate in expressing our experiences, we only succeed in communicating our experience of exclusion. We cannot talk to you in our language because you do not understand it. (Lugones & Spelman, 1983, p. 575)

In one of my earliest collaborations with a 'stranger I met online', Nepalese educator Shyam Sharma (based in the US), we wrote:

[W]e cannot find common bonds if we forget the paradox of trying to find similarity in difference. If differences are to be valued, they may need to be understood in their own terms, the confusions that they create being tolerated, the complexities that they give rise to appreciated. (Sharma & Bali, 2014, n.p.)

We warn of the risks in trying to find common ground across difference, in how it can result in "mimicry of those at the center by those in the peripheries" (ibid).

I have learned from Nancy Fraser's (1995) work about the importance of "parity of participation", through the work of Hodgkinson-Williams and Trotter (2019). How any work we do, and especially collaboration across power differences, cannot be socially just unless we have this participatory parity, where representation and inclusion are not enough, but rather ensuring that all whose voices need to included are able to be there on their own terms, making decisions on an equal footing and not with different levels of power. We know that in academic collaboration, this is not always the case. Sometimes there are hierarchies within institutions, the supervisor co-authoring with a student or subordinate employee; the academic who is the Principal Investigator (PI) on a grant co-authoring with co-PIs, and of course, all of us conducting research, sometimes on or about other humans rather than with them.

And yet, I would not continue to collaborate across borders if the process itself was not, at least occasionally, fulfilling. So much of my collaborative research has been collaborative autoethnography, one of the most participatory approaches to research that I know. Much of my teaching-related virtual collaboration has been social justice focused. In the public, open teaching of *Equity Unbound* (see Zamora, Bali, Cronin and Mehran, in progress), we noticed how open synchronous 'studio visits' between our classes, originally intended to provide rich intercultural experiences for our students, "became unforeseen moments to explore lived experience and discover vulnerabilities in community". Even less visible are the ways in which our private Twitter Direct Messaging conversations became an ongoing lifeline for those of us who are collaborating, such that our collaboration became a seed for nurturing relationships beyond the actual work we were doing.

This book includes stories of collaborations in teaching and research from Africans in networked spaces. There is much to learn from reflecting on our own experiences with collaboration, but also so much insight to gain from the work of peers undergoing similar endeavours and sharing their learning, their challenges, and their triumphs. As you read through these chapters, what messages resonated most with you? How might you approach collaboration differently now?

References

Bakhtin, M. (1984). Toward a Reworking of the Dostoevsky Book. In Caryl Emerson (Ed., transl.) *Problems of Dostoevsky's Poetics*. Minneapolis, MN: University of Minnesota Press, pp. 283-302.

Bali, M. (2016). *Modes of seeking collaboration.* [Weblog post]. https://blog.mahabali.me/social-media/modes-of-seeking-collaboration/

Fraser, N. (2005). Reframing justice in a globalizing world. *New Left Review,* 36, Nov/Dec.

Hodgkinson-Williams, C.A. & Trotter, H. (2018). A social justice framework for understanding open educational resources and practices in the Global South. *Journal of Learning for Development,* 5(3), pp. 204-224. https://jl4d.org/index.php/ejl4d/article/view/312

Lugones, Maria C. & Spelman, Elizabeth V. (1983). Have we got a theory for you! Feminist theory, cultural imperialism and the demand for 'the woman's voice'. *Women's Studies International Forum,* 6(6): pp. 573-581. doi: 10.1016/0277-5395(83)90019-5.

Sharma, S. & Bali, M. (2014, April 4). Bonds of difference: illusions of inclusion. *Hybrid Pedagogy.* https://hybridpedagogy.org/bonds-difference-illusions-inclusion/

Zamora, M., Bali, M., Cronin, C. & Mehran, S. (in progress). Equity Unbound as critical intercultural praxis. For submission to a special issue of *Journal of Applied Instructional Design.*

Index

www.ingramcontent.com/pod-product-compliance
Lightning Source LLC
Chambersburg PA
CBHW061002280326
41935CB00009B/805